KU-313-242

TRAVEL WRITING

Carl Thompson

Routledge
Taylor & Francis Group

LONDON AND NEW YORK

UNIVERSITY OF WINCHESTER
LIBRARY

First edition published 2011
by Routledge
2 Park Square, Milton Park, Abingdon, OX14 4RN

Simultaneously published in the USA and Canada
by Routledge
711 Third Avenue, New York, NY10017

Routledge is an imprint of the Taylor & Francis Group, an informa business

© 2011 Carl Thompson

The right of Carl Thompson to be identified as author of this work has been
asserted by him in accordance with sections 77 and 78 of the Copyright, Designs
and Patents Act 1988.

All rights reserved. No part of this book may be reprinted or reproduced or utilised
in any form or by any electronic, mechanical, or other means, now known or hereafter
invented, including photocopying and recording, or in any information storage or
retrieval system, without permission in writing from the publishers.

British Library Cataloguing in Publication Data
A catalogue record for this book is available from the British Library

Library of Congress Cataloging in Publication Data
Thompson, Carl (Carl Edward)
Travel writing / Carl Thompson. — 1st ed.
    p. cm. — (The new critical idiom)
  Includes bibliographical references and index.
  1. Travellers' writings, English — History and criticism. 2. Travellers' writings,
American — History and criticism. 3. Travellers' writings — History and criticism.
4. Travel in literature. 5. Travel writing — History. I. Title.
  PR756.T72T48 2011
  820.9'491 — dc22
            2010047180

ISBN: 978-0-415-44464-4 (hbk)
ISBN: 978-0-415-44465-1 (pbk)
ISBN: 978-0-203-81624-0 (ebk)

Typeset in Garamond and Scala Sans
by Taylor & Francis Books

Printed and bound by CPI Group (UK) Ltd, Croydon, CR0 4YY

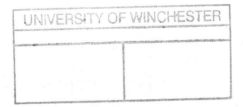
UNIVERSITY OF WINCHESTER

THE UNIVERSITY OF WINCHESTER

Martial Rose Library
Tel: 01962 827306

WITHDRAWN FROM

THE LIBRARY

UNIVERSITY OF

SEVEN DAY LOAN ITEM

To be returned on or before the day marked above, subject to recall.

KA 0385104 4

THE NEW CRITICAL IDIOM

SERIES EDITOR: JOHN DRAKAKIS, UNIVERSITY OF STIRLING

The New Critical Idiom is an invaluable series of introductory guides to today's critical terminology. Each book:

- provides a handy, explanatory guide to the use (and abuse) of the term
- offers an original and distinctive overview by a leading literary and cultural critic
- relates the term to the larger field of cultural representation

With a strong emphasis on clarity, lively debate and the widest possible breadth of examples, *The New Critical Idiom* is an indispensable approach to key topics in literary studies.

Also available in this series:

CONTENTS

Series Editor's Preface

The New Critical Idiom is a series of introductory books which seeks to extend the lexicon of literary terms, in order to address the radical changes which have taken place in the study of literature during the last decades of the twentieth century. The aim is to provide clear, well-illustrated accounts of the full range of terminology currently in use, and to evolve histories of its changing usage.

The current state of the discipline of literary studies is one where there is considerable debate concerning basic questions of terminology. This involves, among other things, the boundaries which distinguish the literary from the non-literary; the position of literature within the larger sphere of culture; the relationship between literatures of different cultures; and questions concerning the relation of literary to other cultural forms within the context of interdisciplinary studies.

It is clear that the field of literary criticism and theory is a dynamic and heterogeneous one. The present need is for individual volumes on terms which combine clarity of exposition with an adventurousness of perspective and a breadth of application. Each volume will contain as part of its apparatus some indication of the direction in which the definition of particular terms is likely to move, as well as expanding the disciplinary boundaries within which some of these terms have been traditionally contained. This will involve some re-situation of terms within the larger field of cultural representation, and will introduce examples from the area of film and the modern media in addition to examples from a variety of literary texts.

ACKNOWLEDGEMENTS

Sadly there is not space to thank everyone who has helped me over the long gestation of this book. But I would especially like to mention Polly Dodson and Andrea Hartill at Routledge for commissioning the book, and Emma Nugent for patiently steering me through the process of getting it to press. John Drakakis has been an exemplary editor, and I've benefited enormously from his suggestions and guidance. Jonathan Hope, Claire Jowitt and Betty Hagglund read large portions of the present volume in draft form, and gave much useful advice on both style and content. I'm also very grateful for the assistance given by many generous colleagues at Nottingham Trent University, including Abigail Ward, Dan Cordle, Sharon Ouditt, Anna Ball, Cathy Clay, Siobhan Lynch, Rob Burroughs and especially Tim Youngs. In addition, I wish to thank all the students who have taken the 'Travel Writing: Texts, Contexts and Theory' module that Tim and I run at NTU, for their many stimulating questions over the years. Michael and Valma Thompson, and Oscar and Angus Macrae have as always been immensely supportive throughout this project. Finally, I'd like to dedicate this volume to my sister, Ceri Thompson, who is the most travelled member of the family, and by far the best teller of travel tales.

1

INTRODUCTION

Travel writing is currently a flourishing and highly popular literary genre. Every year a stream of new **travelogues** flows from the printing press, whilst travel writers like Michael Palin, Bill Bryson and Paul Theroux regularly feature in the bestseller lists in both Europe and America. The reading public's appetite for the form has also prompted publishers to reissue many old out-of-print travel books in series such as Random House's Vintage Departures and Picador's Travel Classics. As a result, armchair travellers today can indulge their taste for the exotic, or for adventure, or simply for news of the wider world, by drawing on a vast array of both contemporary and historical travel books. These books recount journeys made for almost every conceivable purpose, to well-nigh every destination in the world. Their authors range from pilgrims, conquistadors and explorers to backpackers, minor celebrities and comedians undertaking a madcap jaunt on some inappropriate mode of transport; and they range also from 'serious' writers, seeking to make a significant contribution to art or knowledge, to hack writers and dilettantes happy to churn out the most superficial whimsy. Yet if the term 'travel writing' encompasses a bewildering diversity of forms, modes and itineraries, what is not in question is the popularity of the genre as a whole: recent decades have undoubtedly witnessed a travel writing 'boom', and this boom shows no signs of abating in the near future.

As well as enjoying commercial success, travel writing has seen its literary status rise in recent decades. For much of the twentieth century at least, the genre was usually dismissed by literary critics and cultural commentators as a minor, somewhat **middle-brow** form. However, travel writing's reputation rose sharply in the latter part of the century, with the appearance of a new genera-tion of critically acclaimed travel writers such as Paul Theroux, Bruce Chatwin, Ryszard Kapuscinski and Robyn Davidson. Also leading the way in this regard was the prestigious British literary journal *Granta*, which ran several travel-themed special issues in the 1980s and 1990s, and thereby played 'a vital part in establishing … travel writing as the popular literary form it has become' (Jack 1998: viii). Implicit in *Granta*'s championing of the form was the assumption that travel writing is a genre espe-cially reflective of, and responsive to, the modern condition. We live, after all, in an era of increasing **globalisation**, in which mobility, travel and cross-cultural contact are facts of life, and an everyday reality, for many people. Tourism, for example, is now one of the largest industries in the world. At any given moment, moreover, a significant portion of the global population is on the move not through choice, or for recreation, but through necessity, as they are displaced through economic hardship, environmental disaster or war. In these circumstances, travel writing has acquired a new relevance and prestige, as a genre that can provide important insights into the often fraught encounters and exchanges currently taking place between cultures, and into the lives being led, and the subjectivities being formed, in a globalising world.

Over the same period, academic interest in travel writing has also increased dramatically. Scholars and students working in several different disciplines have found the genre relevant to a broad range of cultural, political and historical debates. This is a development especially associated with the spread of what has come to be termed '**postcolonialism**', or '**postcolonial studies**', in many branches of the humanities and social sciences. Broadly speaking, the aim of postcolonial studies is to comprehend, and to contest, the pernicious consequences of the vast European empires of the nineteenth and early twentieth centuries. The European imperial project, and the global capitalism it promoted, laid the foundations of our modern, globalised world. It brought about cross-cultural contact, and the relocation of individuals and peoples, on a massive scale. It also did much to establish the enormous inequalities that currently exist between the different regions of the world, and especially between the developed 'West' and less developed 'Rest', in terms of wealth, health and technological advancement. Postcolonialist scholars have accordingly sought to understand the processes that first created, and now perpetuate, these inequalities, and they have also concerned themselves more generally with questions relating to how cultures regard and depict each other, and how they interact. These are research agendas for which travel writing is an immensely useful resource. From the fifteenth to the twentieth centuries, the genre played an integral role in European imperial expansion, and the travel writing of this period is accordingly highly revealing of the activities of European travellers abroad, and of the attitudes and **ideologies** that drove European expansionism. Similarly, modern travel writing can yield significant insights into the ideologies and practices that sustain the current world order.

It is not just the rise of postcolonial studies, however, that has brought about the recent burgeoning of academic interest in travel writing. In the aftermath of 1970s 'second-wave' feminism, many historians and literary critics have investigated women's contribution to a genre that superficially seems strongly associated with men, although women have in fact been prolific producers of travelogues, especially in the nineteenth and twentieth centuries. The genre has also featured in literary studies in debates about canonicity, and the relationship between aesthetic and functional forms of writing: the 'literary' and the 'non-literary'. In social sciences such as Geography, Anthropology and Sociology, meanwhile, the recent interest in travel writing is partly a consequence of theoretical and methodological debates as to the forms of knowledge and enquiry most appropriate to each discipline. All three disciplines to some extent evolved out of travel writing, engaging in enquiries that once were principally associated with, and articulated in, the genre known in English as '**voyages and travels**'. Institutionalised in the academy in the nineteenth century, however, they sought to distinguish themselves from more anecdotal and subjective forms of travel writing by espousing scientific methodologies and modes of discourse. But with the so-called 'cultural' or 'literary turn' of the 1970s, the supposedly scientific objectivity of the geographic or ethnographic text was called into question (see Rapport and Overing 2002: 236–45); and this has in turn prompted an ongoing reassessment of the role of travel writing as a vehicle for geographic, **ethnographic** and sociological knowledge.

These are just some of the larger debates and research contexts that have drawn scholars to the travel writing genre. Yet if travel writing is now seemingly as popular with academic readers as it is with general readers, it should be noted that these two audiences are not entirely in step with each other, or in accord in their attitudes to the genre. The commercial success currently enjoyed by the genre would seem to suggest a straightforward enjoyment of travel writing amongst the reading public. Yet much of the scholarly discussion of travel writing has been undertaken in a pronounced spirit of critique, and indeed censure, rather than celebration. Witness the judgement passed by Debbie Lisle, a specialist in International Relations, in her study of contemporary British and American travel writing. Lisle laments that there is 'something *wrong* with travel writing in general' (2006: xi, emphasis in the original), and is moved to ask, 'Why … are travelogues still being written in our supposedly "enlightened" age? And why are they still so popular?' (2). She condemns the genre on the grounds that it encourages 'a particularly conservative political outlook that extends to its vision of global politics' (xi), and other commentators have concurred in this assessment of the form's intrinsic bias. Thus Patrick Holland and Graham Huggan, in what is perhaps the best recent survey of contemporary travel writing, suggest that the genre is often 'a refuge for complacent, even nostalgically retrograde, middle-class values' (1998: viii). Robyn Davidson, meanwhile, believes that

the recent surge of popular interest in the genre is underpinned
by nostalgia for a period

> when home and abroad, occident and orient, centre and periphery
> were unproblematically defined. Perhaps [travel books] are popular for
> the very reason they are so deceptive. They create the illusion that
> there is still an uncontaminated Elsewhere to discover.
>
> (2002: 6)

These commentators would contest the *Granta* view that contemporary travel writing offers us powerful insights into the
modern, globalised world. Instead, they regard the form as typically seeking not to reflect or explore contemporary realities,
but rather to escape them. In an age when many cultures and
societies are less homogeneous than they once were, and when
many people possess what is sometimes termed a 'hyphenated'
identity (British Asian, for example, or African American), distinctions between 'them' and 'us', 'home' and 'abroad', seem less
sharp than they used to. Travel writing responds to this situation,
it is alleged, by reinstating a firm sense of the differences that
pertain between cultures, regions and ethnicities, and by dealing
in stereotypes that are frequently pernicious. And by doing so, it is
suggested, the genre usually delivers a consoling, self-congratulatory
message to the privileged, middle-class Westerners who are its
principal readership.

As this will suggest, the recent wave of academic interest
in travel writing should not necessarily be regarded as a straightforward endorsement or celebration of the form. Whilst travel
writing undoubtedly constitutes a useful resource in a range of
ongoing scholarly debates, many researchers seek to read individual
travelogues 'against the grain', so to speak, so as to decipher and
critique their larger **ideological** implications and geopolitical consequences. This is the case not only with contemporary but also
with historical travel writing, where scholars have generally been
most concerned to trace the genre's complicity in the crimes and
injustices inflicted by European imperialism; its contribution to
the racist beliefs and ideologies that were so common in the high
imperial period, for example, and its role in promoting racial and

cultural supremacism. When one combines these critiques of both past and present travel writing, accordingly, it would seem that the current academic verdict on the genre is fairly damning. Travel writing, one might easily surmise from much of the recent scholarly literature on the topic, is a somewhat distasteful and morally dubious literary form; and even if it is not intrinsically so, then this is seemingly an appropriate verdict on how most writers have historically used the genre.

However, travel writing also has academic defenders. Mark Cocker, for example, declares that 'travel is one of the greatest doors to human freedom, and the travel book is a medium through which humans celebrate this freedom' (1992: 260). This is perhaps a little vague and grandiloquent; it certainly begs many questions as to who historically has been able to exercise this freedom, and the extent to which such freedom may come at the expense of others. Discussing the travel writers associated with *Granta*, meanwhile, Jim Philip suggests that the best recent travel writing works to foster an internationalist vision, and implicitly, a cosmopolitan attitude that encourages tolerance, understanding and a sense of global community. Or as Philip puts it, 'it may be possible ... to read these texts as a site of the emergence, however tentatively, of a new kind of international *society* ... capable both of figuring and of opposing those forces of capital which have preceded it upon the global scene' (White 1993: 251, emphasis in the original). Holland and Huggan, for their part, soften their often trenchant critique of contemporary travel writing with an acknowledgement of the form's 'defamiliarizing capacities' (1998: viii). They suggest that travelogues may serve as 'a useful vehicle of cultural self-perception', thereby showing 'readers the limits of their ambition and remind[ing] them of their responsibilities' (xiii). With regard to the travel writing of earlier eras, similarly, some scholars have pointed out that travelogues may vary greatly in the extent of their complicity with European imperialism, and that their consequences were not always wholly baleful and exploitative. As Dennis Porter has written, whilst European travel writing at its worst has often been 'a vehicle for the expression of Eurocentric conceit or racist intolerance', at its best the genre has also constituted a worthy attempt 'to overcome cultural distance through a protracted act of understanding' (1991: 3).

As this will suggest, the recent burgeoning of academic interest in travel writing has been accompanied by considerable controversy and debate about the merits and morality of the genre. The purpose of the present volume, it should stressed, is not to adjudicate in these arguments over the ethical implications of travel writing. Rather, it aims to equip readers to form their own opinion on several key debates currently associated with the genre. To this end, the volume is organised around some of the principal issues or themes in the recent scholarly literature on travel writing. Chapter 2 discusses the basic but complex issue of how we define travel writing, and considers the many different forms that the genre can take. Chapter 3 then offers a brisk overview of the evolution of travel writing, or at least of Western travel writing, from the ancient period to the present day, whilst Chapter 4 addresses the problems of authority and reliability connected with travel writing, exploring the diverse strategies by which writers have historically attempted to convey, and readers to assess, the truthfulness of travel accounts. Chapter 5 considers the autobiographical aspects of travel writing, and examines the diverse ways in which travelogues can become an exploration not so much of the wider world, as of the traveller's own selfhood and subjectivity. Perhaps the most fraught debate currently attendant on travel writing is then discussed in Chapter 6, that of the ethical and political implications of travel writing's fundamental agenda of offering images and representations of other peoples and other cultures. And finally, Chapter 7 considers how issues of gender and sexuality impinge on travel and travel writing; it addresses firstly the extent to which travel writing has often constituted a highly masculinised medium of self-expression and self-fashioning, before going on to discuss the many women who have nevertheless utilised the genre to their own ends, and the constraints that they have had to negotiate in so doing.

The volume focuses principally on travel writing produced in what one can loosely call 'the West': that is to say, Europe and North America, and the cultural tradition stretching back to the Ancient Greeks to which modern Europeans and Americans, rightly or wrongly, lay claim. Further to this, the focus also falls mainly on travel accounts written in English by British and American travellers, and on the British and American contexts for those accounts. Travel writing has of course been produced by non-Western cultures (see, *inter alia*, Plutschow 2006; Euben 2008), and within the Western tradition there have been many travelogues produced by travellers of French, German, Italian and other national origins (see Polezzi 2001; Forsdick 2005; Martin 2008). As Loredana Polezzi has noted, this non-Anglophone travel literature has received comparatively little attention in British and American studies of travel writing, which have tended 'to marginalize texts written in languages other than English, for readerships other than English-speaking ones' (2001: 1). The present volume perpetuates this tendency, although it does at least seek to alert readers to important examples of travel writing produced in non-English speaking cultures. Yet the themes and issues broached in the chapters that follow are undoubtedly relevant to every form of travel text, in every culture and every period. In addressing these topics, therefore, the volume will equip readers with a conceptual framework, and a critical vocabulary, that should prove useful whatever form or tradition of travel writing they are interested in, and whatever disciplinary perspective they adopt on the genre.

2

DEFINING THE GENRE

To travel is to make a journey, a movement through space. Possibly this journey is epic in scale, taking the traveller to the other side of the world or across a continent, or up a mountain; possibly it is more modest in scope, and takes place within the limits of the traveller's own country or region, or even just their immediate locality. Either way, to begin any journey or, indeed, simply to set foot beyond one's own front door, is quickly to encounter difference and otherness. All journeys are in this way a confrontation with, or more optimistically a negotiation of, what is sometimes termed **alterity**. Or, more precisely, since there are no foreign peoples with whom we do not share a common humanity, and probably no environment on the planet for which we do not have some sort of prior reference point, all travel requires us to negotiate a complex and sometimes unsettling interplay between alterity *and* identity, difference *and* similarity.

One definition that we can give of travel, accordingly, is that it is the negotiation between self and other that is brought about by movement in space. Like all such definitions, of course, this is inevitably somewhat reductive, and begs innumerable further questions. For example, are all forms of movement through space really to be regarded as travel? What of a trip to the local shops? Or a quick visit to one's neighbours? And if some journeys are not to be classified as 'travel', at what point, and according to what criteria, does that label become appropriate? Equally, do we need to distinguish between various types of travel, and between different sorts of traveller? How do the journeys undertaken by a tourist differ from those made by an explorer or a refugee? Are some forms of travel more praiseworthy or more valuable than others? These are all valid questions. For the time being, however, I shall set them aside so as to offer, on the basis of the minimal definition of *travel* just outlined, an equally minimal definition of *travel writing*.

If all travel involves an encounter between self and other that is brought about by movement through space, all travel writing is at some level a record or product of this encounter, and of the negotiation between similarity and difference that it entailed. Sometimes the encounter will be described directly in the writing, which will accordingly offer a narration of the events that occurred during the writer's travels. In other instances, the encounter itself will only be implicit in the writing, as it offers an account not of the actual travelling but of just the new perspectives or the new information acquired through travel. In certain extreme forms, indeed, the writing might consist of nothing more than a simple list or catalogue of new data gathered on the journey. Even travel writing in this sparse, **non-narrative** mode, however, is underpinned by, and emerges from, an encounter between self and other precipitated by movement. Consequently, all travel writing has a two-fold aspect. It is most obviously, of course, a report on the wider world, an account of an unfamiliar people or place. Yet it is also revelatory to a greater or lesser degree of the traveller who produced that report, and of his or her values, preoccupations and assumptions. And, by extension, it also reveals something of the culture from which that writer emerged, and/or the culture for which their text is intended.

Again, this is obviously a definition which begs many questions. For example, are all the forms of writing that can emerge from the travel experience to be classified as travel writing? Some readers will not be inclined to class a mere list or catalogue of data as travel writing, and a similar hesitation will probably be felt towards many other texts that undoubtedly have their origins in, and to some extent report back on, a traveller's negotiation of otherness. What of highly specialised academic treatises in fields like geography and anthropology? What of bulletins and articles sent back to newspapers and magazines by foreign correspondents? What of a novel such as Graham Greene's *A Burnt-Out Case* (1961), which is based on Greene's own visits to leper colonies in the Congo? Or even Henry James's novels, which one might not immediately associate with travel but which all reflect James's exposure to the cultural differences between America and Europe? Are all of these texts to be regarded as travel writing in some form, or should they be seen as distinct from travel writing? And if we take the latter course, by what criteria do we exclude these texts from the travel writing genre?

As these questions will suggest, it is no easy matter to provide a neat and unproblematic definition, or delimitation, of what counts as travel writing. The term is a very loose generic label, and has always embraced a bewilderingly diverse range of material. This is especially the case as one moves back in time, to consider travel writing in its earlier manifestations. Simultaneously, and partly as a result of this intrinsic heterogeneity, travel writing has always maintained a complex and confusing relationship with any number of closely related (indeed, often overlapping) genres. As Jonathan Raban notes,

> travel writing is a notoriously raffish open house where different genres are likely to end up in the same bed. It accommodates the private diary, the essay, the short story, the prose poem, the rough note and polished table talk with indiscriminate hospitality.
>
> (1988: 253–54)

Other commentators emphasise not only the genre's formal diversity, but also its thematic and tonal range. Thus Patrick Holland and Graham Huggan, surveying travel writing in the late twentieth century, stress that the form can embrace everything 'from picaresque adventure to philosophical treatise, political commentary, ecological parable, and spiritual quest', whilst simultaneously 'borrow[ing] freely from history, geography, anthropology and social science'. The result, they suggest, is a 'hybrid genre that straddles categories and disciplines' (1998: 8–9).

One consequence of this heterogeneity and hybridity is that it is often hard to define where 'travel writing' ends and other genres begin, such as autobiography, ethnography, **nature writing** and fiction. The boundaries of the travel writing genre are in this way fuzzy, rather than firmly fixed: what we class as travel writing, and what we exclude from the genre, are perennially matters of debate, and may vary according to the questions we bring to bear on the genre. Accordingly, the present chapter does not seek to identify any universal or essential features supposedly possessed by *all* forms of travel writing, beyond the minimal definition given earlier. Nor does it lay down any rules as to what is 'really' or 'properly' travel writing, and what is not. Instead, it begins by discussing the taxonomic debates that have surrounded the genre in recent academic discourse, and the various ways in which the term 'travel writing' has been defined by scholars. Thereafter, it explores two key areas of ambiguity and dispute that have always been attendant on the form, so much so that they are almost constitutive of the generic category 'travel writing'. These are, first, the relationship between fact and fiction in travel writing, and, second, the question of the literary value and intellectual status of travel writing; and by mapping these debates, the chapter seeks not so much to define 'travel writing', as to convey a sense of the diverse forms and modes that the genre has taken historically.

EXCLUSIVE AND INCLUSIVE DEFINITIONS OF 'TRAVEL WRITING'

In my local bookshop, there is a whole floor designated as 'Travel'. It stocks, at a rough estimate, several thousand publications, the majority of which are guidebooks: *Lonely Planets*, *Rough Guides* and the like. The guidebooks occupy approximately two-thirds of the available space on the floor, with the rest being given over to three sub-sections entitled 'Maps', 'Travel Photography' and 'Travel Literature'. 'Maps' is self-explanatory, whilst 'Travel Photography' consists chiefly of beautiful images of exotic locations, reproduced in an expensive, 'coffee-table' format. In 'Travel Literature', meanwhile, we find book-length accounts of journeys that have already been made, and the personal narratives of famous and not-so-famous travellers ranging from Marco Polo and Columbus through to contemporary figures such as Bruce Chatwin, Dervla Murphy, Bill Bryson and Michael Palin.

Clearly, there is a wealth of travel-related material available in the shop. Yet it is equally clear that these different sorts of publication relate to travel, or are about travel, in very different ways. So are they all to be regarded as 'travel writing'? Unfortunately, there is little scholarly consensus on the matter. Some commentators take the term 'travel writing' to mean just the material that tends to be classified in bookshops as 'Travel Literature'; this is perhaps especially the case in studies concerned principally with modern travel writing, and with travel accounts produced in the twentieth and twenty-first centuries. Other critics, meanwhile, use the label 'travel writing' in a much more expansive and inclusive sense, so as to include not only all the travel-related publications outlined earlier, but also many other forms of travel-related document or cultural artefact.

An influential advocate of the more narrow and exclusive conceptualisation of the term 'travel writing' is the critic Paul Fussell. Fussell's *Abroad: British Literary Travelling Between the Wars* (1980) was a seminal study of travel writing which did much to focus critical attention on a genre often previously dismissed as insignificant and sub-literary. At the same time, *Abroad*, along with Fussell's subsequent *Norton Anthology of Travel* (1987), introduced into the scholarly discussion of both travel and travel writing a set of taxonomical distinctions and categories that are still widely used today, although there are also many scholars who find them deeply problematic. For Fussell, the term 'travel writing' implicitly equates with the literary form he prefers to call the 'travel book', although he acknowledges that other terms such as 'travelogue' are also sometimes used. Whatever name one uses, however, Fussell insists that the proper travel book needs to be sharply distinguished from other forms of travel-related text, such as the exploration account and especially, the guidebook.

Hence his magisterial declaration that 'just as tourism is not travel, the guidebook is not the travel book' (1987: 15); and as we shall see, Fussell is a critic much given to emphatic pronouncements as to what counts as 'real' travel and 'real' travel writing.

So what formal and/or thematic features define, for Fussell, the proper 'travel book'? Essentially what he means by this term is the material classified in many bookshops as 'travel *literature*'. These publications are almost invariably extended prose **narratives**, often broken up into chapters, and in this way they generally resemble novels, visually and formally, far more than they resemble guidebooks (or at least, modern guidebooks). In the latter, there may be sections of prose narrative, but these are usually kept short, and interspersed with maps, tables, lists, symbols and other non-narrative modes of presenting information. Travel books, meanwhile, may include illustrative material, such as maps or pictures, but usually these elements are secondary to the main prose narrative, and a much smaller proportion of the text is given over to them.

Further to this, the narrative offered by a travel book will almost invariably be a retrospective, first-person account of the author's own experience of a journey, or of an unfamiliar place or people. What is more, the personal or subjective aspect of that narrative is often very pronounced, as we are made keenly aware not just of the places being visited, but also of the author's response to that place, and his or her impressions, thoughts and feelings. For this reason, Paul Fussell suggests that the form is best regarded as

> a sub-species of memoir in which the autobiographical narrative arises from the speaker's encounter with distant or unfamiliar data, and in which the narrative – unlike that in a novel or a romance – claims literal validity by constant reference to actuality.
>
> (1980: 203)

This emphasis on an autobiographical narrative, and the author's personal experience of another people or place, again distinguishes travel books from guidebooks, since in the latter the writer (or quite possibly, the team of writers) usually dispenses with any direct account of the research trips required to produce the text.

It is the practical information gathered on these trips that is of paramount importance in a guidebook, not the personal experiences of the author(s). In most travel books, however, it is evidently assumed that we will find the author, and his or her distinctive sensibility and style, as interesting as the place they are visiting. This contrasts not only with the modern guidebook, in which authors are usually more self-effacing, but also with many forms of travel document or text in which the emphasis is overwhelmingly on presenting information about the place being described. The latter tend to be classified by Fussell as accounts of 'exploration' or 'discovery', and to be seen accordingly as a genre distinct from the true or proper travel book.

Closely entwined with Fussell's insistence that the true travel book has a pronounced personal or subjective element is the understanding that the agenda in the travel book is not merely functional or practical. Rather, the emphasis in these texts upon foregrounding the author's distinctive sensibility and style is felt to confer upon the travel book a literary dimension. The travel book, accordingly, is for Fussell usually a first-person account of travel that may be read for pleasure, and for its aesthetic merits, as much as for the useful information it provides. Style is thus as important as content in these texts. Again, this is an emphasis that sets them apart from guidebooks and other more functional forms of travel account or document, in which questions of style and aesthetic pleasure are subordinated to the main imperative of relaying information efficiently and accurately.

Finally, in the definition cited earlier, Fussell suggests that the travel book may be contrasted with a novel or **romance** by its claim to 'literal validity' and its 'constant reference to actuality'. By this, Fussell means that travel books profess to be a representation of a journey, and of events on that journey, *that really took place*. Thus they are, in short, a non-fictional rather than fictional form. Or as Mary Campbell puts it, 'the travel book is a kind of witness: it is generically aimed at the truth' (1988: 2–3). According to this criterion, fictive depictions of travel in novels such as Joseph Conrad's *Heart of Darkness* (1902) or Laurence Sterne's *Sentimental Journey* (1768) are not to be classed as travel books. Clearly they are closely mimicking or borrowing from the form by providing a first-person narration of the protagonist's journey, yet as Fussell and other critics have pointed out, the generic 'contract' that exists between the authors and readers of novels is usually significantly different to that which operates between the authors and readers of travel books. Whilst fiction may indeed describe real-life events, the reader understands that the writer is not obliged to recount those events accurately. They may be embellished or adapted or used selectively; interwoven with them, more often than not, will be scenes that are wholly the product of the writer's imagination. In the travel book, however, such embellishments and outright inventions are more problematic. Generally speaking, travel writers do not have the same licence as novelists simply to make things up; to do so is to risk one's narrative being classed as fiction, or worse, as fraudulent.

That said, this seemingly clear distinction between the non-fictional travel book and the fictional novel *about* travel is actually a lot more problematic than one might initially assume. It is also highly problematic to suggest, as Fussell often seems to, that it is only travel books of the sort he describes which can be considered travel writing, or at least 'proper' or 'real' travel writing. Setting both these issues aside for the time being, however, the 'travel book' as defined by Fussell undoubtedly corresponds to one very important and prominent branch of the travel writing genre, in modern times at least. And Fussell has further useful insights to offer as to the appeal of these travel books. Obviously they will usually be educative to some degree, offering their readers interesting observations about the peoples or places visited by the author. At the same time, however, as Fussell astutely notes, the modern travel book also offers its reader something akin to the narrative pleasure of a novel or romance, notwithstanding its claim to be a non-fictional genre. Often, for example, these accounts are underpinned, either explicitly or implicitly, by the mythic motif of the quest. Thus the travel book typically begins with the narrator setting out from his or her home, either in search of some specific goal or else generally seeking adventures, new experiences and interesting stories. On the road, and occupying the liminal position of traveller, the narrator undergoes important, possibly life-changing experiences, before returning home to be reintegrated into his or her own society. Usually, moreover, he or she returns enriched, either literally or metaphorically, by the journey; after all, the very fact that a narrative is subsequently produced is implicitly a statement that these adventures had some significance. Thus for Fussell, borrowing his terminology from the critic Northrop Frye, the travel book can be understood as a form of 'displaced quest romance' (1980: 209). 'Displaced', because the quest elements are translated from the fantastical realm of pure romance or myth into a reality that is usually more mundane than the world we encounter in romance. He further suggests that these 'displaced romances' come in two main modes: a '**picaresque**' mode, in which the emphasis is simply on relating a sequence of adventures and misadventures, and an '**elegiac**' or '**pastoral**' mode, in which the emphasis is on seeking out the last vestiges of a vanishing way of life, or a culture perceived as less complex and less stressful than the traveller's own.

These, then, are some of the key features of the genre that Paul Fussell labels the 'travel book', but that I would want to call more precisely the *modern* or *literary* travel book. Before explaining why I make this qualification, however, it should be noted that this is a form of writing that admits of enormous diversity, even as it conforms, more or less, to the definition just given of it. In the first place, and most obviously, travel books may vary greatly in the destinations they describe and the itineraries they recount; and in this regard, it is worth noting that whilst many travel writers set off for far-flung regions, there is also a well-established literature of 'home travels', in which writers variously celebrate, lament or poke fun at their compatriots, and at the state of their own nation (see Moir 1964; Kinsley 2008). More significantly, however, modern travel books also exhibit a remarkable range in terms of style and tone, form and structure, the personae adopted, the degree of 'literary' aspiration, and in much else besides. The genre admits of both very serious and very humorous writing, and tonally can encompass everything from earnest polemic to inconsequential whimsy, from poetic lyricism to crude farce. It also spans the complete spectrum of what one might term '**highbrow**', 'middle-brow' and '**low-brow**' writing. That is to say, some travel books clearly aspire to the status of 'literature', through the gravity of the topics they discuss or the sophistication of their writing, whilst others make no such cultural claim, being unashamedly exercises in easy reading and/or sensationalism.

Structurally, there can be a similar degree of variation. Although most modern travel books will recount an actual journey undertaken by the author, and organise their narratives according to the itinerary of this journey, this is not always the case. Some will not describe any actual travelling, but just a period spent residing in an unfamiliar place: William Dalrymple's *City of Djinns* (1993), for example, which recounts a year spent in Delhi, India. In travel books that do narrate a journey, meanwhile, that journey can be given a very different degree of prominence in the narrative. Sometimes it will figure greatly, and be the object of significant and sustained attention in the text. On other occasions, however, it will seem largely incidental, as the writer uses the travel theme as little more than a peg on which to hang a series of essays or reflections, which may well be largely unrelated to the journey being undertaken. The extent to which the narrative focuses on, or reveals, the narratorial self may also vary greatly. For Fussell, as we have seen, the travel book is a 'sub-species' of memoir, and as we shall see in Chapter 5 there are indeed many travel books which seem principally concerned to narrate a journey into the self. Yet the genre also includes accounts like Jan Morris's *Venice* (1960), in which the author is highly self-effacing, so that personal information is only revealed occasionally, and usually indirectly, as a by-product of the observations being made about the destination.

Finally, while many modern travel writers are clearly chiefly concerned to afford their readers entertainment and aesthetic pleasure, be it in the form of broad comedy or fine, elegant writing, there are also some whose concerns are more urgent and pragmatic. Some modern travel books seem closer in spirit to investigative journalism than to memoir or fiction: Norman Lewis's *The Missionaries* (1988), for example, or George Monbiot's *Poisoned Arrows* (1989). In these accounts, any desire to entertain the reader is arguably secondary to the more important aim of reporting the dubious practices of US missionaries in Latin America (in Lewis's case), or the extent of environmental devastation in Indonesia (in

Monbiot's case). As this suggests, different travelogues can strike a very different balance between informing and entertaining the reader. Some are much more literary in aspiration, or entertainment-oriented; others, meanwhile, lean more towards reportage and journalism.

It will be apparent that the **modern travel book** is a flexible genre encompassing some highly diverse material. Its variant forms, indeed, arguably begin to stretch and problematise the definition of the genre advanced by Fussell. And as one looks back at the travel writing produced in earlier eras, further difficulties arise with Fussell's definition of the travel book; or alternatively, with any suggestion that we can equate travel writing in its entirety with the form Fussell calls the travel book. Prior to 1900, in the English-speaking world at least, contemporaries usually talked of a genre called 'voyages and travels', rather than 'travel writing' or the 'travel book'. The term 'voyages and travels' embraced an enormous diversity of travel-related texts, that took a variety of different forms and served many functions: ships' logs; travellers' journals and letters; the reports of merchants or spies or diplomats; accounts of exploration, pilgrimage, and colonial conquest and administration; narratives of shipwreck; accounts of captivity amongst foreign peoples and much else besides. Some of these texts can be understood as travel books, if by travel books we simply mean first-person, non-fictional accounts of travel. But in many other regards, they are often not much like the travel books we are used to today, or the travel book as defined by Paul Fussell.

Fussell, it will be recalled, defines the travel book as a 'sub-species of memoir', a definition justified by the pronounced emphasis on the narratorial self that characterises most modern travel books. Surveying material from the 'voyages and travels' era, however, this tenet about the form is swiftly confounded, or at least, complicated. Most travel books written before the late eighteenth century will strike modern readers as remarkably impersonal and un-autobiographical, even when they are written in the first person. Typically, the emphasis falls not on the subjective thoughts and feelings of the writer, but on the information gathered during the journey: the topography of foreign countries, for example, or details of their customs, military capabilities, and principal trading commodities. In some cases, it is still appropriate to regard these narratives as a form of memoir, although we potentially misread them if we approach them with expectations formed by modern travel books, and so fail to recognise the very different rhetorical conventions governing the literary presentation of the self in earlier eras. In other cases, however, it would seem to make little sense to consider these travel books as memoirs. There are accounts of voyages and travels, for example, in which the first-person narrative is just the flimsiest of frameworks, perhaps no more than a few sentences at the beginning and end of a text, between which the writer inserts the data accumulated during travel. The generic label also embraced many accounts which offer no personal narrative of a journey at all, just information relative to travel or to foreign places. Thus Richard Hakluyt's *Principall Navigations* (1589; 2nd edition, 1598–1600), generally regarded as the first great compendium of travel writing in English, includes a document which is simply a list of all the items needed to undertake a successful whaling expedition.

Other distinctions and definitions central to Fussell's conceptualisation of the 'travel book' are also confounded when one goes back to the 'voyages and travels' era. The clear distinction between travel book and guidebook, for example, often breaks down in travel accounts published before 1800, as writers include passages of highly practical advice to prospective travellers within a more personal and 'literary' narrative. Many of these accounts also blur Fussell's strict demarcation between, on the one hand, texts arising from travel that principally follow a functional agenda, and on the other, more aesthetically oriented travel books. Broadly speaking, most 'voyages and travels' texts were far more concerned to disseminate useful data than the modern travel book – hence the comparative impersonality of tone noted earlier. At the same time, however, this emphasis did not necessarily preclude them from being received with great pleasure by many readers. In this regard, the opposition that Fussell seeks to establish between the aesthetic and the functional is both simplistic and anachronistic. We may see works that are principally concerned to give us information as outside the domain of proper 'literature', but earlier eras seem to have defined this category more expansively, embracing as 'literary' many texts that today strike us as very dry and factual.

Hence the importance of prefixing an adjective such as 'modern' or 'literary' to Fussell's notion of the travel book. There were plenty of publications concerned with travel or about travel, not to mention an abundance of unpublished travel-related material such as letters and journals, prior to the nineteenth century, but many of them do not conform with Fussell's definition of the form. But what then should we call all these earlier accounts of travel, if they are not travel books in the sense defined by Fussell? And even if they are not exactly 'travel books', should we still classify them as 'travel writing'?

For Fussell, and for other critics who adopt his taxonomic categories, these texts are regarded as emerging from an era, and an activity, that is designated 'pre-travel' (see Fussell 1987: 21; Blanton 2002: 4–5). Or alternatively, they describe them as emerging from an era not of 'travel' but of 'exploration' (see Fussell 1980: 37–39). This is understood to be an age in which the information gathered by the traveller was still very much at a premium. This agenda, it is suggested, makes the travel writing of this era an essentially utilitarian and functional form, which is unconcerned with any presentation of the authorial self in the text, or with any self-conscious crafting of the text as an aesthetic artefact. Yet this is a far from satisfactory schema, for many reasons. Most notably, it frequently leads Fussell to the somewhat absurd proposition that there was no travel writing, and indeed, no 'proper' travel, before about 1750. For Fussell, we should note, the term 'travel' is rightfully applied to just some forms and expressions of human mobility, and it is not every human being who has made a journey who qualifies, in Fussell's eyes, for the honorific title of 'traveller'. At various points, accordingly, his definitions of real travel deny this status to, *inter alia*, the Spanish conquistadors, and to refugees, exiles and other forms of displaced people. Elsewhere, espousing a distinction frequently made by modern commentators on travel, he also suggests that modern tourists are not to be classed as true travellers. Whole epochs are similarly dismissed by Fussell. Thus he asks of the Ancient period, 'there is plenty of movement from place to place, but is

UNIVERSITY OF WINCHESTER
LIBRARY

there really travel?' (1987: 21). He answers in the negative, producing a rather circular rationale to justify this assessment. As we shall see in the next chapter, classical writers such as Herodotus and Pausanias certainly produced texts that are in diverse ways either the product of travel, or about travel. Yet none of these texts meet Fussell's criteria for the travel book, and from this apparent absence of 'proper' travel books Fussell deduces that there were no genuine travellers in the Ancient world.

In part, Fussell is here engaged in a very useful discrimination between different sorts of human mobility. But to refuse to categorise explorers, conquistadors, refugees, tourists and so forth as types of traveller arguably flies in the face of common sense and the customary usage of the terms 'travel' and 'traveller'. What is more, Fussell's rather rarefied notion of what constitutes 'real' or 'proper' travel is frequently shot through with personal prejudices that smack of elitism and sexism. For Fussell, it seems, there was only a tiny epoch of human history when anyone travelled in the 'proper' sense: roughly, the nineteenth century and the first half of the twentieth century, when people began to have the leisure to undertake travel simply for travel's sake, but before a modern, mass-touristic infrastructure emerged to excessively stage-manage the journey. Proper travel, Fussell repeatedly insists, is no longer possible: the best we can hope for now is what he terms 'post-tourism' (1987: 753–57). Even when it was possible, moreover, proper travel was seemingly a male rather than a female accomplishment. Or so one might infer from Fussell's writings, which generally pay little attention to women travellers and travel writers.

Fussell, then, defines 'proper' travel in a decidedly narrow and exclusive fashion, and he derives from this definition of proper travel an equally narrow definition of the proper 'travel book', one that excludes many types of writing that have certainly been regarded in earlier eras as 'travel writing', or at least, as 'voyages and travels'. Unsurprisingly, therefore, some critics have found Fussell's definitions of 'travel', 'traveller' and 'travel book' too simplistic to adequately account for or describe what has always been a highly protean genre. Many critics accordingly define the genre in a broader, more inclusive fashion, especially when they are dealing with the travel writing of earlier periods. Zweder von

Martels, for example, suggests that the term 'travel writing' can embrace material ranging 'from guidebooks, itineraries and routes and perhaps also maps to ... accounts of journeys over land or water, or just descriptions of experiences abroad' (1994: xi). In this way von Martels sees guidebooks and travel books not as starkly opposed genres, as Fussell does, but as two branches of the same genre, and this seems historically justified when one takes a longer view of the form. One might add here that a historical perspective similarly problematises any sense of a sharp and intrinsic distinction between travel writing and ethnography. Critics such as Fussell who equate the term 'travel writing' with the form I have labelled the modern travel book generally assume that these are two different genres, with travel writing being characterised by a more personal and idiosyncratic approach to the topic in hand, and ethnography by a more scientific methodology and mode of discourse. Prior to the nineteenth century, however, this scientific methodology and style did not exist. Instead, ethnographic information often circulated, and ethnographic enquiry and debate were often conducted, in forms of writing more akin to the modern travel book than the modern ethnographic study.

These historical complexities, and the highly diverse forms of travel-related writing that exist both in our own time and in earlier eras, have led Jan Borm to make a very useful distinction between the 'travel book' and 'travel writing'. The former he defines in more or less the same way as Fussell, as a first-person, ostensibly non-fictional narrative of travel. Unlike Fussell, however, Borm does not insist that the travel book has to be 'literary' and to follow primarily an aesthetic agenda. Borm's notion of the 'travel book' is thus more straightforwardly a formal description than Fussell's. And crucially, Borm does not equate the 'travel book' with 'travel writing' in its entirety. Rather, the latter is understood to be 'a collective term for a variety of texts both fictional and non-fictional whose main theme is travel' (2004: 13). This seems an eminently sensible suggestion, although it risks expanding the category 'travel writing' to such an extent that the term loses any explanatory or descriptive usefulness. After all, movement is one of the most fundamental of human activities, and there is consequently, as Peter Hulme has pointed out, very little 'statuesque literature'

(Hulme and Youngs 2007: 3). That is to say, there are few literary texts that do not make some reference to travel, and/or offer some representation of movement through space. For the French theorist Michel de Certeau, indeed, 'every story is a travel story', and he goes on to suggest that the act of writing is itself, fundamentally and intrinsically, a form of travel, and that travel conversely is always a form of writing (2001: 89).

For de Certeau, then, all writing is travel writing. This is a definition that broadens the generic category of 'travel writing' to such an extent that it becomes meaningless and unhelpful. Yet Borm's essentially thematic definition, which insists only that travel form the 'main theme' of a text, arguably takes us some distance in the same direction. Borm's definition, for example, embraces both fictional and non-fictional texts, and so allows Conrad's *Heart of Darkness* and Sterne's *Sentimental Journey* to be classed as forms of travel writing. This expansion of the genre can perhaps be justified on the grounds that a novel just as much as a non-fictional travelogue may present a highly informative account, born of the author's firsthand experience, of an unfamiliar people or place. Moreover, fictional as well as non-fictional accounts can shape powerfully our perceptions of other peoples and places. *Heart of Darkness*, for example, is arguably the seminal modern account of the Congo; for good and for bad, it has influenced profoundly the West's image of the region, and the attitudes of most subsequent travellers there. For a variety of reasons, then, it may make sense in some discursive contexts to regard both fictional and non-fictional accounts of journeys, and/or of places, as closely related sub-species of travel writing.

Yet if we accept that novels may be a form of travel writing, where do we draw the line? Given that almost all novels will feature journeys of some description, how prominent does the travel dimension in a novel have to be for it to constitute a *main* theme? Must the journeys described have been made by the novelists themselves for their fictions to count as travel writing, or can the genre also include fictional journeys that are wholly imagined by the author? And what of fictions that are clearly born from the author's own travel experiences, but which do not address the travel theme directly, such as some of Henry James's novels?

Furthermore, if one accepts fictional texts as a form of travel writing, what of poetry? Von Martels, interestingly, suggests that poetic as well as prose works can legitimately be considered travel writing (1994: xi). Again, this has some justification on historical grounds, given that Hakluyt includes in *Principall Navigations* 'Letters in verse, written by Master George Turberville, out of Muscovy 1568'. Yet it potentially expands the genre vastly, opening up whole new areas of debate as to what does and does not count as travel writing. Turberville's poem is essentially a versified list of observations about the Russian people, and insofar as its agenda is principally ethnographic rather than aesthetic, it seems easily assimilable to the travel writing genre. But what of more overtly literary poems such as Byron's *Childe Harold's Pilgrimage* (1812–18), or Elizabeth Bishop's *Questions of Travel* (1956)? Or even Wordsworth's 'I wandered lonely as a cloud'? Poems such as these give us first-hand accounts of journeys that we assume to have some basis in reality, and to be rooted in the experience of the 'I' of the poem. So can we categorise them as travel writing?

It should also be noted that von Martels tentatively classifies maps as a form of travel writing. One might protest that maps cannot be classed as a form of writing, since they principally employ visual modes of representation. But they can of course be construed as 'texts', insofar as they are artfully constructed representations of the world that are often ideologically charged and laden with larger cultural meanings. In this respect, accordingly, one might plausibly include maps in the travel writing genre. Yet if one includes maps one presumably also has to include other visual media such as paintings and sketches, photographs, television programmes and films; and so not only *Heart of Darkness*, but also Francis Ford Coppola's filmic reworking of Conrad's novella, *Apocalypse Now* (1979), arguably becomes a form of travel writing. Many readers, no doubt, will baulk at defining the genre so broadly. Yet it is worth noting that academic conferences on travel writing, and specialist journals such as *Studies in Travel Writing* and *Journeys*, will sometimes include papers focusing on depictions of travel, or of other peoples and places, in film, art and other visual media. Their inclusion reflects the fact that the representations offered in these media often work in similar ways, and with similar effects, to the representations offered in more obviously literary forms of travelogue; and for this reason it is in some contexts both useful and appropriate to subsume film, photography and so forth into the broader category 'travel writing'.

As this will suggest, it is possible to define 'travel writing' very broadly indeed. As a consequence, and given the range of material that has historically been classified as 'travel writing' or 'voyages and travels', there is probably no neat and all-encompassing definition of the form that one can give. The genre is perhaps better understood as a constellation of many different types of writing and/or text, these differing forms being connected not by conformity to a single, prescriptive pattern, but rather by a set of what the philosopher Ludwig Wittgenstein would call 'family resemblances'. That is to say, there are a variety of features or attributes that can make us classify a text as travel writing, and each individual text will manifest a different selection and combination of these attributes. Central to the genre, undoubtedly, is the form that both Fussell and Borm label the 'travel book': that is to say, the first-person, ostensibly non-fictional narrative of travel. But as we have seen, this is a branch of travel writing that in itself encompasses enormous variety, and so comes in more forms than some critics (notably Fussell) will acknowledge. Around the central form of the travel book, meanwhile, there circulates a still greater range of texts that can all potentially be understood either as branches and sub-genres of travel writing, or else as separate genres closely cognate with travel writing, and indeed sometimes merging into it: guidebooks, itineraries, novels with a pronounced travel theme, memoirs, writings of place, descriptions of the natural world, maps, road movies and much else besides.

Thus the boundaries of the travel writing genre are fuzzy, and there is little point in policing them too rigidly. But within this larger, looser generic label, one may certainly talk with greater precision of specific modes and sub-genres of travel writing: the medieval *peregrinatio* ('pilgrimage narrative'), for example, or the early modern 'relation', or the eighteenth-century exploration narrative, or the guidebooks of different eras, or indeed the modern travel book, which often draws upon and adapts all these different precursors and companion forms. Each of these sub-genres of travel writing, at each moment of its development, has its own history, its own rhetorical conventions, and its own role in the larger culture of which it is a part. And often it is important that we are attentive to these specific, sub-generic traditions and agendas, if we are not to read the various forms of travel writing inappropriately or anachronistically.

TRAVELLERS' TALES: FACT AND FICTION IN TRAVEL WRITING

However expansively one wants to define the category 'travel writing', a central branch of the genre is certainly the 'travel book', the first-person narrative of travel which claims to be a true record of the author's own experiences. Yet as so often with this protean and slippery genre, there are ambiguities and complexities attendant even on the seemingly straightforward statement that the travel book is a non-fictional form. For all travel writers find themselves having to negotiate two subtly different, and potentially conflicting, roles: that of reporter, as they seek to relay accurately the information acquired through travel, and that of story-teller, as they seek to maintain the reader's interest in that information, and to present it in an enjoyable, or at least easily digestible way. And the necessary negotiation of these two roles ensures that the distinction between 'fiction' and 'non-fiction' in travel writing is not as clear-cut as one might initially assume.

All examples of travel writing are by definition textual artefacts, that have been constructed by their writers and publishers. As Peter Hulme puts it, in a useful formulation, they have at the very least to be 'made', even if they are not supposed to be 'made up' (Hulme and Youngs 2007: 3). One cannot simply record the continuous flow of sensory experience that occurs as one travels; the sheer quantity of data would be overwhelming, as would the utter insignificance of most of it. Even in a form with the apparent immediacy of a travel journal or diary, a writer necessarily picks out significant recent events, and organises those events, and his or her reflections on them, into some sort of narrative, however brief. Travel *experience* is thus crafted into travel *text*, and this crafting process must inevitably introduce into the text, to a greater or lesser degree, a fictive dimension. At the very least, the inevitable filtering of the original travel experience gives a writer considerable scope to be, if not exactly deceitful, certainly economical with the truth. Thus there have been many travel writers over the years who have not deemed it necessary to inform readers that their journey was made with a companion, or companions, or possibly even a whole support team. In some cases, this information was suppressed so as to make the journey seem a more heroic undertaking; and here the careful tailoring of the travel account clearly pushes the text in the direction of fiction, even if the writer does not perpetrate any outright inventions or falsehoods.

In such ways, then, travel writing will often commit significant sins of omission that problematise its status as a wholly factual, truth-telling genre. At the same time, it is often guilty of sins of commission, and of subtle or not-so-subtle elements of fabrication in the telling of the travel tale. In the modern travel book especially, most episodes are clearly written up retrospectively by the writer, rather than being written on the spot. The writer may well have a good memory of the original events; quite possibly, indeed, he or she will also draw upon notes taken at the time. But obviously, there is again considerable scope for such recreated episodes to take on a fictive colouring. In some cases, the writer will opt for a narrative mode of '**showing**' rather than '**telling**', electing not just to report an encounter retrospectively, but rather to reconstruct it on the page in a more vivid and novelistic fashion. Atmosphere will be created through description and imagery; thoughts, feelings and motives may be imputed to other participants in the scene, possibly through devices such as **free indirect discourse**. Dialogue, meanwhile, will sometimes be rendered directly, as if the writer remembered the exact words spoken in a conversation, although this is of course highly unlikely unless the traveller was simultaneously taking notes, or in more recent times using some sort of audio or video device. Insofar as they utilise such literary devices, travel writers are arguably not so much reconstructing as constructing their experiences; inevitably what they offer their readers is a somewhat fictionalised rendering of their journeys.

A degree of fictionality is thus inherent in all travel accounts. Yet the extent to which travel writers weave fictional elements into their texts can of course vary greatly. At one end of the spectrum there are those writers who broadly seek to record faithfully their experiences, but who must necessarily edit, reconstruct, and so subtly distort, those experiences in the process of fashioning their narrative. At the other end of the spectrum, meanwhile, there are many writers who have more wilfully invented details and anecdotes. There is a long history of hoax travel narratives, for example, and these fake accounts in turn span a spectrum from playful literary experiments such as Thomas More's *Utopia* (1516) or Jonathan Swift's *Gulliver's Travels* (1726), which were always meant to be recognised as fictions, to more deliberate deceptions and frauds such as George Psalmanazar's *Historical and Geographical Description of Formosa* (1704). Even when travel writers recount journeys that did genuinely take place, moreover, there have been many authors who have fabricated some incidents and encounters, or exaggerated them, so as to capitalise on the reading public's perennial hunger for wonders, exotic curiosities and sensational titbits.

This is the further sense in which travel writers are often as much story-tellers as reporters. It is not just that they always have necessarily to construct their narratives; it is also that, historically, they have often had a pronounced propensity for tall tales and intriguing or amusing anecdotes. In Ancient Greek culture, revealingly, Hermes was the god of both travellers and liars. As this will suggest, travel writing has often been the focus of profound **epistemological** anxieties, as both writers and readers confront the difficult problem of distinguishing fact from fiction in the written text. Wrestling with this problem, and concerned to dissociate themselves from more fanciful or excessively subjective travel accounts, some modes of travel writing have developed protocols and stylistic conventions intended to reassure readers as to the reliability of the information they purvey. These will be discussed in more detail in Chapter 4. For other travel writers, meanwhile, this blurring of the boundary of fact and fiction, and the freedom to interweave story-telling and reportage, is arguably part of the attraction of the form. Thus recent decades have witnessed, at the more literary end of the genre, a wave of travel writing that one might broadly characterise as **postmodern** in outlook and expression. In travelogues of this type, the most famous examples being perhaps Bruce Chatwin's *In Patagonia* (1977) and *The Songlines* (1987), the traveller-narrators often seem to cast themselves in the role of trickster-figures. Self-consciously aligning themselves with travel writing's long tradition of tall tales and hoaxes, they playfully confound our conventional categories of fiction and non-fiction, in order to explore the competing claims of imagination, reason and moral responsibility in our engagement with the world.

It will be apparent that the label 'non-fiction', when applied to travel writing at least, is somewhat simplistic, and often in need of considerable qualification. For this reason, Paul Fussell would rather understand the genre as offering a '"creative" mediation between fact and fiction' (1980: 214). Or as Patrick Holland and Graham Huggan would have it, drawing upon the theoretical work of Hayden White (1976), most travel narratives should be regarded as 'fictions of factual representation' (Holland and Huggan 1998: 10), texts that for the most part offer us only the illusion of being faithful representations of the world, when in fact they are inevitably selective and fictive to some degree. Recognition of this fact should not lead us to assume that everything in a travelogue is made up, nor does it necessarily discredit the information that travelogues provide about the wider world. Yet clearly we always need to keep in mind that the apparent truthfulness and factuality of a travelogue is always to some degree a rhetorical effect; and we must remember also that any form of travel text is always a constructed, crafted artefact, which should never be read naively as just a transparent window on the world.

THE CULTURAL AND INTELLECTUAL STATUS OF TRAVEL WRITING

'Experience sought for the sake of writing about it may produce reporting, or travel books, but it is not likely to produce literature.' This comment by the American novelist Wallace Stegner (quoted in Kowaleswki 1992: 2) reflects a widespread attitude to travel writing in our culture today. The genre may well be popular, but more often than not it is often viewed dismissively by critics, possibly because of that very popularity. In our contemporary hierarchy of genres, travel writing sits significantly below more esteemed genres such as the novel. Hence, perhaps, the unease that some travel writers feel about being identified with the form. Jenni Diski, for example, admits that 'something about the idea of being a travel writer distresses me' (2006: 1). Bruce Chatwin was similarly uncomfortable with the label 'travel writer'; he fought a long and ultimately unsuccessful battle with his publishers to have *The Songlines* classified as fiction rather than travel writing. Even Paul Fussell feels compelled to ask, 'is there not perhaps something in the genre that attracts second-rate talents?' (1980: 212). He insists, however, that the genre has produced some literary masterpieces, instancing works such as Robert Byron's *The Road to Oxiana* (1937).

If modern travel writing in this way generally seems to fall short of full literary status, so too is it usually denied much credibility or authority as a scientific or intellectual discourse. As we have seen, the form straddles many generic boundaries, often moving into territory also covered by a broad range of academic disciplines, such as natural history, geography or anthropology. When this happens, however, modern travel books can usually be distinguished from more formal academic treatises by virtue of their more personal and more idiosyncratic approach. The result will often be a somewhat anecdotal account, pitched at the general reader, which eschews the arcane technical jargon and the more rigorous and systematic methodologies found in academic literature. Nigel Barley's *The Innocent Anthropologist: Notes from a Mud Hut* (1983) neatly illustrates this aspect of the genre. Barley is a professional anthropologist, and his narrative is an account of a period spent doing fieldwork amongst a West African tribe, the Dowayo. But his anthropological findings were presented more formally in *Symbolic Structures: An Exploration of the Culture of the Dowayo* (1983). This is a daunting structuralist ethnography, pitched at academic professionals, which keeps its focus very much on the object of academic enquiry, the Dowayo themselves. *The Innocent Anthropologist*, meanwhile, focuses in equal measure on the Dowayo and on Barley's experience of doing fieldwork amongst them. A far more accessible account of his fieldwork, it consists chiefly of a series of funny stories about Barley's time with the tribe; few serious anthropological conclusions are offered. For this reason it sits in the 'Travel' section of bookshops, not in the 'Anthropology' section.

Travel writing's relationship with ethnography is replicated in its relationship with most other academic disciplines. The genre has a resolutely amateur or dilettante aspect, or at least, it does in the twentieth and twenty-first centuries: as we shall see, this was not always the case in earlier periods. As a consequence, travel writing is generally perceived as not being at the cutting edge in terms of the factual information it provides. It is probably fair to say that if we were seriously concerned with science, or political debate, or the latest news from around the world, travel writing would not be the forum in which we would do our research or conduct our discussions. It is as if it is too 'literary' to qualify as a serious contribution in these areas, whilst simultaneously, and a little paradoxically, it is too factual and not literary enough for those readers and writers who prefer more obviously imaginative works such as novels. On both sides of its twin agenda of informing and entertaining, therefore, travel writing seems a rather second-order exercise; and consequently, it is very much a minor literary form in the eyes of many critics and commentators.

It must be stressed, however, that the dismissive attitude outlined earlier is principally directed towards travel writing in its modern, literary form; that is to say, towards the (sub-)genre defined earlier as the modern travel book. As we have seen, it is possible to take a more expansive view of the genre, whereby modern ethnography becomes simply one mode of travel writing, rather than a separate genre to be sharply distinguished from it. The same may be said for many other scientific texts which recount various types of fieldwork and travel. Further to this, it should also be noted that travel writing has not always been regarded as such a minor, inconsequential form. In this regard, as in many others, there are significant differences between what we now label 'travel writing' and the earlier, more eclectic genre known to contemporaries as 'voyages and travels'. In the eighteenth and nineteenth centuries, for example, 'voyages and travels' were central to the canon of respectable, desirable reading. The genre of course included many accounts that were regarded as superficial, or luridly sensational, yet at its best the form was felt to provide a wholly satisfactory blend of literary pleasure and useful knowledge. In part, this was because many travelogues of this period were at the forefront of scientific and intellectual enquiry, with explorers like James Cook, Mungo Park and Charles Darwin making important new geographical, zoological and ethnographical discoveries, and domestic travellers like Arthur Young making compelling interventions in contemporary social and economic debates. And in part, this different attitude to the genre derived from subtle differences in taste and aesthetic expectation. Eighteenth-century writers and readers do not seem to have perceived the same schism between imaginative and factual modes of writing as their modern counterparts, and so felt less anxiety about classing travel narratives as 'literature'. Some reasons why this attitude to travel writing evolved into our modern attitude to the genre will emerge over the course of this volume; for now, however, it will suffice to stress that the genre has not always held the somewhat minor, marginal status that it holds today.

3

TRAVEL WRITING THROUGH THE AGES

AN OVERVIEW

Around 1130 BCE, an Egyptian priest named Wenamon made a voyage from Thebes to Lebanon, to purchase for his temple a consignment of cedar wood. The trip was a disaster: Wenamon was robbed, chased by pirates and at one point almost killed, when he himself was mistaken for a pirate. Yet it did have one important outcome. Wenamon subsequently wrote a report on his misadventures, and that report has survived, albeit in a fragmentary condition; it constitutes, according to the historian Lionel Casson, 'the earliest detailed account of a voyage in existence' (1974: 39).

As this will suggest, travel writing has a long history, stretching back into antiquity. Indeed, if we expand our definition of the genre to include tales of travel passed on by word of mouth, it doubtless extends into prehistory. Human beings have probably always told stories about journeys made by themselves or their ancestors. In some cases, as in the still-surviving 'Songlines' of the Australian Aboriginal peoples, these stories may have combined practical usefulness with religious or spiritual observance, detailing routes through a landscape whilst simultaneously registering and reverencing the mythic significance of every landmark along that route. More generally, we can assume that they served variously to entertain, to pass on important knowledge, and to maintain the collective memory of tribal groups. But whatever their function, vestiges of older oral traditions are certainly apparent in some of the earliest written treatments of the travel theme, such as the *Epic of Gilgamesh* (c.1000 BCE), Homer's *Odyssey* (c.600 BCE), and the Biblical books of Genesis and Exodus (which reached their final written forms in the fifth century BCE).

Although a fictive account of a largely legendary traveller, it is *The Odyssey* that inaugurates the Western tradition specifically of travel *writing*. That is to say, it is both one of the earliest written accounts of travel, and also the first text that exerted a significant influence on subsequent travel literature, both fictional and non-fictional. The poem's episodic structure, its thematic focus on misadventure and problematic homecoming, and its presentation of its traveller-protagonist as a crafty, sometimes morally questionable individual, all provided templates that were taken up by many later writers, in connection with accounts of both real and imagined journeys. In what follows, accordingly, my principal concern is to trace from *The Odyssey* onwards the evolution first of European, and then subsequently, after the European settlement of America, of what I shall term Western travel writing.

THE ANCIENT WORLD

People travelled in ancient times for diverse reasons: to make war, or to escape it; to conduct trade by land or sea; to visit religious shrines and oracles; and to administer and maintain the various empires of the Ancient world, from the Egyptian through to the Roman. And from as early as 1500 BCE, it seems, some were travelling simply for recreational reasons, making visits to the Sphinx, the Great Pyramid and similar destinations principally in a spirit of sight-seeing (see Casson 1974: 32).

All this activity gave rise to a number of forms of travel-related text. Amongst the most basic and functional were the documents known as *periploi* in Greek, or *navigationes* in Latin (in the singular, *periplus* and *navigatio*). These provided navigational directions for sea captains. Usually they consisted of little more than a bare list of ports and coastal landmarks, together with an estimate of the distance between them; occasionally they might interweave a more detailed description of the voyage that had first reconnoitred this route. Equivalent documents existed for overland journeys, and were known in Latin as *itineraria* (singular, *itinerarium*).

More elaborate forms of travel writing are chiefly to be found, in the Classical era, in works that blur modern generic categories. Herodotus has been called the 'Father of History', but he can also be regarded as a travel writer, since his account of the Greco-Persian wars in *The Histories* (c.431–425 BCE) draws significantly on his own travels around the Mediterranean and Black Sea, and includes lengthy ethnographic digressions on the cultures he encountered. Strabo's *Geography* (c.7–24 CE) similarly includes information drawn from the writer's own journeys, along with many reports from other travellers. Pausanias's *Description of Greece* (c.155–80 CE), meanwhile, seems close in spirit to a modern guidebook, offering detailed accounts of Greek antiquities and rituals.

None of these works, however, offer the reader any sort of re-creation in writing of the original travel experience. Typically, they just provide the information garnered during the author's personal travels. This is the norm in most travel-related writings of the Ancient era, which seldom conform to our modern notion of the 'travel book' as a first-person narrative of travel. One exception, however, is Horace's poem 'A Journey to Brundisium', in Book 1 of his *Satires* (c.35 BCE). This lively travelogue in verse offers a much more personal travel account, in which the narrator recounts some of the hardships and misfortunes which befell him along the way, and in this regard it provided an important model for travel writers in later eras.

One of the earliest accounts of Christian pilgrimage, the *Pilgrimage of Egeria* (c.381–84 CE), also places more emphasis on the travelling self, and on the details of the journey, than was usual in this period. Egeria, sometimes known as Aetheria, was a woman, possibly a nun, who travelled from Spain or Western Gaul to

Jerusalem. An account of her journey, in the form of a long letter to her compatriots, subsequently circulated in manuscript, and is thus the earliest first-person, non-fictional narrative of travel we know of in the Western tradition. As the following passage shows, it provides a fairly detailed account of Egeria's itinerary in the Holy Land:

> We reached the place on the Jordan where holy Joshua the son of Nun sent the children of Israel across, and they passed over, as we are told in the book of Joshua the son of Nun. We were also shown a slightly raised place on the Jericho side of the river, where the children of Reuben and Gad and the half tribe of Manasseh made an altar. After crossing the river we came to the city of Livias, in the plain where the children of Israel encamped in those days.
>
> (Wilkinson 1999: 113)

As this will suggest, the focus of Egeria's narrative falls principally on the spiritual significance of the landscapes through which she moves, and on the devotional practices of the people she encounters, rather than on her personal thoughts and feelings. As a result, it still seems to modern eyes a rather impersonal form of travel writing, even though it is cast in the first person.

There are also many fictive treatments of travel in Classical literature. *The Odyssey* has been mentioned already, but the Greek romances of late antiquity, by Heliodorus and others, also often set their protagonists wandering through the Mediterranean world and beyond, to encounter shipwreck, kidnap by pirates and similar misfortunes. And Lucian's *True History* (written between 160 and 185 CE) is arguably the first parody of travel writing; in a satire on the preposterous and fantastical claims made by many travellers in this era, it recounts a voyage to the moon.

MEDIEVAL TRAVELLERS AND TRAVEL WRITING

The medieval era, like the Classical era, produced an abundance of travel-related texts. Once again, however, few of these texts conform closely to our modern notion of the travel book. Rather, the reports of travellers are often woven into medieval geographies, natural histories, bestiaries and 'books of wonders'. The continents of Asia and Africa especially were a source of fascination to readers in Europe, and gave rise to a rich, if often highly speculative, literature. Very few of these accounts, however, are first-person narratives of travel in which the writer recounts his or her own experience. Typically, they are compendia of information, in which the observations of Classical authorities such as Herodotus and Pliny are combined with more recent reports that have filtered back, often via a series of intermediaries, to the centres of intellectual activity in Europe. As a consequence, many medieval travel texts seem to modern readers a curious blend of the factual and the fabulous, as they combine plausible descriptions of foreign peoples and places with accounts of monstrous or miraculous beings that are clearly projections of European fears and fantasies, such as winged centaurs, dog-headed men and Amazons.

First-person accounts of actual travels occur most commonly in this era in the form of the 'peregrinatio', or pilgrimage narrative. Feudal society did not encourage much personal mobility, but pilgrimage was one form of culturally sanctioned travel, and by the later Middle Ages something akin to a tourist industry had emerged, catering for pilgrims visiting Rome and the Holy Land, and to many local sites of religious significance. Geoffrey Chaucer's *Canterbury Tales* (c.1387) provide a vivid depiction in verse of the medieval pilgrimage. For real-life pilgrims, numerous handbooks were available, offering practical and devotional advice to would-be travellers, and some of these guides were written by authors who had themselves made the pilgrimage. As with the fourth-century *Pilgrimage of Egeria*, however, the element of travelogue is often strictly subordinated to the text's practical and religious concerns. Typically, there is little effort to record the events of the actual journey, or the traveller's subjective thoughts and feelings. Nor do these accounts usually evince much interest in the natural world, or in the other cultures encountered during the journey. In such a strongly Christian era, an excessive interest in such secular matters might potentially be classified as the sin of *curiositas* (curiosity). It was the education of the soul that was the text's first concern, a homiletic agenda that often makes the medieval pilgrimage narrative little more than a compilation of passages from the Bible.

Not every traveller in the medieval era was a pilgrim, of course. Within Europe, men might also travel on church business, or as merchants, diplomats, soldiers and scholars; women, meanwhile, would sometimes accompany husbands and fathers in their travels, and on occasion undertook journeys on their own. The Crusades took many Christian Europeans to the Near and Middle East, and many more gained some familiarity with the region through subsequent chronicles of events there. Missionaries and embassies were also periodically sent still further afield, to places such as China, India and Africa. It was a diplomatic mission to the court of the Mongol emperor Kublai Khan that produced the most famous travel account of this period, the *Travels of Marco Polo*, which circulated in various versions, and under various titles, from the late thirteenth century onwards. Polo's description of the wealth and sophistication of China, as set down in writing by the romance-writer Rustichello da Pisa, fascinated the age, although it also provoked much scepticism and incredulity in contemporary readers.

After Marco Polo's *Travels*, the most influential and widely circulated travel narrative of the late middle ages was the *Travels of Sir John Mandeville* (c.1356). This account, originally written in Anglo-French, begins as a guide for pilgrims to the Holy Land, supposedly based on the author's own travels in that region, but then extends beyond the Middle East to discuss China, India and well-nigh the whole world known to medieval Europeans. Although the narrator claims firsthand experience of these places, many details and anecdotes clearly derive from earlier sources, both Classical and medieval. But whether the account is just a digest of other works, or whether its author made at least some of the journeys recounted here, is less certain. It is also unclear whether the narrative was seriously intended as an encyclopaedic summing-up of the geographical knowledge of the age, with the traveller-persona of 'Sir John Mandeville' being invented to provide a coherent narrative thread through this mass of information, or if it was in fact meant to be a parody of contemporary travel writing, in the spirit of Lucian's *True History*.

If pilgrimage is the most common paradigm in medieval travel and travel writing, another important, and closely related, motif in this era is that of the chivalric quest. Quest romances detailing the exploits of the knights of Arthur and Charlemagne, by Chretien de Troyes and others, became popular in Europe from the twelfth century onwards; and whilst these were fictive, literary renderings of the travel theme, they established personae and narrative conventions which subsequently influenced many real travellers, and which accordingly came to be adopted in many genuine, non-fictional travel accounts.

Forms of travel writing also existed in other cultures in this period. In Chinese literature, the genres known as the *yu-chi*, or lyric travel account, and the *jih-chi*, or travel diary, were taking shape as early as the eighth century CE, and truly began to flourish from the eleventh century onwards. In the Islamic world, meanwhile, the *rihla*, or book recounting travel, began to emerge (see Euben 2006). Its greatest exponent would be the Moroccan *qadi*, or judge, Ibn Battutah, whose *Travels* (c.1355) describes an epic, 75,000-mile peregrination around North Africa, India, China and South East Asia.

EARLY MODERN TRAVEL WRITING

The four voyages of Christopher Columbus, undertaken between 1492 and 1504, constitute a watershed in the history of European travel and travel writing, and a key point of transition from medieval to early modern attitudes, practices and conventions. It was the accounts of Marco Polo and Mandeville that inspired Columbus to seek out the fabulous wealth of the Far East; yet by sailing westwards to reach China, and thereby arriving at America, he dealt a considerable blow to the medieval world-view, and to its trust in the authority of Classical texts. One result of Columbus's startling discoveries was accordingly a new emphasis on the act of eye-witnessing, of seeing for oneself and establishing facts through **empirical** enquiry rather than through reference to the great authors of the past. Increasingly, philosophers such as Sir Francis Bacon sought a radical reorganisation of knowledge and the principles of intellectual enquiry, insisting on the importance not only of an empirical approach, but also of an **inductive** method; that is to say, they emphasised the need to accumulate facts about the world prior to any attempt to deduce the laws underpinning natural phenomena. By promoting this intellectual agenda, philosophers such as Bacon laid the foundations of modern science, and they also exercised a profound influence on the development of Western travel writing.

Columbus's voyages inaugurated an era of European discovery, led in the first instance by the navigators of Spain and Portugal. Vasco da Gama sailed from Lisbon to India via the Cape of Good Hope in 1497; in the same year, Amerigo Vespucci pushed beyond the Caribbean islands discovered by Columbus, to reach for the first time the mainland of South America; and in 1519, Ferdinand Magellan led the first successful circumnavigation of the globe. The English for their part made a somewhat belated contribution to these maritime endeavours. Francis Drake made the first English circumnavigation between 1577 and 1580, and the 1570s also witnessed the first significant English attempts to explore the New World, led by Martin Frobisher and Humphrey Gilbert, and later by figures such as Walter Ralegh and Henry Hudson.

These ventures were driven not by intellectual curiosity, but rather by a keen awareness of the opportunities they opened up for trade, conquest and colonisation, and also by the religious imperative of converting heathen peoples to Christianity. In the Treaty of Tordesillas in 1494, the Pope assigned the newly discovered lands beyond Europe to Portugal and Spain; the former quickly established a lucrative empire in India, South East Asia and Brazil, and the latter did likewise in central and South America. This division of the globe was contested by France, England and later Holland, who all strove to establish their own overseas dominions. Ralegh led a first, unsuccessful English settlement at Roanoke, Virginia in 1584, before the English established a second, successful colony at Jamestown, Virginia, in 1607. This was followed in 1620 by the Pilgrim Fathers' settlement at Plymouth, Massachusetts. Ralegh would also lead two voyages to Guyana in South America, in 1594 and 1616, where he sought to discover El Dorado, the fabled city of gold.

These enterprises stimulated a wave of travel-related writings and documents. Aided by the spread of the printing press, maps, surveys and reports relating to the new discoveries and conquests quickly circulated in Europe, notwithstanding the attempts often made by governments to control publication of economically and strategically sensitive material. Travel writing in all its different forms gained immensely in importance, as politicians, merchants and navigators sought information to enable further expeditions. To cater to this need, and in some cases to arouse commercial and colonial ambitions amongst their compatriots, editors and publishers began to issue large-scale collections of travel accounts and documents: notable examples include Giovanni Batista Ramusio's *Navigationi et Viaggi* (*Voyages and Travels*; 1550), Richard Hakluyt's *Principall Navigations, Voyages, Traffics and Discoveries of the English Nation* (1589, with a greatly expanded second edition appearing 1598–1600) and Samuel Purchas's *Hakluytus Posthumus, or Purchas His Pilgrimes* (1625).

In this way, there began to take shape the genre that would be known for several centuries as 'voyages and travels'. As discussed in Chapter 2, this was always a highly heterogeneous generic designation, but as a result of the growing emphasis on empirical enquiry and eye-witness observation, it was a genre increasingly centred on the report, or 'relation', of someone who had actually made the journey themselves. That said, few of the leading figures in this age of discovery produced their own narratives. An exception here was Walter Ralegh's *Discoverie of the Large, Rich and Bewtiful Empyre of Guiana* (1596), which will be discussed in more detail in Chapter 5. Usually, however, it was left to junior members of an expedition to write up its progress and findings. Thus it was the astronomer and mathematician Thomas Harriott, a participant in Ralegh's Roanoke venture, who published *A Brief and True Report of the New Found Land of Virginia* (1588). A detailed account of the marketable commodities to be found in the colony, and also of the customs of the native Algonkians, it has been described as 'Elizabethan England's most sophisticated and influential travel book' (Sherman 2002: 26).

It was not only the New World that was the focus of travellers' accounts in this era. Information was also eagerly sought about the countries and cultures of the 'Old World', Europe, the Middle

East, Asia and Africa. Travel from the British Isles to the European continent and beyond became more difficult after the Reformation, which created a rift between Protestants and Catholics, and also brought an end to many forms of pilgrimage in Protestant regions. Yet there were still many travellers who ventured abroad and subsequently recounted their experiences in print. Examples include Thomas Coryat, author of *Coryat's Crudities, Hastily gobled up in five monethes travels* (1611), and seemingly the first writer to travel primarily for the sake of writing up the experience; Fynes Morison, whose *Itinerary* (1617) described ten years of travel through Europe and the Middle East; and William Lithgow, whose *Rare Adventures & Painfull Peregrinations* (1632) describe travels across Europe and as far afield as North Africa, Palestine and Egypt. As this brief list will suggest, most writers of travels in this period were men; there are no published accounts by women, reflecting both the fewer opportunities women had to travel in this era, and also the much greater difficulties they faced in becoming authors.

Coryat's Crudities is an early example of what one might regard as a 'literary' mode of travel writing, a text that is meant to be enjoyed as much for its style, and for the playful self-presentation of its author, as for the information it contains. In most other travel writings of this era, the focus is very much on the traveller's findings, and the useful data they were able to relay back to readers at home. In this they were guided by a burgeoning advice-literature, which issued directions on how to travel to best advantage, and the sort of information to record. An example is Sir Francis Bacon's 1625 essay, 'Of Travel', which urged travellers to keep journals, and to attempt to learn the language of the country they were visiting.

The momentous discoveries of the early modern era inevitably sparked reflection and commentary amongst writers in Europe. In particular, the encounter with native Americans, and the often brutal treatment these natives received at the hands of Europeans, prompted much philosophical and ethical debate. Bartolomé de las Casas's *Brief Account of the Destruction of the Indies* (1552) was a powerful indictment of the conduct of the Spanish conquistadors. It greatly influenced the French thinker Michel de Montaigne, whose essay 'On Cannibals' (1580) questioned the supposed superiority of European civilisation to native American 'savagery'. Closer to home, many English commentators pondered the advisability of travel to the continent. By the latter part of the sixteenth century, it was becoming increasingly common for the sons of aristocrats and gentry to be sent to France and Italy to complete their education. This practice would evolve in time into the eighteenth-century Grand Tour. But critics argued that travel abroad simply exposed impressionable young men to moral dissolution, foreign affectation and Catholicism.

These themes and debates also rippled through the imaginative literature of the period. In fiction, Thomas More mimicked the new travel accounts to great satiric effect in *Utopia* (1516, and originally published in Latin), inventing an imaginary new culture that could serve as an unsettling mirror to European society. A later fiction, Joseph Hall's *Mundus Alter et Idem* (*Another World and the Same*; 1605), similarly deployed the conventions of contemporary travel literature, but did so to critique the very idea of travel, suggesting that it was a pointless and morally dangerous exercise. Also in fiction, a new genre or mode appeared that was very much predicated on travel, and that would provide a potent model in later years for some travellers and travel books. Reflecting in part the loosening of feudal bonds, and parodying the more idealistic aspirations of chivalric quest romance, picaresque fictions set a rootless, and usually disreputable, protagonist 'on the road', to encounter a sequence of adventures and misadventures. The genre was Spanish in origin, and arguably achieved its greatest expression in Miguel de Cervantes's mock-heroic epic, *Don Quixote* (1605). But it quickly spread throughout Europe; an early English example is Thomas Nashe's *The Unfortunate Traveller* (1594). On the stage, meanwhile, plays such as *The Travels of Three English Brothers* (1607), by John Day, William Rowley and George Wilkins, celebrated the achievements of Englishmen abroad, whilst Shakespeare's *The Tempest* (1611) is at one level a subtle reflection on contemporary colonialism.

THE LONG EIGHTEENTH CENTURY, 1660–1837

'Few books have succeeded better of late than voyages and travels' (quoted in Leask 2002: 13). As this comment by Vicesimus Knox in 1778 suggests, travel writing proliferated in the eighteenth century, gaining a prestige and popularity which it maintained until well into the nineteenth century. This was a period in which travel books were read both for intellectual profit and for literary pleasure. Many were at the cutting-edge of contemporary scientific, political and moral debate; others again were in the vanguard of some of the period's most important aesthetic develop-ments. The genre also worked a crucial influence on the evolution of other literary forms in this era, such as poetry and the novel.

The proliferation of accounts of voyages and travels reflects the fact that this was an era of ever-increasing mobility, as across Europe feudalism gave way to a more commercial, embryonically capitalist society. At the same time, the technologies and infra-structures that enabled travel steadily improved. To cite just two of these advances, in 1765 John Harrison designed a chronometer that for the first time enabled longitude to be determined at sea; whilst by the early nineteenth century, the steam engine was being utilised as a means of motive power, firstly in ships and then on land, in the railway. As a consequence, more people were travelling, both within Europe and beyond, as the European exploration and colonisation of the globe continued apace. The steady expansion of print culture, moreover, meant that an increasing number of these travellers were able to publish accounts of their journeys.

For convenience, one can group the key developments in travel and travel writing in the eighteenth and early nineteenth centuries under two main headings: exploration and tourism. For much of this period, however, these two forms of travel and travelogue were less sharply distinguished than we might today assume. At the beginning of the period especially, almost all travellers were supposed to set out in search of useful knowledge, regardless of whether they were travelling recreationally or in some professional capacity, and regardless of whether they were travelling within the British Isles, or to Europe, or to some more remote destination pre-viously unvisited by Europeans. Travel as an information-gathering exercise was regarded as crucial arm of the New Science of the late seventeenth century, and to this end the Royal Society, founded in London in 1660, did much to promote travel and coordinate the activities of travellers. Also influential in the English-speaking world in this regard was the empiricist philosophy propounded by John Locke, most notably in his *Essay Concerning Human Understanding* (1690). For Locke, knowledge was generated above all by experience of the world, and as a consequence travel was soon regarded as 'something like an obligation for the person conscientious about developing the mind and accumulating knowledge' (Fussell 1987: 130).

The influence of the Royal Society is apparent in one of the most popular and influential travel narratives of the period, William Dampier's *New Voyage Round the World* (1697). Dampier had sailed extensively in the Caribbean and the South Pacific as a 'privateer': essentially, a member of a non-naval vessel licensed to plunder Spanish shipping, Britain being at war with Spain at the time. In the course of his adventures, however, he had also made copious notes on the natural history of the regions he visited, and the customs of their inhabitants. At the instigation of the President of the Royal Society, these were written up into an account that established a new standard for exploratory travel writing, combining a keen eye for detail with a plain, unembellished prose style.

The New Science's inductive agenda, and its desire to accumulate a comprehensive knowledge of the natural world, received further stimulus with the publication in 1735 of *Systema Naturae* (*The System of Nature*), by the Swedish naturalist Linnaeus. In this work, Linnaeus established a classificatory system that could seemingly be used to catalogue the whole of the natural world, and this **taxonomic** project was eagerly taken up in the latter half of the eighteenth century. The three voyages of Captain James Cook to the Pacific Ocean (1768–80) inaugurated an era of more overtly scientific exploration by European and American travellers. Especially noteworthy amongst these 'explorers', as they came to be known, are James Bruce, Mungo Park and Francois Le Vaillant in Africa; Louis Antoine de Bougainville and the Comte de La Perouse in the South Pacific; Matthew Flinders in Australia; Alexander von Humboldt in South America; and in North America, Alexander MacKenzie. In 1803, moreover, the first significant US exploratory venture got underway, Meriweather Lewis and William Clark's overland expedition to America's Pacific coast.

Much of this exploration was state-sponsored, or financed by organisations with close ties to contemporary policy-makers, such as, in Britain, the African Association, founded in 1788. Accordingly, it needs always to be kept in mind that although many explorers in this period trumpeted the purely scientific motivation for their travels, the knowledge and specimens they brought back were usually intended to be put to practical use, and to be harnessed to the larger economic and strategic goals of the European great powers. In this spirit, for example, Sir Joseph Banks, one of the principal patrons of exploratory endeavour in Britain, arranged the transportation of plant species around the emergent British empire, and instigated the use of Botany Bay in Australia as a penal colony. Banks was also instrumental in getting many accounts of British exploration into print, and these soon became one of the most popular branches of the voyages and travels genre.

If the scientifically motivated explorer was one distinctive new type of traveller to emerge over the course of the eighteenth century, another was the 'tourist'. The term had been coined by the end of century, although initially it held none of the pejorative connotations that it sometimes has today. For many years, indeed, to be a tourist was a mark of conspicuous privilege. At the beginning of the period, the only form of tourism widely practised was what had been dubbed in the late seventeenth century the 'Grand Tour': that is to say, an extended visit, lasting sometimes as long as two years, to the European continent, and especially to France and Italy. This was a rite of passage for many young male aristocrats. The ethos and aims of the Grand Tour are well exemplified in Joseph Addison's *Remarks on Several Parts of Italy* (1705), which for many years became a virtual handbook for the Grand Tourist. As well as acquiring foreign languages, the young traveller was supposed to gather useful information, in the empirical spirit of the New Science. He was also meant to visit the many remains of Roman antiquity, so as to complete his training in the classics, which in this era were seen as a key benchmark of taste and cultivation. Or at least, this was the agenda that a young tourist was *supposed* to follow. In practice, many devoted themselves to more frivolous or dissolute pursuits, for which they often found themselves lampooned by hostile commentators and satirists.

If it began as an elite practice, however, tourism was increasingly taken up by the emergent middle classes. From the 1760s especially, the number of middle-class travellers to the continent rose sharply. And when in the 1770s the domestic tour to regions within Britain became fashionable, this new mark of status became available to an even wider portion of British society. The growing appetite for tourism brought with it a diversification of touristic tastes, interests and itineraries. Some tourists clung to the classicism of the traditional Grand Tour; others preferred to seek out regions seemingly little touched by contemporary modernity. Many were drawn to the Scottish Highlands by the hugely popular *Ossian* poems (1760–65) of James McPherson, which lent a glamour both to the landscape and to the traditional customs of its inhabitants. Perhaps the most famous of these travellers was Samuel Johnson, whose *Journey to the Western Isles of Scotland* (1775) records Johnson's keen interest in the vanishing way of life of the Highland clans. He was accompanied by James Boswell, who later published his own *Journal of a Tour to the Hebrides* (1785).

If the influence of the *Ossian* poems encouraged a greater aesthetic appreciation of landscape, this new taste was also stimulated by the cult of the picturesque, promoted most vigorously by the Reverend William Gilpin, who from 1782 published a series of 'picturesque tours'. Other tourists, meanwhile, espoused an 'improving' agenda. Following the lead of Arthur Young, who from 1768 published a series of 'farmer's tours', they aimed to identify and disseminate good agricultural practice, so as to boost the British economy. Whether 'picturesque' or 'improving' in their tastes, however, many of these tourists ventured into print, making the late eighteenth and early nineteenth centuries, in Dorothy Wordsworth's words, a '*tour*-writing and *tour*-publishing age'. Most of these published accounts were by men, but there were also increasing opportunities for women both to travel and publish travelogues in this period. Only one travel account by a woman seems to have been published before 1763, Elizabeth Justice's *A Voyage to Russia* (1739), although there were of course many female travellers who kept journals or wrote letters not intended for publication: examples include Celia Fiennes in

Britain, and Sarah Kemble Knight in America. Between 1763 and 1800, however, some twenty female-authored travelogues appeared, by Mary Wortley Montagu, Ann Radcliffe, Mary Wollstonecraft and others (Turner 2001: 127). After 1800, meanwhile, the number of published female travel writers rose even more dramatically, as figures such as Anna Jameson, Maria Graham and Frances Trollope made noteworthy contributions to the genre.

For the writers of touristic travelogues, travel writing's traditional remit, that it report back useful knowledge, became ever harder to fulfil. Increasingly, there were few places in the British Isles, or in the standard Grand Tour circuit in Europe, that had not already been extensively described. One response to this predicament was to foreground the personality of the traveller, focusing less on the places visited and more on his or her subjective impressions of those places. A key influence here was Laurence Sterne's novel *A Sentimental Journey* (1768), which inspired a host of real-life imitators. These '**sentimental**' tourists sought emotional adventures that could demonstrate both their own sensibility and the fundamental benevolence of all mankind; their accounts, meanwhile, pioneered new techniques for writing about the self, and for expressing the flux of inner thoughts and feelings. It was not only touristic travelogues that adopted these techniques. Part of the appeal of Mungo Park's enormously successful *Travels in the Interior Districts of Africa* (1799), for example, was its interweaving of sentimentalist elements into the more rigorous style of an exploration narrative, as Park recorded his own affective responses to some of the predicaments he encountered.

The burgeoning of touristic travel and travel writing prompted much hostile commentary. By the early nineteenth century, the tourist had come to seem emblematic of modernity, and of the more commercial and consumerist society brought into being by the Industrial Revolution. As greater numbers began to travel recreationally, moreover, and as extensive infrastructures developed to cater to them, tourism itself began to seem an industry. In the 1830s, the publishing firms of Baedeker in Germany and John Murray in Britain began producing guidebooks for tourists in a recognisably modern form. And in the 1840s, Thomas Cook introduced the concept of the package holiday, in which an agent organised most aspects of the journey for the traveller. As tourism developed in this way, many tourists increasingly felt the need to differentiate themselves from other tourists. They sought out new styles of travel, and alternative destinations, so as to demonstrate their moral superiority and greater discrimination in taste. The beginnings of a modern 'backpacker' mentality, for example, is apparent in the late eighteenth-century vogue for 'walking tours'; eager 'pedestrians' included William Wordsworth and Samuel Taylor Coleridge (see Jarvis 1997). Lord Byron's poetic travelogue *Childe Harold's Pilgrimage* (1812–18), meanwhile, became a handbook for travellers anxious to feel they were not merely tourists, teaching them how to respond to even the most hackneyed tourist destination with a poet's heightened sensibility.

There were of course travellers and travel accounts in this period which were neither touristic nor exploratory. Perennially popular at all levels of print culture, for example, were accounts by castaways, shipwreck victims, and captives held hostage by barbarous tribes and hostile foreign regimes (see Baepler 1999; Colley 2002; Thompson, 2007b). An early American example of this genre is Mary Rowlandson's *The Sovereignty and Goodness of God* (1682), which recounts a period spent as a prisoner of the Wampanoag Indians in Massachusetts. In some variants this was a sensationalist literature that simply dealt in horrific suffering; in other versions, however, it was deeply infused by Protestant traditions of **spiritual autobiography**, often presenting a traveller's ordeal as the route by which an errant individual rediscovered God. Another sort of religious traveller was also becoming more common by the end of the period. The Evangelical revival of the late eighteenth and early nineteenth centuries led to the establishment of a number of missionary societies, and accounts of missions to 'heathen' tribes soon became another popular strand of the voyages and travels genre. Many in the Evangelical movement also campaigned vigorously for the abolition of slavery, and as part of this campaign published the memoirs of ex-slaves such as Olaudah Equiano and Mary Prince; since these life-stories often described numerous journeys and enforced relocations, they arguably constitute the first modern travel writing by men and women of African descent, in the Western tradition at least.

It was also in this period that a distinctively American tradition of travel writing began to emerge, after the creation of the USA in 1776. Prior to that there had of course been many travel accounts produced both by colonists and by European visitors to the continent: notable examples include Thomas Harriott, John Smith and John Bartram. After independence, however, travellers who defined themselves as American began to explore both their own nation and the wider world, and the accounts they produced played an important role in forming a sense of nationhood. As Judith Hamara and Alfred Bendixen have noted, 'travel and the construction of American identity are intimately linked' (2009: 1). The USA is after all a nation founded by immigrants, which subsequently expanded westwards across the North American landmass, and eventually across the Pacific to Hawaii. Accounts by explorers, settlers, naturalists and missionaries did much to facilitate this expansion, whilst simultaneously giving voice to the young nation's growing sense of cultural identity. Also contributing to this enterprise were the accounts of US travellers who journeyed around the more settled, Europeanised regions of the Eastern seaboard, and indeed those who travelled overseas, since as always the encounter with other cultures required travellers to define more clearly their own values and affiliations. Notable US travel accounts from this period include De Crèveceour's *Letters of an American Farmer* (1782), the naturalist William Bartram's *Travels* (1791), and Washington Irving's various writings on both Europe and the American frontier (published between 1819 and 1837).

All this activity in the spheres of travel and travel writing was inevitably reflected in other forms of writing. As Paul Fussell notes, the imaginative literature of the age 'is full of travelling heroes enmeshed in journey plots' (1987: 129). The modern novel, indeed, arguably came into being as an imitation of contemporary travelogues. Daniel Defoe's *Robinson Crusoe* (1719) is a fictional version of the spiritual-autobiographical shipwreck narratives mentioned above, whilst Jonathan Swift's *Gulliver's Travels* (1726) is in part a parody of the voyage narratives produced by William

UNIVERSITY OF WINCHESTER
LIBRARY

Dampier and similar figures. Later novelists such as Henry Fielding and Tobias Smollett, meanwhile, produced many variations on the picaresque theme, in works such as *Joseph Andrews* (1742) and *Humphrey Clinker* (1771).

It was not just subject matter that these novelists derived from contemporary accounts of tours, voyages and travels: the new modes of realism that distinguish the novel from the earlier romance are significantly indebted to the plain, descriptive style developed by Dampier and others, in response to Royal Society guidelines. The descriptive rigour of contemporary exploration narratives is also an influence on much Romantic poetry later in the century, as more precise observation replaced neo-classical generalities. The theme of travel, and the traveller persona, are also central to many Romantic poems, from Coleridge's 'Rime of the Ancient Mariner' (1798) to Wordsworth's *Prelude* (1805) and *Excursion* (1814), and Byron's *Childe Harold*.

THE VICTORIAN AND EDWARDIAN PERIODS, 1837–1914

In the nineteenth century the empires of the principal European powers expanded massively, to reach their zenith in the early twentieth century. Across the same period, the USA established and consolidated its territorial control of the 48 contiguous states, and added Alaska and Hawaii to the Union in 1867 and 1898 respectively. The acquisition, governance and in some cases settlement of these new European and US dominions generated innumerable travel-related writings, from explorers, soldiers, sailors, surveyors, missionaries, merchants, scientists, colonial administrators, diplomats, journalists, artists and many others besides. As this list of occupations will suggest, the types of text they produced varied greatly, encompassing memoirs, literary travelogues, newspaper reports, campaigning tracts and a mass of purely functional documents intended for highly specialist audiences such as scientists, economists and policy-makers. Yet all of this material arguably constitutes a form of travel writing, if one accepts the looser definition of the genre outlined in Chapter 2. And almost all of it worked, sometimes directly, sometimes subtly and indirectly, to facilitate European and US expansion in this era. This was a period, for instance, in which the emergence of a spurious 'science' of race in the European and American academy bred a more pronounced sense of innate superiority amongst Europeans and (white) Americans, who increasingly regarded themselves as the bearers of civilisation, enlightenment and progress to supposedly primitive peoples. There were of course some dissenting voices, yet most of the travel-related writings outlined earlier were deeply suffused with these notions of cultural and racial superiority, and worked to inculcate them in their readership.

One of the most important forms of travel writing in this era of high imperialism was the exploration narrative. From Charles Darwin's *Voyage of the Beagle* (1839) to Alfred Russel Wallace's accounts of the Amazon basin and the Malay archipelago (1853 and 1869 respectively), and from David Livingstone, Richard Burton and Henry Morton Stanley's descriptions of the African interior to the long tradition of polar exploration associated with figures like Franklin, Peary, Amundsen and Scott, the reports of explorers supplied the intellectual centres of Europe and America with an abundance of highly useful geographical, natural-historical and ethnographic information about well-nigh every region of the globe. At the same time, they also gripped the popular imagination. Explorers came to be regarded as emblematic figures, ideal types of imperial masculinity who embodied the highest ideals of science and Christian civilisation. As we shall see in Chapter 6, their travel experiences were increasingly rendered in a stirring style that drew significantly on the literary techniques and idioms developed in another burgeoning nineteenth-century genre, the imperial adventure stories that one associates with writers like Frederick Marryat, Rudyard Kipling and Rider Haggard, and with the *Boy's Own* magazine. These fictional tales of adventure in turn often drew on contemporary accounts of exploration for their settings and plots. Thus the two overlapping genres came to function as an 'energising myth of English imperialism', in Martin Green's phrase (1980: 3) – that is to say, they worked to legitimate the imperial project to domestic audiences, whilst simultaneously inspiring readers with fantasies of the heroic exploits they might themselves perform in distant regions of the world.

Travel writing in less adventurous modes also proliferated in this period. Tourism flourished as never before, and a tourist infrastructure that guaranteed travellers a comparatively safe and comfortable journey was consolidated and steadily extended in both Europe and the USA. By the latter part of the century, it was possible to travel by train all the way from Paris to Istanbul, in modern-day Turkey, on the famous *Orient Express*. Many of the travellers who took up these new travel opportunities were stirred to write accounts of their experiences. As always with travel writing, they did so in a great variety of styles, and espoused a broad range of interests and approaches. Some offered fairly lightweight, superficial 'sketches' or 'recollections' of picturesque or exotic regions; others sought to reflect more insightfully on the destinations they had visited. Whatever their degree of intellectual or artistic accomplishment, however, many of these travellers evinced a desire to get 'off the beaten track', and to avoid the usual tourist itineraries (see Buzard 1993). This agenda was driven partly by a Romantic desire to visit sites of unspoilt natural beauty, and/or cultures seemingly untouched by modernity. A desire to escape the stifling moral codes of the Victorian era was also a factor for some travellers. Many Americans and North Europeans, accordingly, sought both authenticity and sensuality in the sunny climes of Italy and the Middle East. In this spirit, for example, A.W. Kinglake's hugely popular *Eothen* (1844) presented the Middle East as a place where a young man might be free of the humdrum chores of domestic life, whilst for writers like Gérard de Nerval and Gustav Flaubert the region became the site of alluring erotic adventures.

Attempts to get off the beaten track were also often motivated by a desire to escape one's fellow tourists, who thronged in unprecedented numbers to established destinations. Another recurrent feature of many Victorian travelogues, accordingly, is an **anti-touristic** rhetoric that seeks to distinguish the author from the more vulgar tourist 'herd'. This impulse is also one reason why the inward turn in some modes of travel writing, as discussed earlier in relation to Sterne, becomes even more marked in the Victorian era. By shifting attention away from the scenes being witnessed and on to the narratorial self that was doing the witnessing, many Victorian travel writers sought to signal a sensibility, and an intellectual and emotional cultivation, superior to that of other tourists.

This last development is also bound up with the emergence, in the nineteenth century, of the more self-consciously 'literary' mode of travel writing that I earlier labelled the modern travel book. In this regard, it is significant that the Victorian era saw many writers with established reputations in other literary genres take up the travelogue form. Thus the French novelist Stendhal wrote *Memoirs of a Tourist* (1838), whilst Charles Dickens produced *American Notes* (1842) and *Pictures from Italy* (1846), and Mark Twain the hugely popular *The Innocents Abroad* (1869). Many of these literary travelogues were intended to be read as much for the quality of the writing they contained, and for the insights they offered into the idiosyncratic personalities of their authors, as for the useful information they contained about the places being described. Or, alternatively, they claimed to capture impressionistically or poetically the 'spirit' of a place or culture, rather than offer a comprehensive, factual account of it. Thus in one branch of the travel writing genre, it was style and aesthetic effect rather than factual information that was increasingly prioritised by writers, and valorised by critics and readers.

Women writers also made a significant contribution to the travel writing genre in the Victorian period, although this required them to negotiate the highly constraining norms of femininity that operated in this era (see Morgan 1996; Schriber 1997). Figures like Isabella Bird, Marianne North, May French Sheldon, Mary Kingsley and Anna Leonowens ventured well beyond the standard tourist circuits of their day. Some of these women, indeed, were engaged in activities close in spirit to exploration, although they did not usually present themselves in this light: the heroic title of 'explorer' was a male preserve in this period. Yet Bird and Kingsley were eventually admitted as Fellows to the Royal Geographical Society and the Anthropological Society respectively, in recognition of their contributions to natural history and ethnography. The majority of female travellers, like the majority of male travellers in this period, were of course far less adventurous than figures like Bird and Kingsley. Many nevertheless produced accounts of their travels, covering the spectrum from largely inconsequential sketches and reminiscences to more substantial interventions in contemporary aesthetic, intellectual and political debates. Notable writers in this regard include Flora Tristan, Isabelle Eberhardt, Catherine Parr Traill, Harriet Beecher Stowe, Harriet Martineau, Louisa Ann Meredith, Gertrude Bell and Edith Wharton.

As in earlier periods, finally, the travel theme, and the depiction of foreign peoples and places, was also frequently taken up by writers working in more obviously imaginative or fictive genres. The assumptions of cultural and moral superiority that under-pinned the European imperial project are powerfully critiqued in Joseph Conrad's *Heart of Darkness* (1902), for example, although the novella is itself not free of prejudicial attitudes to Africa and Africans. Herman Melville in *Typee* (1846) and R.L. Stevenson in his South Sea tales are amongst the many writers of fiction who take the South Pacific and its inhabitants as their theme; and Rudyard Kipling's *Kim* (1901) is just one of many novels which brought India vividly to life for European and American readers. Travel is also a frequent theme and motif in much poetry in this era, in works such as A.H. Clough's *Amours de Voyage* (1848), Walt Whitman's 'Song of the Open Road' (1856), and even, in a more symbolic and/or nonsensical vein, Arthur Rimbaud's 'Le bateau ivre' ('The Drunken Boat'; 1871) and Edward Lear's 'The Owl and the Pussy Cat' (1871). As always, these fictive and poetic accounts of travel often drew on contemporary travel writing not only in their content but also in their style, form and imagery. And as always, some of these literary texts exercised in turn a significant influence on subsequent travel accounts, by shaping travellers' attitudes to other peoples and places.

TRAVEL WRITING FROM 1914 TO THE PRESENT

With the creation and steady expansion of the European and American railway networks, from the mid-nineteenth century onwards, a wholly new mode of transportation became widely available in these two continents. The railway journey introduced travellers to a new sense of speed, and a new sense of disorientation, as the landscape in the immediate foreground of a window-view sped by in a blur. It also radically adjusted the Western sense of space and time and, by so doing, Wolfgang Schivelbusch (1986) has argued, it played a key role in generating a distinctively modern, industrialised mode of consciousness. The tyranny of distance was further defeated in the twentieth century by the motor car and the aeroplane, two new technologies of travel which again introduced travellers to new sensory experiences. And as the use of trains, planes and automobiles steadily grew across the twentieth century, so travel increasingly became a mass activity, available to almost all members of Western society; a development that some commentators have regarded as a laudable democratisation of travel, and others as a deplorable vulgarisation.

These new technologies contributed significantly to a dramatic increase in what one might label global interconnectedness, the sheer volume of exchanges and transactions between the different regions and different cultures of the world. In this regard, it is worth noting that our modern age of globalisation has its origins in the late nineteenth- and early twentieth-century era of high imperialism, when the constant capitalist quest for new markets, products and resources established many of the global networks of trade and travel that exist today. The first major cultural movement in the West in the twentieth century, Modernism, is very much a product of the more mobile and more globalised society that thus came into being. Writers and artists such as T.S. Eliot, Ezra Pound, James Joyce, Joseph Conrad and Pablo Picasso were themselves émigrés, living much of their adult lives outside the nations of their birth. With its emphasis on fragmentation, unexpected juxtapositions and abrupt jumps from one image to another, meanwhile, much Modernist literature and art bears the imprint of the faster lifestyle and the disorientating kinesis that is seemingly characteristic of modernity. Many Modernist writers and artists were also deeply fascinated by the 'primitive' societies described by explorers and anthropologists, and by primitive artefacts and artworks, examples of which had accumulated in the metropolitan centres of the West as a consequence of imperialism. In the wake of Sigmund Freud's theories of psychoanalysis, these works were frequently regarded in the West as expressive not only of human society in an earlier stage of cultural development, but also of primal desires and appetites that were repressed or sublimated in Western art and culture. Viewed in this way, so-called primitive art was often disturbing yet liberating to European and American sensibilities, and for artists such as Picasso it pointed the way to new modes of artistic expression.

Given this larger context, it is unsurprising that travel writing flourished in the years between the First and Second World Wars, both in experimental, Modernist modes and in more traditional forms. Critically acclaimed travelogues of the 1920s included T.E. Lawrence's *The Seven Pillars of Wisdom* (1922), D.H. Lawrence's *Sea and Sardinia* (1921) and *Mornings in Mexico* (1927) and André Gide's *Voyage au Congo* (*Voyage to the Congo*; 1927). The genre also remained popular with the general reader, with middle-brow travel writers such as Rosita Forbes, H.V. Morton and Richard Halliburton achieving great commercial success. Travel writing's appeal grew still further in the 1930s, which is often regarded as a golden age of literary travel writing, especially in Britain (see Fussell 1980). In a decade that witnessed a global economic depression, the rise of totalitarianism in Europe, and ultimately the outbreak of the Second World War, the travelogue seemed to enable a more direct engagement with worldly affairs and with politics than was possible in the traditional literary genres. Figures such as George Orwell, Graham Greene, Evelyn Waugh, Peter Fleming, Robert Byron, Ernest Hemingway, Rebecca West and Freya Stark accordingly took up the travel writing genre, and utilised it to diverse ends: as a form of political and cultural commentary (in the case of Orwell and West); as a source of comic adventures (Fleming and Waugh); or as a means of exploring subjectivity, memory and the unconscious (Greene). Robert Byron's *The Road to Oxiana* (1937), meanwhile, creates a dazzling collage-like effect through its interweaving of fragmentary notes, brief vignettes and a variety of documentary sources such as passport visas and newspaper cuttings; this formal inventiveness has led some critics to hail the book as the greatest masterpiece of 1930s travel writing, and indeed, of travel writing generally (see Fussell 1980: 95; Chatwin 1989: 286). Formal experimentation was also to the fore in W.H. Auden and Louis Macniece's *Letters from Iceland* (1937), and Auden and Christopher

Isherwood's *Journey to a War* (1939), both of which mingle verse and prose.

The strong British tradition of literary travel writing was continued in the post-war era by writers such as Eric Newby, Norman Lewis, Colin Thubron, Jan Morris and Patrick Leigh Fermor, and also by the Irish writer Dervla Murphy. Their travelogues obviously embrace a variety of interests and tonal registers: Lewis's travel writing, for example, is often journalistic in style, while Fermor and Thubron typically adopt a more effusive, lyrical voice. Yet prevalent in much British travel writing of both the 1930s and the post-war era is a self-deprecating persona, and a strategy of understatement that presents the narrator in ironic and belated counterpoint to the more overtly heroic travel writing of Victorian explorers like Stanley and Burton. There is also a distinctly patrician air to this branch of travel writing, amongst the male writers especially. Many were privately educated at elite schools, and had strong links with the political and cultural establishments of their day; their freedom to roam the globe was accordingly predicated to some extent on the privileges accruing from their social standing. More or less contemporaneously, however, Jack Kerouac pioneered in America a very different idiom in travel writing. Although ostensibly novels, works such as *On the Road* (1951) and *Dharma Bums* (1958) were clearly lightly fictionalised accounts of Kerouac's own travel experiences; they established a picaresque, low-life agenda, and a fast-paced 'hipster' style that would become the hallmarks of a self-consciously alternative, counter-cultural tradition in travel writing.

Whilst literary and journalistic travelogues flourished in the twentieth century, another branch of the travel writing genre – the narrative of scientific exploration – gradually fell into abeyance. In this regard, Apsley Cherry-Garrard's *The Worst Journey in the World* (1922), a description of Robert Falcon Scott's ill-fated Antarctic expedition in 1910–13, arguably represents the culmination of, and an elegy for, the nineteenth-century cult of the explorer. The conspicuous heroics of figures like Stanley, which was predicated in part on an immense self-belief as to the West's intellectual and moral superiority over the rest of the world, became increasingly unpalatable after the horrors of two world

wars, and during the era of decolonisation that followed the
Second World War. Increasingly, moreover, there remained fewer
and fewer 'undiscovered' regions that required exploration. And
where exploratory work of this sort was required, it was increasingly
undertaken by professional scientists and social scientists who
were usually concerned to distinguish their writings from those of
mere travel writers. Thus Claude Lévi-Strauss, perhaps the most
influential anthropologist of the twentieth century, declares
bluntly at the beginning of *Tristes Tropiques* (*Sad Tropics*; 1955): 'I
hate travelling and explorers' (1973: 1). He means he detests
writers who produce colourful narratives of their personal travel
experiences, full of incident, anecdote and subjective impressions,
rather than simply presenting, in methodologically rigorous fashion, the ethnographic data and theories generated by their travels.
In the case of *Tristes Tropiques*, this is a somewhat paradoxical
declaration; as Lévi-Strauss immediately acknowledges, he does
'tell the story of [his] expeditions' in this particular volume, and
is thus himself writing a sort of travelogue (1973: 1). Most of his
writings, however, are aimed at scientific specialists rather than the
general reader, and eschew the anecdotalism and **subjectivism** that
was by now strongly associated with travel writing.

This development was already underway in the nineteenth
century, when there were many in the scientific establishment
who looked askance at what they perceived as the showmanship
and sensationalism of figures like Stanley and Burton. Yet in that
period there were still many accounts in which genuinely new scientific and ethnographic information was integrated within a narrative that simultaneously gave literary pleasure to the reader. This
synthesis became increasingly hard to maintain in the twentieth
century, especially after the Second World War, although there
were arguably some writers who tried to keep alive this agenda:
Wilfred Thesiger is perhaps an example. Instead, the vast array of
interests and agendas catered to by the older 'voyages and travels'
genre was divided up between, on the one hand, the different
scientific and social-scientific disciplines in the academy and, on
the other, the spheres of literature and popular entertainment.
This may in part explain why the very term 'voyages and travels'
gave way, around the start of the twentieth century, to our

modern label for the genre, 'travel writing'. The change in terminology was accompanied by a loss in intellectual status and cultural prestige, as the term 'travel writing' came to mean, in the eyes of many commentators, just the more literary, journalistic or middle-brow forms of travelogue.

As a consequence, and notwithstanding the success of the 1930s generation of writers, travel writing was firmly relegated in the twentieth century to the status of a 'minor' genre. The genre's critical and commercial fortunes seem especially to have flagged in the decades immediately after the Second World War. Critical and popular interest in the form was rekindled, however, in the late 1970s. This period witnessed a flurry of commercially successful, and in some cases highly innovative travelogues, the most significant being Paul Theroux's *The Great Railway Bazaar: By Train through Asia* (1975) and *The Old Patagonian Express* (1979), Peter Matthiesen's *The Snow Leopard* (1975), Bruce Chatwin's *In Patagonia* (1977) and Robyn Davidson's *Tracks* (1980). This period also saw the publication of Edward Said's *Orientalism* (1978). A groundbreaking academic study of the way in which Western writers habitually depicted the cultures of the so-called 'Middle' and 'Far' East, *Orientalism* was enormously influential in awakening scholarly interest in travel writing, a genre that had previously been little studied.

Since Said, whose influence will be discussed in more detail in Chapter 6, the academic study of travel writing has burgeoned. So too, of course, has the travel writing genre itself. The spread of the internet, for example, has arguably produced a wholly new mode of travel writing in the form of the travel 'blog', or weblog. Bypassing the traditional need for publication in print culture, travel blogs represent a subtle re-negotiation of the boundary between public and private communication. They have also greatly escalated the volume of travel writing being yearly produced, although of course the quality of this on-line material varies enormously. And so travel writing continues to flourish and to reinvent itself, both in new media and in more traditional forms, so as to reflect new patterns of global travel, and new global concerns.

4

REPORTING THE WORLD

In most of its forms, travel writing's principal business has been to bring news of the wider world, and to disseminate information about unfamiliar peoples and places. Yet there are many layers of mediation between the world as it really is, and the world as it is subsequently rendered in travel writing. The scenes and incidents we encounter in a travelogue necessarily come to us in a filtered form, refracted first through the perceiving consciousness of the traveller, and secondarily through the act of writing, the translation of 'travel experience' into 'travel text'. As discussed in Chapter 2, this translation involves at the very least a selective process whereby the writer prioritises some aspects of the travel experience over others, in accordance with authorial preference and generic requirement. As a result, even forms of travel writing that strive for accuracy and objectivity offer only a partial depiction of the world, and an incomplete picture of a far more complex reality.

Like a lens, therefore, travel writing necessarily distorts the world even as it brings it into view. At the same time, however, recognition of the distortions always inherent in the medium should not lead to a wholesale dismissal of its habitual claim to truthfulness and factuality. In this regard, Patrick Holland and Graham Huggan's assessment of travelogues as essentially *'fictions of factual representation'* (1998: 10; my emphasis) is perhaps too vehement a critique. It is arguably a valid judgement on the modern travel book, a distinctly literary mode of travel writing that usually prioritises the aesthetic pleasure it gives the reader over the accuracy of the information it relays. But in other modes, and other eras, such a blunt equation of travel writing with fiction is more problematic. In particular, it obscures the extent to which travel writing has often constituted an adequate, if never an absolutely accurate, form of knowledge for its readers. Thus many travel accounts have helped subsequent travellers to make the same journey, providing vital information as to navigational routes over land and sea, and the language and customs of distant peoples. More dubiously, empire-builders have often found this information sufficient to their ends, gleaning from the genre useful intelligence on a range of strategic, economic and cultural issues. For travel writing to be practically useful in this way, there must presumably be some correspondence between the details given in a travelogue and the facts 'on the ground', so to speak; some travelogues, at least, must have some purchase on the reality of the places and cultures they describe. And to the extent that these correspondences exist, a travelogue is not simply a fiction or fabrication.

Poised in this way between fact and fiction, travel writing presents its readers with distinctive challenges that are broadly speaking **epistemological** in nature. That is to say, readers have always had to wrestle with questions relating to the validity of the knowledge seemingly offered by travel writing. How, for example, can one gauge the reliability of a travel account? How can one sift accurate observation from inadvertent misperception, or worse, wilful deception? And how can one adjudicate between two very different accounts of the same people or place? By what criteria do we regard one description as more trustworthy than another? These epistemological anxieties translate in turn into a rhetorical challenge for the writers of travel accounts. How can readers be persuaded of the truthfulness of a traveller's observations? How can the travel text 'obtain credit' with its readers, convincing them that it is an authoritative source of knowledge about the world and its inhabitants?

The present chapter explores some of the ways in which the readers and writers of travel accounts have sought to address these concerns, focusing especially on the various strategies by which travellers have tried to present themselves as reliable sources of information. Prior to discussing these strategies, however, the chapter will tease out in more detail some difficulties and dilemmas that have always been attendant on travel writing's role as witness to the wider world.

DISCOVERIES AND WONDERS: SOME PERENNIAL PROBLEMS IN TRAVEL WRITING

> My intention and my subject in this history will be simply to declare what I have myself experienced, seen, heard and observed, both on the sea, coming and going, and among the American savages, with whom I visited and lived for about a year.
>
> (Léry 1992: 3)

So states the French traveller Jean de Léry at the outset of his *Histoire d'un voyage fait en la terre du Bresil* (*History of a Voyage Made to the Land of Brazil*; 1578). It is an emphatic reminder of the most basic fact underpinning the authority of Léry's text and, indeed, the authority of all travellers – namely, that Léry has had personal experience of the scenes he is going to describe. The authority all travellers claim for themselves is thus that of the eye-witness, someone who has observed for him- or herself what others have only learnt about secondhand, through the reports of intermediaries. Such 'autopsy' (Greek for 'self-seeing', seeing for oneself) has long been privileged as a route to knowledge in Western culture. An early advocate of this 'autoptic' principle, or method, was the Greek historian Herodotus, who may also be regarded as one of the first travel writers insofar as he endeavoured to base his accounts of Egypt and other regions on his own observations rather than on hearsay. Thereafter, the value which has been placed on the reports of travellers has fluctuated; as we shall see, evidence or information acquired empirically has been more highly regarded in some periods than in others. Yet for the travellers themselves, a key means of asserting the accuracy and importance of their accounts has always been through reference to this autoptic principle, and through a vigorous insistence on their eye-witness status. For this reason, first-person verb forms will often be found even in modes of travel writing that are otherwise very impersonal; phrases such as 'I visited' and 'I saw' serve in part a rhetorical function, marking the text as a statement from someone who was actually present at the scenes described.

This appeal to the authority of the eye-witness, however, is not without its problems for travellers and travel writers. If on the one hand it lends the traveller's report an authoritative status, on the other it may also render the traveller an object of suspicion. Rooted as it is in personal experience, the traveller's account will often contain details that cannot be confirmed by any other witness, and that cannot receive external verification. The audience to any traveller's tale must therefore frequently defer to the traveller, taking on trust his or her report. This requirement to trust the traveller, however, may engender scepticism rather than belief. As audiences have often recognised, it is easy for travellers to exploit the privileged, eye-witness position that they claim for themselves. It was proverbial in the seventeenth century, for example, that 'Travellers may tell Romances or untruths by authority' (quoted in McKeon 2002: 100). The proverb is an acknowledgement that the traveller's classic retort – 'You weren't there!' – has frequently been a licence to embroider the facts or to invent outright falsehoods. Hence the habitual linkage, in many different cultures and epochs, between travellers and liars, and the equally widespread equation of the terms 'traveller's tale' and 'tall tale'.

The longstanding association between travellers and liars, however, is not just a consequence of the many hoaxes and deceptions practised by travellers over the years. It also derives from a further predicament that perennially faces travellers as they attempt to describe people and places unknown to their readers: namely, the fact that these people and places may be so far beyond the ken of the audience, and may appear so strange or exotic, that they beggar belief back home. The historical record throws up many travellers who have been for this reason disbelieved, even as they sought to relate faithfully their experience. The eighteenth-century Scottish traveller James Bruce was one such victim of audience incredulity. Bruce visited Abyssinia (modern-day Ethiopia) in the late 1760s, at a time when the country was little known to Europeans. He returned with a stock of colourful stories about the bizarre practices of this ancient, complex culture, including most notoriously the claim that the Abyssinians sometimes ate meat cut from living cattle. Readers and commentators back in London, however, regarded Bruce's account of the Abyssinians as preposterous and implausible, and he was soon being lampooned on the stage as 'MacFable'. Yet in time, later travellers to Abyssinia would corroborate many of Bruce's observations.

Bruce's initial failure to obtain credit with his audience was partly the consequence of the over-blown, self-aggrandising account he gave of his exploits amongst the Abyssinians. Yet it also reflects a failure in that audience to grasp, and to accept as genuine, cultural practices that were radically different and 'other' to their own. And whenever travellers have to describe events and phenomena that significantly confound the expectations of their audience, they are liable to be dismissed in this way, and labelled frauds and liars. As the editor of one seventeenth-century travel account grumbled, 'they who never saw more than their own Village, never imagine that Steeples are of any other fashion than their own' (quoted in McKeon 2002: 111).

Travellers themselves, of course, have often been confounded by their encounters with radical difference, and have frequently struggled to comprehend phenomena that surpass or overturn all previous expectations. For this reason, travel can be a deeply estranging experience, as the traveller is set adrift from the security of inherited norms and categories. Somewhat paradoxically, this estrangement may often be expressed, in part at least, by wonderment. As critics such as Mary Campbell (1988), Stephen Greenblatt (1991) and Anthony Pagden (1993) have observed, wonder constitutes a recurrent theme, and a stock **trope**, in travel writing. Wonder may be defined as the emotional and intellectual response that occurs when a traveller is confronted with something that temporarily defies understanding, and that cannot easily be assimilated into the conceptual grid by which the traveller usually organises his or her experience. The mixture of awe and bafflement that ensues will often operate at a pre-rational, even somatic level. Travellers report being rooted to the spot, or struck dumb in amazement; and the latter condition is one reason why tropes of inexpressibility and linguistic inadequacy are another commonplace in travel writing, with writers frequently protesting that even retrospectively they cannot find the words to convey fully their experience. Wonder is in this way an affective category with strong links to the **sublime**. Like the sublime, moreover, wonder is often a curious, unsettling amalgam of awe, fascination and fear. And as both Greenblatt and Pagden emphasise, it does not necessarily signal approval or pleasure; rather, 'wonder precedes, even escapes, moral categories' (Greenblatt 1991: 20). Thus the moment of dumbstruck wonder may as easily resolve itself into disgust and horror as into delight.

As this will suggest, in the encounter with the truly new and unknown, travellers will often face great difficulties simply comprehending their own experience, and what exactly it is that they have witnessed, even before they attempt the equally difficult task of describing that experience to others. To a great extent, of course, these two challenges, of comprehension and of communication, go hand in hand: to make sense of the travel experience will be simultaneously to arrive at a terminology and a conceptual framework that one can then use to recount that experience to others. In both enterprises, moreover, the same underlying methodology is often apparent. As Anthony Pagden has emphasised, in their endeavours to make sense of their encounters, and thereafter to describe them, travellers often proceed by a 'principle of attachment' (1993: 17) – that is to say, the traveller must seek to attach unknown entities to known reference points, and to familiar frameworks of meaning and understanding. Or to invoke a different vocabulary often used by Pagden and other critics, the 'incommensurable' must be rendered 'commensurable', by the finding of some common ground that can be used to measure and make meaningful what is otherwise simply baffling and alien.

This 'principle of attachment' can operate in many different ways, and at a variety of different levels. The most basic device at the traveller's disposal in this regard is perhaps the simile, which is accordingly a rhetorical figure much used in travel writing. Through the use of simile, travel writers can establish a point of comparison that frames the unknown in terms of the known, as in the following passage from William Dampier's *New Voyage Round the World* (1697):

> [The guava fruit] grows on a hard scrubbed Shrub, whose Bark is smooth and whitish, the branches pretty long and small, the leaf somewhat like that of a Hazel, the fruit much like a Pear, with a thin rind.
>
> (Dampier 1703: 222)

Simile is here utilised in its most simple form, to pick out points of visual resemblance between on the one hand, the guava and, on the other, the hazel and pear, plants more familiar to Dampier's readers. This is a strategy commonly adopted by travellers. It is not without its hazards, however. In medieval and early modern travelogues especially, Mary Campbell has suggested, simile is often used excessively to create 'perverse collages' which destroy 'the coherence of the alien subject in order to transmit a visualizable image' (1988: 70). Moreover, it was probably the use of simile in this way that generated some of the hybrid monsters described in ancient and medieval geographies, as slippages occurred from similitude to a supposed statement of fact, possibly because of errors in scribal transmission. One medieval 'wonder book', for example, informs us that 'there are on the Bryxontis wild animals which are called Lertices. They have ears of a donkey and wool of a sheep and feet of a bird' (quoted in Campbell 1988: 70). This grotesque-sounding beast probably evolved out of an original eye-witness account that *likened* its ears, fur and feet to those of a donkey, sheep and bird respectively.

There are many other methods by which travellers and travel writers can 'attach' the unknown to the known. The scientific knowledge operative in a given period, for example, may constitute a key conceptual framework by which the traveller seeks first to comprehend, and subsequently to communicate, the new and the other. Examples of this mode of attachment are obviously most plentiful in the eighteenth and nineteenth centuries, when more overtly scientific forms of travel begin to develop in Europe, but an interesting earlier example is provided by Marco Polo when he reports the existence of unicorns in Java. Modern readers might assume that this is a gesture towards the romance genre, and that Polo is simply inventing this detail to lend an air of the marvellous to his tale. Yet the truth here is probably more complex. Medieval natural history assumed the existence of unicorns; they are included, for example, in many bestiaries of this period. And there were horned quadrupeds not utterly dissimilar to unicorns to be found in the Indonesian archipelago in this period. What Polo (or his informant) probably saw was the creature that modern zoology would label the Sumatran rhinoceros. Having no concept of the rhinoceros, however, Polo 'attached', or assimilated, the animal that he saw to the closest matching conceptual category available in his culture: the unicorn.

When they could find no obvious reference point or conceptual category in their own culture for the scenes they witnessed, many European travellers historically have sought comparisons in the accounts of romance and fantasy known to their audiences. This is a more subtle way in which unknown entities and phenomena can be 'attached' to what is more familiar and known. It registers the sense of wonder and incomprehension that the traveller feels, whilst simultaneously finding some sort of reference point, albeit a fictive one, which can help audiences conceptualise the scenes being described. In this way, for example, early modern European travellers often figured the dazzling wealth of the Incan and Aztec empires in terms drawn from romance descriptions of sumptuous, magical palaces (see Greenblatt 1991: 132–33). By this means, also, European travellers could cast themselves, either implicitly or explicitly, as the virtuous knights-errant of romance fiction, protagonists whose heroic quests usually required them to overcome monstrous adversaries: a self-fashioning that often had fateful consequences for the native Americans who found themselves unwittingly cast in the latter role.

In various ways, then, travellers often proceed by some sort of 'principle of attachment', both as they seek to make sense of their experience, and as they seek to convey that experience to the reader. This is arguably all that a traveller can do when faced with the new and the different, yet at the same time it is an epistemological and descriptive procedure that can be highly problematic. In the first place, the truly new and the radically different will often ultimately resist recuperation in this way. Many travellers have complained that comparisons and analogies do not suffice to convey the true nature of the thing, people or place they wish to describe. Hence the frequency in travel writing of tropes of inexpressibility, as mentioned earlier. Thus the Spanish conquistador Bernal Diaz complained in his *Discovery and Conquest of Mexico* (1576), 'However clearly I may tell all this, I can never fully explain to one who did not see' (1996: 308). Jean de Léry similarly struggles to describe the Tupinamba, and eventually concedes that 'their gestures and expressions are so completely different from ours that it is difficult, I confess, to represent them well by writing or by pictures' (1992: 67). He goes on to suggest that the only way one can really grasp what the Tupinamba are like is by visiting them oneself. Yet this is to renege on the basic premise, and promise, of a traveller's report, and to substitute tautology for description; it leaves Léry somewhat in the position of Mark Antony, in Shakespeare's *Antony and Cleopatra*, when he parodies the conventional traveller's tale by delivering the unhelpful information that the crocodile is 'shaped ... like itself', and is 'just so high as it is' (Act 2, Scene 7).

The principle of attachment, then, may not suffice to make the new and the different comprehensible, either to the traveller or to their audience. Conversely, however, it may also sometimes operate too effectively. Having found some grounds for assimilating the unknown to the known, one temptation is to assume a greater similarity between familiar and unfamiliar entities than is actually the case. It was this assumption, Anthony Pagden points out, that led the sixteenth-century Spanish traveller Gonzalo Fernandez de Oviedo to attribute the practice of human sacrifice to the Taino tribespeople he encountered in America. He had no evidence for this claim; however, he had noticed that Taino men, like the ancient Thracians described by the Latin author Eusebius, took multiple wives, and on the basis of this initial point of resemblance Oviedo ascribes to the Taino other practices attributed to the Thracians, including human sacrifice (Pagden 1993: 24). Thus the necessary process of attaching the unknown to the known may easily lead to a series of what one might call 'over-attachments', and so to a variety of unwarranted assumptions and projections about the new phenomenon under consideration. Travellers and audiences who fall into this trap have in a sense not paid due deference to the intrinsic otherness of a new environment or culture; they have rendered the alien world too quickly comprehensible, and in the process effected a mistranslation of it.

As this will suggest, the traveller's situation is always liable to produce inadvertent misperceptions and unwarranted extrapolations, as he or she struggles to make sense of places and cultures which inevitably blend familiar and unfamiliar aspects. All travellers have only a partial viewpoint on the scenes and events they are witnessing, and insofar as they generalise from their own experience to draw conclusions or make larger observations about a foreign people or place, they are necessarily reliant on the rhetorical trope of **synecdoche**. That is to say, they must take a part as emblematic of a greater whole, since no traveller can survey every inch of a new environment, or become familiar with every member, and every nuance, of a foreign culture. Further to this, the observations they make and the conclusions they reach will inevitably be to some degree subjective, reflecting their own personal tastes, interests and attitudes. Simultaneously, this subjective viewpoint will always have to some extent an ideological aspect, being the expression of attitudes, assumptions and aspirations inherited from the larger culture or subculture of which the traveller is a part. All travelogues can in this way be said to provide not so much a representation of the world as it really is, as the representation of one particular *perspective* on the world. That is to say, they arguably tell us much more about the conceptual matrices, the conscious and unconscious assumptions, and frequently the ambitions of the individuals and communities that produce them, than they do about the people or place they purport to describe.

Mindful of the perspectivalism inevitably attendant on any traveller's report, some communities of travel writers and readers have developed procedural and stylistic strategies designed to minimise the distorting effects of the traveller's subjectivity, and also the distortions inevitably introduced by his or her ideological orientation. Some of these **objectivist** strategies, which are intended to render the information provided by the traveller more objective and so supposedly more accurate, will be discussed later in this chapter; although it is worth noting at once that even seemingly 'objective' forms of travel writing usually reflect, to some degree, a distinctive ideological perspective on the world. However, it is probably fair to say that historically most travel writers and their readers have not been overly troubled by the idea that the traveller's own cultural and ideological position informs and distorts any report of other peoples and places. After all, travel writers and their original, intended audiences have generally shared the same ideological assumptions, and what those audiences have accordingly usually wanted is to see the wider world translated into conceptual and moral categories that they recognise. Of greater concern to most readers of travel writing historically, though, has been the more straightforward issue of whether they are being lied to and deceived. To minimise this possibility, therefore, readers in every period will tend to demand of travel writing that it conforms to prevailing notions of what the historian of science Steven Shapin has termed 'epistemological decorum' (1994: 193). That is to say, if travelogues are to be credited by their readers, they must meet contemporary audience expectations as to what denotes reliability and plausibility in the travel account. And as we shall now see, it has been changes in these expectations, and in protocols of 'epistemological decorum', that have done much to drive the evolution of travel writing, and to produce its diverse modes and forms.

EPISTEMOLOGICAL DECORUM IN TRAVEL WRITING: GAINING THE READER'S TRUST

In medieval times, the plausibility and reliability of travel accounts was usually assessed in relation to the account of the world provided by a well-defined canon of established authorities. This canon comprised, on the one hand, the Bible and the writings of the Church Fathers and, on the other, the works of Classical philosophers, geographers and natural historians such as Aristotle and Pliny. Collectively these texts defined, for both travellers and their audiences, not only the known world but also what was knowable in the world, and what was likely to be true. Medieval travellers were certainly capable, to some degree, of questioning and problematising the prevailing wisdom and inherited conceptual categories of their culture. Marco Polo, for example, may construe the rhinoceros as a unicorn, but he is also able to point out all the ways in which this creature is unlike the conventional understanding of a unicorn: it is ugly, has hair like a buffalo, and crucially, is *not* easily captured by virgins. But generally, in cases where an individual traveller's account contradicted the intellectual orthodoxy of the day, med-ieval readers kept faith with orthodoxy, and judged that report implausible, and probably untrue. Thus 'epistemological decorum' in travel writing, in this period, was closely bound up with con-formity to the canon. The intellectual climate of the time placed less premium on the personal testimony of individual travellers than would later be the case, and it is for this reason that first-person accounts of actual travels form a comparatively small por-tion of what one can loosely define as medieval travel writing. For information on geographic and ethnographic matters, medieval readers were more likely to turn to texts that simply collated the existing canonical knowledge; as a consequence, even writers who had actually visited the people or places in question often eschewed a detailed account of their personal experience, so as to provide instead a compendium of relevant passages from earlier authorities.

As discussed in Chapter 3, the reports of travellers acquired a new prestige and significance in the aftermath of Columbus's discovery of America. In the English-speaking world, philoso-phers such as Sir Francis Bacon and John Locke increasingly stressed the importance of empirical evidence and inductive rea-soning. In this way, new protocols of 'epistemological decorum' took shape over the sixteenth and seventeenth centuries, and these protocols influenced in turn the activities and accounts of many travellers. Thinkers such as Bacon and Locke, and institutions such as the Royal Society, set up in 1660 to promote Baconian principles in science and knowledge, issued numerous directives to travellers, seeking in this way to regulate and systematise not only the sort of information they gathered, but just as crucially, the observational methods they used to gather and record data. These guidelines as to observational techniques influenced in turn the writing of travel texts, with the result that by the late seventeenth century a fairly standardised stylistic and structural template had emerged for the travelogue. Derived from what was perceived to be 'best practice', so to speak, in earlier accounts, this template was intended to authorise the traveller's report as reliable and trustworthy; although as we shall shortly see, it could also be used by mendacious travellers and fraudsters to lend a spurious air of plausibility to their fabrications.

William Dampier's hugely popular, and hugely influential, *New Voyage Round the World* (1697) provides perhaps the best illustration of this new template, and of the protocols of epistemological decorum that underpinned it. Dampier's bestselling account of his thirteen years as a privateer in the Caribbean begins as follows:

> April the 17th 1681, about Ten a Clock in the morning, being 12 Leagues N.W. from the Island *Plata*, we left Captain Sharp and those who were willing to go with him in the Ship, and embarked into our La[u]nch and Canoas, designing for the River of Santa Maria, in the Gulph of St Michael, which is about 200 leagues from the Isle of Plata. We were in number 44 white Men who bore Arms, a Spanish Indian, who bore Arms also: and two Moskito Indians, who always bear Arms amongst the Privateers, and are much valued by them for striking Fish and Turtle, or Tortoise[,] and Manatee or Sea Cow; and five Slaves taken in the South Seas, who fell to our share.
>
> The Craft which carried us was a La[u]nch, or Long Boat, one Canoa, and another Canoa which had been sawn asunder in the middle, in order to have made Bumkins, or Vessels for carrying water, if we had not separated from our Ship. This we joyn'd together again and made it tight; providing Sails to help us along: And for 3 days before we parted, we sifted so much Flower as we could well carry, and rubb'd up 20 or 30 pound of Chocolate with Sugar to sweeten it;

these things and a Kettle the Slaves carried also on their backs after
we landed.

(Dampier 1703: 1–2)

Prior to this opening, it should be noted, a short introduction
serves to establish how Dampier came to be on this island in the
Caribbean, who Captain Sharp is, and the circumstances that
gave rise to the rift between Sharp and Dampier's companions.
The introduction gives this information in a brisk summary;
with the start of the narrative proper, however, we begin to get a
more detailed and precise account of movement, location, and
activity. The narrative is presented in a journal format, and is
clearly based on a log or diary that Dampier maintained at the
time. Dampier, indeed, takes care to emphasise this fact in his
preface. As he explains, the account 'is composed of a mixt relation of Places and Actions, in the same order of time in which
they occurred: for which end I kept a journal of every day's
Observation' (unpaginated).

The keeping of journals was a key directive laid down for travellers
by the Royal Society. It was intended to ensure that observations
were recorded whilst still fresh in the memory, or even whilst
the scenes and phenomena being described were still in front of
the traveller, rather than being hazily remembered at a different
location or later point in time. Accordingly, it soon became
incumbent upon travel writers to demonstrate both that they had
adopted such a disciplined approach to note-taking whilst travelling, and also that their published narrative was largely derived
from these original, on-the-spot observations. Dampier's adoption
of the journal format is intended to reassure the reader on these
points, as is the apparent artlessness of the writing style. For the
most part his prose eschews elaborate tropes and figures of speech,
and whilst his sentences are often long, they typically proceed by
a comparatively simple, **paratactic** accumulation of clauses, rather
than by a more elaborate, **hypotactic** syntax involving numerous
subordinate clauses. His diction, meanwhile, reveals a marked
preference for authentic-sounding vernacular terms, such as, in the
passage above, 'Canoas' and 'Bumkins', over ostentatiously erudite
or elegant phraseology. This use of a plain style corresponds to

Royal Society directives against the use of excessive rhetorical ornamentation in travel accounts. The aim was partly to avoid ambiguity, and thus limit the potential for misinterpretation. Yet this style was also intended to signal that the printed text was indeed a transcription of Dampier's original field notes, rather than an account written up retrospectively, and so potentially falsified or misremembered.

The protocols of epistemological decorum established by the Royal Society influenced not only *how* one recorded one's observations and presented them to the public, but also *what* one observed and recorded. Abstract or metaphysical speculations were to be kept to a minimum, as were subjective impressions, and personal thoughts and feelings. Instead, writers were advised to prioritise the observation of measurable, material phenomena in the external world. Hence Dampier's precise denotations of time, place, number and distance as he charts his movements around the Caribbean. The result is a narrative voice which makes much use of the first-person pronoun, in both its singular and plural forms, yet which nevertheless often seems very unemotive and impersonal. Rhetorically, this works to enhance the sense of Dampier as a dispassionate, rational and therefore reliable eye-witness to events and phenomena. As Jonathan Lamb puts it, the aim is construct a sense of the narratorial self as a 'sturdy platform [for observation], superior to the stresses that might distort its measurement of things, or trouble the sense of its own consistency' (2001: 78). In this way Dampier presents himself as what it is sometimes labelled a 'Cartesian' self or subject, and as an 'I' who seems simply a disembodied 'eye' surveying the surrounding scene; and the term 'Cartesian' here alludes to the influential theory of the self developed by the seventeenth-century philosopher René Descartes, which postulated an absolute division between mind and matter, observing subject and observed object.

Further to this, the Royal Society, and figures associated with it like John Locke and Robert Boyle, followed Bacon's example and published guidelines listing the 'Heads', or categories, of data they would like travellers to gather. Here the emphasis was generally on the acquisition of 'useful knowledge', by which was meant natural-historical and ethnographic information relevant to contemporary scientific debates, or else with an obvious strategic or commercial application. This observational rubric gives rise, in Dampier's *New Voyage*, to an account in which a narrative proper, describing the movements and activities of the narrator, is interspersed with more static passages purely of description. This is what Dampier means when he describes his account as a '*mixt relation* of Places and Actions' (my emphasis). However, it is not simply 'places' that are described in the observational segments of the account, but also a plethora of plant and animal species, along with meteorological phenomena, the customs of the Moskito Indians, and much else besides. Something of the precision of Dampier's descriptive technique in these passages may be gauged from the account of the guava cited earlier in this chapter.

In many cases, it should be noted, these descriptive passages bring together observations that were obviously made over a period of time, and in several different places. They must therefore have been composed retrospectively, from detailed notes made at different moments in time, so Dampier is clearly being disingenuous when he insists in his preface that his observations are related strictly 'in the same order of time' as they were originally made. Yet by situating these observational passages within the larger journal framework, Dampier underscores and seemingly corroborates his claim that all the information he is presenting has been acquired 'experimentally', as he puts it at one point; he means empirically, through personal experience. The narrative portions of the text thus contextualise the passages of static description, allowing readers to understand how Dampier's observations were gathered, and reassuring them of Dampier's status as an eye-witness to the phenomena he describes. Moreover, insofar as the journal format requires Dampier to present something of himself, and offer over the course of his account a degree of personal narrative, it also seemingly allows the reader to assess the overall trustworthiness of the author. The general plausibility of the experiences Dampier relates, the absence of any obviously romantic details such as monsters or supernatural events, and of course the plain style in which he recounts his experiences, all serve to demonstrate that the writer is a sober, reliable individual, not prone to exaggeration, or flights of fancy. And this sense of reliability and scrupulous note-taking, built up over the narrative as a whole, works to authorise each individual observation that Dampier presents to the reader.

Dampier's *New Voyage* went through five editions in almost as many years. Its enormous popularity reflected the extent to which contemporary readers were persuaded of its truthfulness and reliability. Its success in this regard, coupled with the influence of the Royal Society more generally, helped to establish procedural, formal and stylistic paradigms which were widely followed in eighteenth- and early nineteenth-century travel writing, and which to a great extent continue to underpin the genre even today. For the critic Michael McKeon, these paradigms, and the epistemological protocols that give rise to them, are best characterised as 'naïve empiricism' (see McKeon 2002: 100–117). With regard to the writing-up of the traveller's experience, this attitude of 'naïve empiricism' assumes that the most accurate and trustworthy of travel accounts are those that present themselves as fairly direct, unmediated transcriptions of the traveller's original travel notes. An air of artlessness, and the apparent absence of any retrospective narratorial or editorial emendation, thus becomes a key marker of authenticity and reliability in travel writing. It is in this spirit, for example, that the editors John and Awnsham Churchill commend one account in their four-volume *Collection of Voyages and Travels* (1704) for having

> nothing of Art or Language, being left by an ignorant Sailor [...]; and therefore the Reader can expect no more than bare matter of Fact, deliver'd in a homely Stile, which it was not fit to alter, lest it might breed a Jealousy that something had been chang'd more than the bare Language.
>
> (Quoted in McKeon 2002: 109)

Or in the words of Shakespeare's Othello, which were much quoted by eighteenth-century commentators in this context, the travel account should ideally aim to be a 'plain, unvarnished tale' (Act 1, Scene 3) that has undergone as little re-organisation or embellishment as possible in the transition from journal to print.

This air of artlessness and scrupulous, on-the-spot note-taking could of course be an illusion. It is for this reason that McKeon designates the formal and stylistic paradigms outlined earlier '*naïve* empiricism'. For many contemporary readers, Dampier's *New Voyage* ushered in a new era for travel writing, in which the genre shook off its age-old association with fantastical romance to become instead a far more reputable and reliable vehicle for intellectual enquiry and scientific knowledge. Yet as McKeon points out, and as many sceptical commentators pointed out at the time, travel writing in the new style could just as easily be a vehicle for romance and fabrication. However plain and authentic-sounding the prose style, and however detailed the journal entries, there was in fact no guarantee that an account had not been significantly altered in its transition from original diary to published narrative. Modern scholarship, for example, has established that Dampier himself significantly altered some key episodes in his narrative, on occasions condensing several events into one and reworking them so as to cast himself in a better light (see Edwards 1994: 28–30). More worrying still, a journal format and a plain prose style in the published text did not in themselves guarantee that the narrative recounted events which had actually taken place. Daniel Defoe's fictional *Robinson Crusoe* (1719), for example, used the plain style pioneered by Dampier to create a powerful effect of realism, and the illusion of truthfulness. The same narrative conventions could also be exploited by outright fraudsters such as George Psalmanazar, whose best-selling *Historical and Geographical Description of Formosa* (1704) fascinated European readers for several years with its accounts of polygamy, cannibalism and other bizarre practices. Only when the Formosan craze began to abate, however, did the author admit to compiling his narrative out of earlier sources, and making up the more lurid details.

The attitude of 'naïve empiricism' espoused in much eighteenth- and nineteenth-century travel writing, then, does not necessarily produce travelogues that are any more reliable and trustworthy than their predecessors. Yet adherence to the formal and stylistic conventions outlined earlier became in this period a rhetorical necessity for travel writers who wished to be believed. They were a key means by which writers fashioned a successful 'fiction of factual representation', in the phrase Holland and Huggan (1998:10) borrow from Hayden White (1976), and so persuaded readers of their reliability. To flout these conventions was accordingly to risk a sceptical response from the reading public. In this way, however, the prevailing conventions of travel writing often subtly constrained what travellers were able to report. If the yardstick for plausibility in medieval travel writing was set by the canon, and so by the precedents established by prior textual authorities, the new protocols of epistemological decorum tended to gauge plausibility by the prior experience of readers and commentators, and by prevailing audience expectations as to what sorts of phenomena were both possible and likely. A version of what is sometimes termed 'probabilism' thus operated in the reception of travel writing. In this spirit, for example, Samuel Johnson praised Jerome Lobo's Abyssinian travelogue, which he translated into English in 1735, on account of the fact that it contained 'no romantic absurdities or incredible fictions' but only events that conformed to usual expectations of possibility and probability. He further insisted that the travel writer 'who tells nothing exceeding the bounds of probability, has a right to demand that they should believe him who cannot contradict him' (Johnson 1789: 11). Yet as we have seen with the example of James Bruce, travellers have often encountered phenomena and practices which stretch 'the bounds of probability' that normally operate at home. Many travel writers, however, have been aware that their credibility and reputation for trustworthiness could easily unravel on the basis of just one seemingly fantastical detail in their account. As Lady Mary Wortley Montagu complained,

> we travellers are in very hard circumstances: If we say nothing but what has been said before us, we are dull, and we have observed nothing. If we tell anything new, we are laughed at as fabulous and romantic.
>
> (1906: 156)

And so the new agenda and attitude in travel writing, born of the desire to produce a more accurate picture of the world and its inhabitants, sometimes had the paradoxical effect of bringing about the non-reporting of certain sorts of information. The African explorer Mungo Park, for example, is said to have told Sir Walter Scott that he left many remarkable stories out of his acclaimed *Travels in the Interior Districts of Africa* (1799), since he feared suffering the same fate as Bruce.

There were also further limitations attendant on the conventions of naïve empiricism, at least for some eighteenth- and early nineteenth-century travel writers and their readers. The period saw European science become increasingly rigorous and specialised; it also saw a massive expansion in the number of overseas territories administered by the European powers. These were to some extent complementary and connected developments, insofar as the increasing rigour and specialisation of science was partly driven by the need of the colonial powers to acquire a detailed and comprehensive knowledge of the territories they controlled, or sought to control. As a consequence, a new sort of European traveller emerged, the scientific surveyor or 'explorer'. From James Cook onwards, these were often highly trained professionals, whose activities were driven by, and contributed to, the increasingly sophisticated taxonomic and theoretical schema developed by figures like the Swedish natural historian Linnaeus. To aid them in their data collection, these explorers increasingly carried with them a plethora of scientific instruments: sextants, altimeters, thermometers, barometers and even, in the case of the German explorer Alexander von Humboldt, a cyanometer, designed to measure the blueness of the sky. These instruments enabled measurements to be taken with much greater precision, thereby minimising the mediating and potentially distorting influence of the traveller's subjective viewpoint. And this desire to find ostensibly objective techniques of observation and data collection, rather than relying on personal impressions, also led to the growing use, amongst some explorers and surveyors, of statistical or census techniques for gathering information about both the natural world and foreign cultures (see Edney 1997; Leask 2002: 161–66).

These developments contributed to the gradual abandonment, in some branches of travel writing, of the conventions of naïve empiricism outlined earlier. The growing specialisation of science, for example, generated an increasingly technical scientific vocabulary that could not easily be reconciled with the requirement for a plain prose style in the travel account. Increasingly, moreover, exploratory expeditions and surveys generated both more information, and also more data that was purely quantitative, than could be easily incorporated into a readable narrative of the explorer's journey. For such travellers, moreover, a chronological personal narrative was not necessarily the most useful method of structuring their reports, at least when those reports were intended for scientific specialists and colonial bureaucrats. A chronologically ordered report might require readers to work through the whole narrative to glean all the observations relevant to a given topic. Far more useful, accordingly, were accounts which presented their information in a systematic fashion, with the observations relevant to each specific subject area brought together and consolidated in separate sections or chapters. In some cases, these chapters might then be integrated within a larger personal narrative of the traveller's journey. Alternatively, they might be presented as appendices to the personal narrative; this is the strategy adopted in Park's *Travels*, for example, where a long and frequently technical appendix written by the geographer James Rennell provides a digest of the new geographical information garnered through Park's endeavours. In other cases, however, the element of personal narrative was abandoned altogether, to present simply a digest of the traveller's findings, and possibly his or her theoretical reflections, on various topics. Perhaps the most striking example of this tendency in the form is the vast, multi-authored *Description de l'Egypte* (*Description of Egypt*). Commissioned by Napoleon and published in twenty volumes between 1809 and 1818, this provides an exhaustive and methodical account of Egypt's antiquities, its natural history, and its current political and cultural state. However, this information is seldom framed within any sort of narrative of the journeys undertaken to gather it.

In this way some modes of travel writing became increasingly reliant on what one might term objectivist strategies for presenting information and appearing authoritative. Where the traditions of naïve empiricism sought to emphasise the extent to which all observations were rooted in the traveller's eye-witness experience, these new modes typically downplayed or elided this personal dimension, focusing to a greater extent simply on the data gathered by the traveller. In this regard, it is worth contrasting the passage from Dampier's *New Voyage* cited earlier with the following passage from John Barrow's *Travels into the Interior of Southern Africa* (1801):

> The following day we passed the Great Fish River, though not without some difficulty, the banks being high and steep, the stream strong, the bottom rocky, and the water deep. Some fine trees of the willow of Babylon, or a variety of that species, skirted the river at this place. The opposite side presented a very beautiful country, well wooded and watered, and plentifully covered with grass, among which grew in abundance, a species of indigo, apparently the same as that described by Mr Masson as the *candicans*.
>
> (190)

For all that Dampier's account keeps its focus on events and material phenomena in the external world, his observations are framed by a first-person narration that frequently deploys the pronouns 'I', 'we', 'us' and 'our'. Barrow, meanwhile, has excised this first-person framework for much of the passage above. After the initial clause, information is presented more baldly, with little reference to the narratorial self that traversed the African landscape to gather these observations. Thus Barrow presents himself even more emphatically than Dampier as a dispassionate, disembodied 'Cartesian' subject, concerned simply to survey the surrounding scene.

Barrow utilises this impersonal style within a larger narrative structure that broadly tracks the traveller's itinerary. As noted, however, some forms of scientific or bureaucratic travel reports increasingly dispensed with this narrative dimension altogether, producing accounts which simply presented and analysed the information relevant to one specific topic or field, without making any reference to the author's journey. As modern scientific disciplinarity emerged in the mid-nineteenth century, many academic disciplines that had previously relied greatly on travel writing for their data began to strive for this sort of **objectivism** in style and structure, so as to distinguish themselves from more anecdotal, impressionistic forms of travelogue. These objectivist strategies were also adopted in many guidebooks, which similarly began to take on their distinctive modern form in the 1830s. Along with a more impersonal mode of discourse, moreover, many guidebooks and scientific treatises adopted non-narrative or graphic methods of presenting information, such as gazetteers, lists and catalogues, or tables and charts. Again, the rhetorical effect of these devices was an air of a greater objectivity, and so of increased authority. A table or list does not remind readers of the mediating role of a traveller/observer in the way that a personal narrative of travel does, and it obscures the processes by which the knowledge being offered was produced; we are seemingly presented with facts, pure and simple, rather than with just one individual's observations, and his or her interpretation of those observations.

Of course, even these seemingly more objective and authoritative modes of travel writing can be mimicked, by both mendacious and playful writers. Once again, they are not intrinsically any marker of a greater reliability in the travel text, but rather just a different rhetorical strategy for conveying authority and obtaining credit from the reader. Like any form of travel writing, moreover, even such seemingly 'objective' texts necessarily render the world in a partial and to some extent skewed manner, since inevitably they record only some aspects of another people or place. Furthermore, whilst these objectivist strategies in both the collection and representation of data are often intended to overcome the inevitable subjectivity of an individual traveller's viewpoint, the texts that result will still usually possess an ideological dimension. The information that a traveller and his or her culture choose to record, and the methods they use to obtain and present that data, are reflective of a culture's attitudes, assumptions and ambitions towards the wider world. The long lists of 'natural productions' that fill the appendices of many eighteenth- and nineteenth-century exploration narratives, for example, arguably constitute a kind of stock-taking; and here a seemingly objective mode of representation is in fact expressive of, and contributive to, the commercial and colonial agendas that underpinned much European exploration in this era (see Franklin 1979; Pratt 2008).

As this will suggest, the developments in travel writing outlined in this section, and the vigorous debates about the genre which drove those developments, were not undertaken as abstract intellectual exercises, or in a spirit merely of literary experimentation. Indeed, most of the travel texts discussed so far in this chapter should not really be regarded as 'literature', in the principal modern sense of this term. They served more pragmatic ends, although this did not prevent them also being read for pleasure and achieving immense popularity with the reading public. To borrow a useful distinction from Stephen Greenblatt, in these texts we see not the 'imagination at play' but rather the 'imagination at work' (1991: 23), struggling to overcome epistemological and representational problems so as to render travel writing a more effective technology for the transmission of information. This technology was required in the first place for the accumulation of knowledge, and travel writing in this regard played a major role in the emergence of Western science in its modern forms. In the model of scientific enquiry offered by the sociologist Bruno Latour, the traveller's account may be considered one of the 'mobiles', or transportable forms of data, that are brought back from the field to the **centres of calculation** that drive the scientific process (see Latour 1987). These 'centres' might be institutions such as, in Britain, the Royal Society, the Admiralty and the Royal Geographical Society; or they might be individuals, such as Sir Joseph Banks, who travelled on Cook's first voyage and thereafter played a pivotal role in British exploratory activity. Either way, their role was to accumulate and disseminate the data gathered by travellers; to oversee the development of new theories and models in the light of this data; and thereafter to direct further missions to test, extend or put to practical use the new knowledge that had thus been formed.

These scientific endeavours were not conducted in a vacuum, divorced from the *realpolitik* of strategic and economic considerations. From its emergence in the seventeenth century down to the present day, European science has been driven as much by the requirements of the state as by pure intellectual curiosity. Across the same period, travel writing, as a key contributor to the advancement of science, has contributed significantly to the advancement of European power, and to the emergence of the Spanish, Portuguese, French, British and other European empires. The explosion in European travel writing from the fifteenth century onwards constituted a massive accumulation of what Greenblatt has termed 'mimetic capital' (1991: 6), providing a stock of hugely useful descriptions of the world. It was partly this ever-growing body of knowledge, along with superior weapons systems, that gave Europeans a decisive technological advantage over many of the indigenous peoples they encountered round the world; and the implications of European travel writing's complex entanglement with the processes of empire, colonisation and exploitation will be discussed further in Chapter 6.

AUTHORITY AND VERACITY IN THE MODERN TRAVEL BOOK

What, though, of the 'imagination at play' in travel writing? What of the claims to truthfulness made by the modern travel book, the more literary branch of the travel writing genre which has flourished since the nineteenth century, and which today is what most readers recognise as 'travel writing'? Through what strategies and literary devices do the writers of these texts seek to establish their trustworthiness and authority as eye-witnesses and commentators?

Insofar as they wish to convey truthfulness and factuality, modern travel writers have at their disposal all the literary devices and narrative conventions developed by earlier travel writers, and by other modes of travel writing. They may align themselves with the tradition of naïve empiricism, and present their whole narrative as just a lightly edited transcription of notes and journal-entries made 'on the spot'. Alternatively, they may insert into a more obviously polished and written-up account just a few sections marked as 'from my diary' or 'from my notebook', thereby emphasising to readers that the narrative as a whole is grounded in personal experience. They may even utilise some of the more objectivist literary devices described earlier, incorporating into their accounts any number of tables, lists and graphs, so as to suggest that they are giving us plain facts, rather than a more subjective viewpoint.

These are just some of the authenticating, and as it were 'factualising' strategies available to the writers of modern trave-logues, and every travel writer will make their own permutation of the various devices available to them in this regard. Usually in the modern travel book, however, these devices are located within an account that is still structured as a 'mixt relation', in William Dampier's phraseology; that is to say, as a combination of narrative sections, in which the narrator describes the events of the journey and his or her personal travel experiences, and more descriptive sections of commentary and reflection, in which the traveller proffers an interpretation of those experiences, and essays some broader conclusions about the people and places that have been visited. Or as Rob Nixon has put it, we typically find in travel literature today an oscillation between 'an autobiographical, emotionally tangled mode' and a 'semi-ethnographic, distanced, analytical mode' (1992: 15). Thus Ryszard Kapuscinski's travel essay 'The Ambush' opens with the information that 'We were driving north from Kampala, toward Uganda's border with Sudan' (2007: 147) and then proceeds to weave together, on the one hand, a personal narrative of his experiences whilst accompanying a presidential motorcade and, on the other, a series of more general pronouncements about life in this part of East Africa. We are informed, for example, that

> the residents of Kampala speak of their kinsmen from Karimojong (it is at once the name of a place, a people and a person) with distaste and embarrassment. The Karimojong walk around naked, and insist upon this custom, seeing the human body as beautiful (and in fact they are magnificently built, tall and slender). Their intransigence on this score has yet another basis: most of the Europeans who reached them in the early years of African exploration rapidly fell ill and died, from which the Karimojong deduced that clothing causes illness, and getting dressed is tantamount to sentencing yourself to death.

> (2007: 151–52)

This is the 'semi-ethnographic' mode to which Nixon refers, a more impersonal and dispassionate prose style that conveys the sense that the observations being made are not simply the traveller's personal impressions, but rather that they have a general validity, and are an objective statement of fact.

As a medium for presenting information about the wider world, however, the modern travel book has often generated considerable uncertainty and unease in readers; or at least, in more scholarly readers. As we have seen, an epistemological anxiety about the validity of the knowledge provided by travelogues has always haunted travel writing. But in the modern travel book, this age-old anxiety about the truthfulness and accuracy of travel writers is significantly compounded by a range of further factors. In the first place, for example, it is not always clear to what extent the modern travel book actually means to make any sort of truth claim, or undertakes to convey an accurate knowledge of the wider world. As discussed in Chapter 2, the modern travel book is usually both more overtly *autobiographical*, and more self-consciously *literary*, than most of the travelogues discussed so far in the present chapter. This emphasis on autobiography and 'literariness' causes the modern travel book's agenda, and its generic contract with the reader, to be subtly but significantly different from that which operates in other forms of travel writing. In a sense, it ceases to matter as much whether the information we are being given is strictly true. Instead, readers understand that they are reading for the insights they will gain into the writer's distinctive sensibility, and for the pleasure they will gain from an equally individual literary style. Take, for example, the following passage from Bill Bryson's best-selling comic travelogue, *The Lost Continent: Travels in Small-Town America* (first published 1989). Addressing his readers directly, Bryson informs them that when they drive in Kansas, as he has just done, they will frequently find old pick-up trucks pulling out in front of them, only narrowly avoiding a collision. This phenomenon is explained as follows:

> Curious to see what sort of person could inconvenience you in this
> way in the middle of nowhere, you speed up to overtake [the truck]

and see that sitting at the wheel is a little old man of eighty-seven, wearing a cowboy hat three sizes too large for him, staring fixedly at the empty road as if piloting a light aircraft through a thunderstorm. He is of course quite oblivious of you. Kansas has more drivers like this than any other state in the nation, more than can be accounted for by simple demographics. Other states must send them their old people, perhaps by promising them a free cowboy hat when they get there.

(1999: 280)

Clearly, no reader of this passage is going to complain if they subsequently visit Kansas and discover that the roads are not full of pick-up trucks driven by old men in outsize cowboy hats. And this is not just because their journey will have turned out to be less hazardous than Bryson here predicts. Most readers will recognise immediately that this is just an amusing comic riff, which is meant to be appreciated more for its absurdity and exaggeration than for its fidelity to the truth. In other literary travel books, similarly, readers will often recognise that a key agenda in many passages may not be accuracy of representation *per se*, but rather the telling of amusing anecdotes, or the crafting of an overall mood or tone. In these passages, accordingly, the authority that travel writers claim for themselves is not really bound up with the accuracy or otherwise of their accounts: rather it is predicated on whether they hold the reader's attention, either by writing well or by telling an interesting story. They claim, in short, the authority of fiction, and by so doing side-step the requirement that they be strictly truthful in their reporting.

Yet this is not the whole story about the literary travelogue. If on the one hand the genre usually seems to prioritise the aesthetic effects it creates, and the aesthetic pleasure it gives the reader, over the accuracy of its account of the world, on the other hand the modern travel book will also usually present itself as being broadly a factual representation of real experiences and real places. Indeed, many travel writers in this tradition will often suggest that by virtue of their distinctive, uniquely insightful personalities, and/or their fine writing, they are able to offer a portrait of peoples and places that goes deeper, and is ultimately more

UNIVERSITY OF WINCHESTER
LIBRARY

truthful, than those accounts that stick pedantically to matters of clear, observable fact. Thus the writers of more literary travelogues often claim, somewhat paradoxically, the authority both of fiction and of non-fiction. Or as Patrick Holland and Graham Huggan put it, the modern travel book is 'generically elusive, as unwilling to give up its claims to documentary veracity as it is to waive its license to rhetorical excess' (1998: 12). It is this generic ambiguity that has often scandalised commentators, since obviously it creates enormous scope for confusion and misinterpretation, and for readers to construe as fact what was actually only intended as playful conceit or personal opinion.

Further to this, many scholarly commentators over the years have attacked the modern, more literary travel book for the ease with which it enables writers to claim an often unwarranted authority in their pronouncements on other peoples and places. As Holland and Huggan (1998), Debbie Lisle (2006) and others have recently emphasised, the fact of having 'been there', and so having personal eye-witness experience, will often confer a spurious legitimacy on what are actually very superficial and ill-informed accounts of other people and places. All too often, it is suggested, travel writers take what Graham Greene in his Mexican travelogue *The Lawless Roads* (1939) calls the 'tourist view' of a foreign destination, with the result that a whole nation such as Mexico is thought of 'in terms of quiet and gentleness and devotion' largely 'on the strength of one prosperous town on the highway, [and] on the strength of a happy mood' (1981: 42). That is to say, travel writers are notoriously prone to summing up whole cultures, and passing sweeping judgements on other peoples and places, on the basis of just a few personal impressions, or from merely anecdotal evidence.

Once again, this has been an accusation frequently lodged against all forms of travel writing over the centuries, and it derives from the perennial problem, noted earlier in this chapter, that all travelogues must to some extent proceed as a series of synecdoches, whereby parts are taken as representative of a larger totality. As Greene also writes in *The Lawless Roads*: 'How to describe a city? Even for an old inhabitant it is impossible: one can present only a simplified plan, taking a house here, a park there as symbols of the whole' (1981: 41). As we have seen, however, some modes of travel writing, from the seventeenth century onwards, have sought to limit or counterbalance this inevitable tendency in the traveller's report. The protocols of naïve empiricism that emerged over the course of the seventeenth century, for example, aimed to reduce the potential for unwarranted generalisations by insisting that travellers simply observe the material phenomena in front of them, without extrapolating unduly from those immediate observations. (This was, of course, a rubric that was not always observed.) In the nineteenth century, meanwhile, disciplines such as Geography, Anthropology and Sociology developed more overtly scientific and academic modes of travel writing, and so imposed a degree of methodological rigour on travellers working in these traditions. Writers in these branches of travel writing were increasingly required to cross-reference their personal findings against a larger body of established disciplinary knowledge, and to offer a degree of explicit self-reflection on the theoretical assumptions brought to bear on another people or place. By these means, more academic modes of travel writing have sought to counteract the traveller's frequent tendency to rush to hasty and wholly subjective conclusions.

The writers of more literary travel accounts, however, are not obliged to follow any sort of methodological or disciplinary procedure as they formulate their reports of other countries and cultures. That said, many of these writers will often claim a degree of scholarly expertise, making a show of specialist knowledge and academic rigour as they frame their observations. Yet as many critics have pointed out, in 'literary' works aimed at the non-specialist reader one must always keep in mind that any show of scholarship may be simply a facade, and a rhetorical strategy designed to bolster the writer's credibility, rather than an indication of genuine expertise in a given field. Thus Bruce Chatwin's *The Songlines* (1987) presents itself at one level as a fairly scholarly enquiry into mankind's nomadic impulses, yet in the eyes of most professional anthropologists the theory that Chatwin develops, and the account he offers of Aboriginal sacred practices, are both profoundly flawed and inadequate (see Huggan 1991; Shakespeare 1999, 489–90). The anthropologist Neil Whitehead similarly lambasts the apparent ethnographic rigour of Charles Nicholl's Guyanese travelogue *The Creature in the Map: A Journey to El Dorado* (1995); as Whitehead points out, Nicholl provides the reader with numerous 'mistaken linguistic etymologies', and misidentifies at least one of the tribes he encounters (1997: 32).

If some travel writers claim in this way a scholarly authority that is often unjustified, others insist that their authority derives, somewhat paradoxically, precisely from their lack of specialist knowledge. As Holland and Huggan (1998) note, the persona of the 'amateur' or the 'dilettante' is frequently adopted by the narrators of modern travel books. In part, this is a narratorial self-fashioning born of defensiveness and a sense of belatedness; the writers of literary travelogues are often keenly aware that they are following in the footsteps of true explorers, heroic figures who reported real discoveries and made genuine contributions to knowledge. Yet this pose of comparative ignorance may simultaneously invest the traveller with an alternative form of authority. He or she is thus able to present themselves as an 'everyman' figure, and as the ordinary reader's representative in the field; and implicit in this characterisation, usually, is the assumption that it is travellers equipped simply with bluff common sense who produce the most accurate reports, since they are supposedly free of the preconceived ideas, and the entrenched theoretical positions, that might accompany a more specialist knowledge of the region being visited.

In practice, of course, this amateurishness frequently produces a superficial and highly impressionistic account of another people or place. Just as frequently, moreover, such accounts simply reiterate and reinforce many of the prevailing stereotypes and prejudices already circulating in the traveller's culture, notwithstanding his or her claim to be some sort of independent-minded free spirit. As a consequence, Holland and Huggan have suggested that whilst many modern travel books undoubtedly adopt what Rob Nixon has termed a 'semi-ethnographic' mode (1992:15), it is in fact more appropriate to regard them as '*pseudo*-ethnographic' documents (Holland and Huggan 1998: 12; my emphasis), which can seldom be relied on to give us an accurate account of other cultures.

In this way Holland and Huggan, like Lisle and several other recent critics, are generally dismissive of the modern travel book's claim to be a factual genre that presents us with reliable information about the wider world. Yet this is a critique of the form that needs to be qualified in several regards. It is worth noting, for example, that when anthropologists and other academic professionals scoff at the unreliability and superficiality of many travel books, what we are witnessing is to some extent a disciplinary turf war, in which academics wish to assert the superiority of their own modes of travel and travel writing. From their emergence in the nineteenth century onwards, scholarly modes of travel writing such as ethnography have always defined themselves against the supposedly lightweight and anecdotal travel book; this has been a key rhetorical device by which these disciplines have themselves heightened their own air of authority. More recently, however, some anthropologists have questioned whether there is such a clear dividing between, on the one hand, supposedly scientific, objective ethnography and, on the other, the supposedly impressionistic, subjective travel book (see Clifford and Marcus 1986; Geertz, 1988). Or, as Mary Louise Pratt puts it, ethnography has generally been in denial about the extent to which 'its own discursive practices were often inherited from ... other genres [such as travel writing,] and are still shared with them today' (Pratt 1986: 26).

Rethinking ethnography's relationship with the travel book in this way brings with it the implication that travel books may sometimes be a valid source of ethnographic information, even if that information is not always couched in the specialised idiom of the professional anthropologist. Certainly this seems a fair assessment of the many travel writers over the years who have lived long periods amongst the peoples and landscapes they describe, and who clearly have a deep knowledge of, and a great affinity with, those peoples and landscapes. One thinks here of travelogues such as Wilfred Thesiger's *The Marsh Arabs* (1964), which is of course not free from its own prejudices and foibles, but which nevertheless offers an insightful account of the Madan people of southern Iraq. A work such as Hugh Brody's *Maps and Dreams: Indians and British Columbia Frontier* (1981), meanwhile, sits somewhere between a formal ethnography and a travel book, being written to rigorous anthropological standards yet pitched at a more general audience. And finally, Barry Lopez's *Arctic Dreams* (1986), a scrupulously rendered account of the interrelationships between different species in the Canadian Arctic ecosystem, reminds us that the modern travel book will sometimes be rigorously grounded in the natural as well as the social sciences.

It is worth remembering also that claims to scholarly expertise in the modern travel book are not always a façade, or a rhetorical device intended to bolster the writer's authority. Some travel writers really are the experts they claim to be; thus Daniel Everett's *Don't Sleep, There Are Snakes* (2008), a fascinating account of the Piraha people of Brazil, is the work of an academic linguist who has held professorships at several leading universities. In this regard, one must keep in mind the diversity of material embraced by even that subset of travel writing, the modern travel book. There are of course many shallow, inconsequential and sometimes highly prejudicial travel books, yet the genre also encompasses accounts which are far more scrupulously and conscientiously researched, and which accordingly make a significant contribution to our knowledge of the world. At their best, moreover, travel writers in this tradition turn the genre's freedom from formal academic methodologies into an advantage rather than a limitation, using the form to cut across conventional disciplinary boundaries and engage with their theme in a variety of different modes. Lopez's *Arctic Dreams* is again a case in point. It is grounded in impeccable science, yet it also combines that science with both a lyrical, emotional register and a historical perspective. Lopez's aim here is to critique and redress the Cartesian tendency often inherent in accounts that adopt just a scientific perspective on the world. As we have seen, this Cartesian outlook or narratorial position seems to reflect and foster the belief that there is a radical schism between observing subject and observing object. For Lopez and many other environmentally minded travel writers, this is an attitude that is both psychologically damaging and environmentally disastrous; and Lopez accordingly endeavours to convey more fully how self and world, humanity and nature, act constantly upon and shape each other. In this way, the subjectivism permitted in the modern travel book is not always self-indulgent; rather, it may sometimes serve an important philosophical and moral function, exposing and countering the limitations and biases inherent in seemingly more rigorous, academic modes of intellectual enquiry.

5

REVEALING THE SELF

Bill Bryson's bestselling travelogue *The Lost Continent* (1989) at
one level recounts the author's bemused peregrinations around
small-town America. At another level, however, it records a different sort of journey, more subtle and more inward. As Bryson
re-enacts the dreadful vacation trips of his 1950s childhood, he
slowly works through some of his complex, conflicted feelings
towards his recently deceased father. Both journey and narrative
begin with Bryson harbouring some resentment towards the tedium
of his Iowa upbringing, and towards his father for inflicting that
upbringing on him. Yet as the journey progresses, he comes to feel
that Iowa in the 1950s was not such a bad place to be brought
up, certainly in comparison with many regions of the United
States in the late 1980s. In the process, Bryson gradually revises
his opinion of his father and ceases to regard him as a failure for
settling in, and settling for, Iowa. In fact, Bryson senior had
many virtues, and many accomplishments to his name, as his
son's narrative increasingly acknowledges. In this way *The Lost
Continent* charts not only the literal travels of its author, but also
an emotional and psychological journey *within* the author; or
more precisely, an emotional and psychological evolution which is

always likely, in our culture at least, to be construed metaphorically as a journey. And in the absence of any clear goal or destination for Bryson's actual travels, it is principally this inner development that gives shape and aesthetic form to his narrative. It generates for the reader a pleasing sense of closure and completion; we finish Bryson's travelogue feeling that this traveller has at least made some important *self*-discoveries, even if he has not made the great discoveries about the wider world that are perhaps more traditional in travel writing.

Bryson's travelogue thus conforms to the guidelines laid out by an earlier travel writer, Norman Douglas, when he suggests that,

> the reader of a good travel-book is entitled not only to an exterior voyage, to descriptions of scenery and so forth, but [also] to an interior, a sentimental or temperamental voyage, which takes place side by side with the outer one.
>
> (Quoted in Fussell 1980: 203)

This directive is cited approvingly by literary critic Paul Fussell, for whom this marriage of interior and exterior journeys represents the aesthetic ideal in travel writing. Underpinning this literary-critical valuation, it should be noted, is a more general critical assumption that travel writing is usually, or properly, a highly autobiographical form and a genre that is typically just as concerned to explore and present the subjectivity of the traveller-narrator as it is to explore and report the world. Thus Fussell classifies travel writing, or at least the modern travel book, as a 'sub-species of memoir' (1980: 203), whilst for Patrick Holland and Graham Huggan, more evocatively, 'travel narratives articulate a poetics of the wandering subject' and the 'roving "I"' (1998: 14).

As always, however, one must be wary of making over-broad generalisations about a vast and highly protean form. If we accept the larger, baggier conception of the travel writing genre outlined earlier in this volume, we must also accept that there have been historically, and continue to be today, modes of travel writing that do not exhibit any great interest in the subjectivity of a traveller-narrator: the modern guide-book, for example, or some of the scientific forms of travel writing discussed in the last chapter, in which emphasis increasingly falls on the presentation of quantitative data. Putting these exceptions aside, however, it is certainly the case that many modes of Western travel writing, from the late medieval era onwards, evince a growing interest in the autobiographical dimensions and potentialities of the travelogue form. That said, this growing concern with the traveller's personal experience does not seem to have originated in any overtly autobiographical impulse on the part of travel writers, and in its earliest manifestations it seldom reflected a desire to trace in detail the inner world of the travelling self. Rather, it was a development closely bound up with the emergence, from the late medieval period onwards, of the observational and rhetorical protocols discussed in the last chapter; its starting point was a growing desire, and requirement, to emphasise the traveller's eye-witness status, and so give greater credibility to their report. Yet insofar as these protocols brought about a new attentiveness to what travellers had seen and done *themselves*, and correspondingly an increasing readiness to admit first-person narration and subjective thoughts and feelings into the travel text, so in time they precipitated more autobiographical and inward-looking strains of travel writing.

At its most extreme, this tendency in the genre has led to travelogues that are almost wholly about the traveller-narrator, rather than the places visited, as the encounter with the wider world becomes merely a pretext or prompt to narratorial introspection and self-analysis. Such complete self-absorption, however, is uncharacteristic of the genre. More usual are narratives that seek to interweave the inner and outer worlds, mixing ostensibly factual, objective description of the people and places through which the traveller passes with a more openly subjective account of the traveller's own thoughts and feelings over the course of the journey. Hence the combination of narratorial modes that Rob Nixon sees as characteristic of the modern travel book; namely, the oscillation between, on the one hand, a 'semi-ethnographic, distanced, analytical mode' and, on the other, 'an autobiographical, emotionally tangled mode' (1992: 15). Of course, the balance struck between these two modes can vary considerably. In different periods, and in different branches of the genre, travel writers may position themselves at various points along a spectrum that runs from, on the one hand, an extreme subjectivism that concerns itself chiefly with an inner terrain of thought and feeling, memory and imagination and, on the other, an extreme objectivism that seeks to present facts about the world with seemingly little or no narratorial mediation. Yet insofar as most forms of post-medieval travel writing *do* incorporate some elements of personal information and first-person narration, the genre may be regarded as an important branch of what is now often termed '**life writing**'. That is to say, travel writing has frequently provided a medium in which writers can conduct an autobiographical project, exploring questions of identity and selfhood whilst simultaneously presenting to others a self-authored and as it were 'authorised' account of themselves. Moreover, the generic requirement to include an element of personal detail ensures that travelogues will often offer interesting insights into what is sometimes termed an individual's **subject position**, even when travel writers have not deliberately set out to write in such a self-reflective fashion.

The present chapter accordingly explores some of the ways in which travel writing has functioned as a form of 'life writing'. To this end, the central section of the chapter addresses the growing tendency in the genre, from the late eighteenth century onwards, to foreground the narratorial self, so that the traveller becomes as much the object of the reader's attention as the place travelled to. This is a development which makes travel writing more obviously a vehicle for autobiographical writing, and the section considers both the diverse ends to which the genre has been put in this regard, and the diverse strategies and rhetorical techniques that travel writers have employed to represent the self. As noted, however, travelogues need not be explicitly autobiographical in intent, nor do they have to adopt an overtly subjective register, in order to provide revealing insights into the personality of the traveller. Similarly, even travelogues that seem to modern eyes very impersonal and un-autobiographical can sometimes serve as a mode of self-fashioning, by which the writer seeks to project to the wider world a desired identity or persona. The first section of the chapter accordingly explores the extent to which even travelogues written before the 'inward turn' of the late eighteenth century constitute a form of writing about the self, and also a writing *of* the self, notwithstanding the apparent impersonality of many of these texts. And finally, the third section of the chapter addresses the ethical concerns that some critics have recently raised about the centrality of the narratorial self in many travel accounts; it discusses some of the personae most commonly fashioned by travel writers, and considers the rhetorical agendas implicit in these personae, and their larger cultural and ideological implications.

GRAND TOURISTS, PILGRIMS AND QUESTING KNIGHTS: SELF-FASHIONING IN ADDISON'S *REMARKS ON ITALY* (1705) AND RALEGH'S *DISCOVERIE OF GUIANA* (1596)

In Chapters 8 and 14 of his *Remarks on Several Parts of Italy* (1705), Joseph Addison discusses Rome, which he had visited in the course of a tour of France and Italy undertaken between 1701 and 1703. As the capital of the greatest empire in the ancient world, Rome was in many ways the focal point and climactic destination for well-to-do Britons embarking on what had become known as the Grand Tour. The ruling elite of Britain liked to style themselves the inheritors of ancient Rome's power and prestige, and for their sons it was accordingly a rite of passage to visit the most celebrated landmarks of the Roman world, and to peruse the classical antiquities that had survived the passage of time. And nowhere, of course, did these landmark sites and acclaimed relics exist in more abundance than in Rome itself.

Given the importance of Rome in the itinerary of the Grand Tour, the modern reader might expect Addison's account of the Eternal City to convey a sense of the pleasure and excitement he felt when finally he reached this key destination. We might even assume that the period spent in Rome will be rendered in his narrative as some sort of climax or conclusion to the whole journey. Yet this is not the case. There is no build-up, as it were, to Addison's arrival in Rome, neither on the first occasion he arrives there, when he is only able to make a short stay before setting off for Naples, nor on the second occasion, when he returns from

Naples and is at last able to make a more extended visit. Thereafter, Addison gives the reader little sense of what he felt as he viewed the various sites and antiquities of Rome; indeed, there is little direct narration of his personal experience at all. To modern readers, Addison's description of Rome will seem very dry and scholarly, both in tone and tenor. For it consists chiefly of a series of disquisitions on issues such as the aesthetic merits and architectural technicalities of St Peter's church; classical sculpture, and the insights it gives us into topics such as Roman clothing and the musical instruments of the ancient world; Roman funeral practices; and the coins and medals of both the Republican and Imperial eras. For example, Chapter 14 of *Remarks*, where Addison gives his extended account of Rome, begins as follows:

> It is generally observed, that Modern Rome stands higher than the Ancient; some have computed it about fourteen or fifteen feet, taking one place with another. The reason given for it is, that the present city stands upon the ruins of the former; and indeed, I have often observed, that where any considerable pile of building stood anciently, one still finds a rising ground, or a little kind of hill, which was doubtless made up out of the fragments and rubbish of the ruined edifice. But besides this particular cause, we may assign another that has very much contributed to the raising the situation of several parts of Rome: it being certain the great quantities of earth, that have been washed off from the hills by the violence of showers have had no small share in it. This any one may be sensible of, who observes how far several buildings, that stand near the roots of mountains, are sunk deeper in the earth than those that have been on the tops of hills, or on open plains.
>
> (Addison 1705: 300–301)

This passage is a good illustration of Addison's style and narrative technique throughout his account of Rome, and throughout his narrative generally. And as this example will suggest, whilst *Remarks* is structured as a first-person narrative based to some degree on a journal kept by the traveller-narrator, it actually offers the reader comparatively little in the way of a personal narrative of the writer's own experience. Instead, snippets of first-person narration serve simply to frame much longer passages of general observation and speculation, or else to support assertions made in the course of those observations. Thus the opening of Chapter 14, as cited above, was prefaced at the end of Chapter 13 by a single-sentence paragraph informing us that 'half a day more brought us to Rome, thro' a road that is commonly visited by travellers' (Addison 1705: 299). The phrase 'I have often observed', meanwhile, is inserted into the passage above to remind us that Addison's speculations have some empirical basis, yet Addison does not here recount any particular episode in which he personally witnessed the phenomenon he is describing.

It will be apparent that Addison is a far more reticent narrator than we are accustomed to seeing in modern travel books. Attention is firmly focused on the world beyond the self, with the result that Addison himself comes to seem a distinctly dispassionate, and even disembodied presence in his own travel narrative. The account makes little attempt to convey Addison's lived travel experience, as it were, nor does it concern itself with the various sensations, ranging from anticipation and pleasure to discomfort, inconvenience and disappointment, which he must have felt in the course of his travels. A more personal and expressive register, interestingly, *is* evident in the private letters that Addison sent home from Italy. In one letter, for example, he informs a friend that,

> I am just now arrived at Geneva by a very troublesome journey over the Alps where I have been for some days together shivering among the eternal snows. My head is still giddy with mountains and precipices and you can't imagine how much I am pleased with the sight of a plain.
>
> (Quoted in Batten 1978: 18)

Here we do get some sense of Addison's personal travel experience, as the writing seeks to render how his circumstances impinged upon him both physically and emotionally. In *Remarks*, however, the same journey across the Alps is described thus:

> I came directly from Turin to Geneva, and had a very easy journey over Mount Cenis, though about the beginning of December, the

snows having not yet fallen. On the tip of this high mountain is a large plain, and in the midst of the plain a beautiful lake, which would be very extraordinary were there not several mountains in the neighbourhood rising over it.

(1705: 444)

There then follows a rather abstract discussion of Italian lakes in general, and the way they are described in Latin poetry. The comparatively emotive register utilised in the letter gives way, in the published account of the tour, to a far less personalised style and narrative focus. This narratorial reticence is typical of most travelogues before the latter part of the eighteenth century; or at least, of most travelogues designed for circulation beyond an immediate circle of family and friends. Travel writers generally strove to convey a sense of themselves as impassive, trustworthy observers of the external world; as 'Cartesian' selves, in the parlance discussed in the last chapter. And consequently, published travel accounts seldom included much personal detail or narratorial interiority, even when the account was presented to the public as a journal, diary or letter, narrative forms that we might assume to be inherently intimate and autobiographical.

This impersonal style does not necessarily indicate that the travellers of earlier eras felt things less keenly than we do today, or that they were configured emotionally and psychologically in some fundamentally different way to ourselves. There is of course plenty of historical and anthropological evidence to suggest that concepts of the 'self', and of human individuality, can vary greatly across different cultures and periods. However, one needs to exercise some caution before ascribing the impersonality of most pre-modern travelogues to the notion that earlier travellers possessed a sense of self radically different from that which operates in modern Western culture. The further one goes back in time, of course, the more plausible this claim becomes; an early medieval traveller such as Egeria, for example, emerged from a culture so very different from our own that it is likely she must also have had a profoundly different sense of her own selfhood and individuality (see Campbell 1988: 20–33). Yet the lack of focus upon the narratorial self we find in many pre-1750 travel accounts also derives, to some extent, from differences not so much in the travellers themselves as in the generic conventions associated with the travelogue form. The chief duty prescribed for almost all travel writers before the late eighteenth century was that they bring back useful knowledge. It was this utilitarian agenda alone that was felt to justify venturing into print and demanding public attention; and consequently, for a travel account to dwell too much on the traveller's personal feelings and impressions smacked of presumption and vanity, and was likely to earn the writer a rebuke for being, in eighteenth-century parlance, too 'egotistical'. Even Addison's *Remarks* was censured in some quarters in this regard. As Charles Batten notes, at least one anonymous pamphlet of the day poked fun at Addison for including information about operas he had seen, and for recounting an incident in which he had from a distance mistaken linen spread out on the ground for a lake (see Batten 1978: 12–13). Such details, it seems, were felt to be too incidental and inconsequential for a published account of travels.

Given this impersonality of style, Addison's *Remarks* will not seem very autobiographical to modern readers. Certainly, it is not concerned with what is generally felt today to be the key agenda that defines autobiographical writing; namely, a conscious attempt on the part of the writer to explore his or her selfhood and identity, to express the contours of their inner world of thought and feeling, and to reach an understanding of the influences and circumstances that shaped them. Yet it should also be remembered that autobiographical writing is usually a Janus-faced activity, which looks in two directions simultaneously. On the one hand, it requires an inward scrutiny, as the writer attempts to reach some sort of self-understanding; on the other hand, it is also often undertaken with at least one eye on the writer's prospective audience, and with a constant awareness of the persona that the writer wishes to present to that audience. And in this latter sense at least, even seemingly impersonal travelogues such as Addison's *Remarks* arguably constitute a form of autobiographical writing. For whilst Addison makes little explicit reference to himself in the course of his narrative, his narrative nevertheless implicitly serves to fashion a public persona for the author.

What Addison's account signals most obviously, of course, is that the author has made the tour of Italy. As noted already, this was an important rite of passage amongst the political and cultural elite in the eighteenth century, since the tour was felt by many to play an important, formative role in the development of taste and good judgement. As Samuel Johnson remarked, 'a man who has never been to Italy is always conscious of an inferiority, from not having seen what it is supposed a man should see' (Boswell 1791: vol. 2, 61). Addison's *Remarks* demonstrates that he need feel no such inferiority, whilst simultaneously, his reticence as a narrator signals a traveller, and a writer, whose principal concern is not vainglorious self-promotion, but the acquisition of useful knowledge for the benefit of British society as a whole. Further to this, the persona that Addison projects is also a matter of the topics that he chooses to discuss. We might assume today that the topics addressed in *Remarks* simply reflect Addison's personal interests, but again, this is perhaps anachronistic; as Batten has emphasised, it is more accurate to say that Addison engages with those subject-areas deemed appropriate for the travelogue in this period. For contemporary readers, moreover, some of these topics were subtly coded in ways that we may not recognise today. For example, Addison provides a detailed account of the political and economic affairs of most of the city-states he visits. In the eyes of most eighteenth-century reviewers and critics, however, it was not every writer who was licensed to pass comment in this way on political and economic matters. Women who ventured an opinion on these topics, for instance, were likely to be censured, or at best patronised. It was not every writer, equally, who could discuss classical poetry in as much detail as Addison does; for the most part, it was only the members of a very privileged, masculine elite, the recipients of what was termed a 'liberal education', who were well read in Latin literature. By discussing such topics in his narrative, accordingly, Addison simultaneously asserts and demonstrates his status as a well-educated, public-spirited gentleman, someone who is both equipped and entitled to discuss matters of public importance.

Even a comparatively impersonal travel account such as Addison's *Remarks*, then, may function as a form of self-fashioning, enabling writers to craft and project a distinctive identity for themselves. There are occasions, moreover, when we can detect in travelogues produced before the late eighteenth century a more conspicuous element of overt self-fashioning, notwithstanding a similar reluctance to focus directly on the narratorial self. For example, the image of the author presented in Sir Walter Ralegh's *Discoverie of the Large, Rich and Bewtiful Empyre of Guiana* (1596) seems carefully calculated to win back the favour of his monarch, Elizabeth I of England. Elizabeth had banished Ralegh from court when she discovered his illicit marriage to one of her ladies-in-waiting, and to redeem himself in the Queen's eyes Ralegh led in 1595 an expedition to South America. His aim was discover the fabled city of Manoa, or as it has become known to posterity 'El Dorado', which was rumoured to possess spectacular wealth; and Ralegh's ultimate goal was to annexe that wealth for England, in emulation and defiance of Spain's colonial presence in the region. Unfortunately, however, the venture was a failure. Notwithstanding the title of his account, Ralegh did not 'discover' any 'large, rich and bewtiful empyre' in the region, he merely brought back hearsay reports that such a realm might exist further inland. Gifted with much greater literary skills than most travel writers of this period, however, Ralegh contrived ingeniously to turn this failure to his advantage when subsequently he wrote up the expedition.

Ralegh himself, in a prefatory letter, indicates the figure that he wishes to cut in the main narrative of his account. In this preface, he expresses the wish that his abortive venture will receive 'the gracious construction of a paineful pilgrimage' (Whitehead 1997: 121). This is a canny rhetorical manoeuvre, which attempts to shift readerly attention away from what the expedition achieved in terms of tangible, worldly goals. Instead, it implies that the journey was worthwhile insofar as it brought about a spiritual, existential transformation in the travellers; pilgrimages, after all, traditionally involve a renovation of faith, and also a shriving of past sins through the pilgrim's readiness to countenance discomfort and pain in the course of their journey. That said, the pilgrimage motif is not invoked at any point in the main body of Ralegh's narrative, nor does Ralegh ever concern himself with any sort of introspective analysis of how he was changed by his travel experiences. Like

Addison's *Remarks*, Ralegh's *Discoverie* will strike modern readers as an outward-looking, comparatively objectivist text, which by today's standards allots little narrative space to the subjectivity of the narrator. Although written in the first person, its first-person pronouns for the most part govern simple statements of movement and action; they chiefly relate where the party went, what they did and what they saw, rather than reflecting on what was thought and felt about these discoveries. Like Addison, moreover, Ralegh's principal concern throughout his account is to relay the information that he has acquired, for example about the different indigenous tribes in the region, and about Spanish activities there.

At the same time, however, Ralegh's failure to return with any really significant new discoveries about the region produces what Neil Whitehead terms a 'drive to narrativity' in his account of the expedition (1997: 63). That is to say, the progress of the journey, rather than simply the results of the expedition, had to be fore-grounded to a greater extent than was usual in this period. This in turn allowed, or required, Ralegh to recount something of the ordeal he and his men endured. We learn accordingly of how the party's clothes 'hung very wet & heavy on our shoulders' because of the stifling heat (187), and of their exhaustion and fear as they navigated the labyrinthine waterways of the Orinoco basin:

> When three more days were overgone, our companies began to despair, the weather being extreme hot, the river bordered with very high trees that kept away the air, and the current against us every day stronger than the last ... The further we went on (our victual decreasing and the air breeding great faintness), we grew weaker and weaker when we had most need of strength.
>
> (Whitehead 1997: 160–61)

Yet whilst Ralegh's own mood and physical condition can be inferred from passages like this, he seldom describes himself directly. The way in which these distressing circumstances impinged on Ralegh personally, and indeed his private inner world of sensation, thought and feeling throughout the whole expedition, goes largely unrecorded in *The Discoverie*.

It is presumably passages such as the one cited above that are meant to evoke for the reader the notion of a suffering pilgrimage, in which a penance is made for past sins. Or alternatively, they may bring to mind the figure of a questing knight, the protagonist perhaps of one of the chivalric romances that were hugely popular at Elizabeth's court, someone who undergoes discomfort and danger in pursuit of a noble goal. In the latter regard, it is perhaps significant that Ralegh also takes care to inform us that he imposed a strict rule of sexual abstinence on his men. By this detail, he both distinguishes the English from the allegedly more rapacious Spanish, and also signals his own ability to resist sexual temptation. Again, this is behaviour befitting a romance hero such as King Arthur or Sir Galahad, who were renowned for their chastity and honour; and it was also information calculated to appease Elizabeth, who had of course fallen out with Ralegh over a sexual misdemeanour, when he married without her permission. Yet it must be stressed once more that whilst Ralegh seems to want us to construe his journey as a pilgrimage or chivalric quest, it is for the most part left to the reader to make this interpretation of his South American experiences. Ralegh does not dramatise or articulate *within* his narrative any sort of transformation of the travelling self; this is merely implied by the brief reference to pilgrimage in the prefatory letter. As with Addison, the literary and cultural conventions of his day preclude such overt self-description, and self-fashioning, in the travelogue; to have used the form in this way would have seemed a significant breach of generic decorum. In time, of course, the generic expectations pertaining to travel writing would change significantly in this regard, and this is a development we shall now explore.

WRITING THE SELF: TRAVEL WRITING'S INWARD TURN

Early in his European travelogue, *A Tramp Abroad* (1880), Mark Twain describes the views available, by day and by night, from Heidelberg Castle in Germany:

> Behind the Castle stands a great, dome-shaped hill, and beyond that a nobler and loftier one. The Castle looks down upon the compact

brown-roofed town; and from the town two picturesque old bridges span the river. Now the view broadens; through the gateway of the sentinel headlands you gaze out over the wide Rhine plain, which stretches away, softy and richly tinted, grows gradually and dreamily indistinct, and finally melts imperceptibly into the remote horizon.

I have never enjoyed a view which had such a serene and satisfying charm about it as this one gives.

The first night we were there, we went to bed and to sleep early; but I awoke at the end of two or three hours, and lay a comfortable while listening to the soothing patter of the rain against the balcony windows. I took it to be rain, but it turned out to be only the murmur of the restless Neckar, tumbling over her dikes and dams far below, in the gorge. I got up and went into the west balcony and saw a wonderful sight. Away down on the level, under the black mass of the Castle, the town lay, stretched along the river, its intricate cobweb of streets jewelled with twinkling lights; there were rows of lights in the bridges; these flung lances of light upon the waters, in the black shadows of the arches; and away at the extremity of all this fairy spectacle blinked and glowed a massed multitude of gas jets which seemed to cover acres of ground; it was as if all the diamonds in the world had been spread out there. I did not know before, that a half mile of sextuple railway tracks could be made such an adornment.

(Twain 1997: 10)

Twain's descriptive strategies here can be usefully compared with Addison's account of Rome, as cited earlier. Addison, it should be noted, would probably not have commented on the views from the castle: a taste for such views, and an aesthetic appreciation of landscape, is seldom evident in travel writing prior to the late eighteenth-century vogue for the 'picturesque'. Had he done so, however, it is likely that he would have simply informed the reader that Heidelberg has many fine views, both in the day and at night. This is of course very different to the register and narrative technique adopted in Twain's account. The word 'I' becomes much more prominent than it ever is in Addison's account, as Twain endeavours to give us not just a report of information gathered over the course of his journey, but also a rendering of his personal, lived experience *during* that journey. To enable this the narrative mode is one of showing rather than telling, according to the terminology often used in studies of prose fiction. That is to say, Twain does not simply relate retrospectively, and in a baldly summarising manner, what he feels are the key points to be made about the views from Heidelberg Castle; instead, he recreates or dramatises the act of taking those views, so that the reader to some extent shares the experience with him. Thus the first paragraph in the passage earlier is in the present tense, and tracks the movement of Twain's eye as it pans out, so to speak, towards the horizon. The description of Heidelberg at night, meanwhile, is contextualised by an account of how Twain first came to see that view, after waking in the middle of the night. As with the description of the daytime view, moreover, the account of Heidelberg at night strives to recreate the view for the reader, itemising its key features in some detail, and in a metaphoric language that aims to convey vividly not so much objective facts about the external scene, as the subjective *impressions* created in the spectator. Thus the town appears to this spectator a twinkling 'fairy spectacle', whilst the gas-jets by the railway tracks resemble diamonds strewn across the ground.

Set against Addison's *Remarks* or Ralegh's *Discoverie*, *A Tramp Abroad* clearly constitutes a much more personalised, and in a loose sense of the term, a more obviously autobiographical type of travel writing. Twain foregrounds the narratorial self to a much greater extent than either Addison or Ralegh, and as he does so we encounter a mode of travel writing concerned not simply to present information about the wider world, but also to dramatise something of the complex and subtle interactions that necessarily occur between self and other, the traveller and the world, in the course of travel. As with Twain's interest in landscape, this is a subjectivist agenda in travel writing, and a personalised style, that can be traced back to the latter part of the eighteenth century. More specifically, it is chiefly a product of those larger literary and cultural movements that we now call sentimentalism and Romanticism. Both of these movements, whose most famous proponents in English literature are, respectively, the novelist Laurence Sterne and the poet William Wordsworth, fostered a greater interest in the interior workings of consciousness and the self. They were also much concerned with the role played by feeling and emotion, as well as purely rational thought, in shaping an individual's engagement with the world; and these sentimental and Romantic interests led in turn to the adoption of a more subjective and emotive register in many literary genres. Travel writing was no exception in this regard; indeed, in some branches of the genre, including most notably the literary form of travel writing that is the modern travel book, a degree of subjectivism soon became the norm, as writers increasingly felt licensed to inform readers of their subjective impressions, and their personal thoughts and feelings, as these arose during their journeys.

From the late eighteenth century, then, travel writing starts to look inwards as well as outwards. At the same time, however, this new concern with the travelling self could be pursued in several different ways, and it has since the eighteenth century encompassed a variety of styles and techniques for writing about the self. For example, the extent to which travel writers articulate their inner world of thought and feeling can vary considerably. In many travelogues, this inward scrutiny and subsequent self-expression does not go much further than a simple declaration of what the traveller thought and felt at various junctures. Thus the prospect from Heidelberg castle elicits from Twain the comment that he had 'never enjoyed a view which had such a serene and satisfying charm about it'. In more extreme forms, however, this inward gaze may become an attempt to chart the flux of consciousness in the course of travel. An important early model in this regard was Laurence Sterne's fictional travelogue *A Sentimental Journey* (1768). In passages such as the following, in which the traveller-narrator Yorick describes his reaction to a hotel-keeper who he fears is about to over-charge him, Sterne uses a disjointed syntax and snippets of soliloquy to track in detail the ebb and flow of his traveller's moods.

> I looked at Monsieur Dessein through and through – eyed him as he walked along in profile – then, *en face* – thought he looked like a Jew – then a Turk – disliked his wig – cursed him by my gods – wished him at the devil –

And is all this to be lighted up in the heart for a beggarly account of three or four louis-d'ors [a unit of French currency], which is the most I can be over-reached in? Base passion! said I, turning myself about, as a man naturally does upon a sudden reverse of sentiment – base, ungentle passion!

(Sterne 1987: 39)

Although a fiction, *A Sentimental Journey* introduced techniques for the representation of the self that greatly influenced many writers of genuine travel accounts, including explorers such as John Ledyard and Mungo Park. Sterne's example also licensed a much more digressive, wide-ranging form of travelogue, in which the narrative focus often wanders far away from the actual scenes in front of the traveller. Again, this digressiveness in the form was to some extent a consequence of the new dispensation that permitted a more detailed portrayal of the interior world of the traveller. Consciousness, after all, is not bound by space and time in the same way as the body, and the traveller's physical presence at a site will often be a spur for memories, reflections and imaginings that lead far away from their immediate surroundings. In *A Tramp Abroad*, for example, Twain records at one point how he took a walk through a forest in Germany. Whilst describing this walk, however, Twain recollects how he 'fell into a dreamy train of thought about animals which talk, and kobolds, and enchanted folk, and the rest of the pleasant legendary stuff' (1997: 11). This train of thought leads Twain to recall a story that he was told fifteen years previously, in California, about talking blue-jays; and as this story is recounted, over some six pages, so those woods in Germany disappear entirely from the reader's view.

A striking example of this digressive tendency in the modern travel book occurs in W.G. Sebald's *Die Ringe des Saturn* (*The Rings of Saturn*, 1995; English translation, 1998). Ostensibly an account of a walking trip through the landscapes of coastal East Anglia, *The Rings of Saturn* in fact uses the literal, exterior journey principally as a means of mapping an interior landscape. The description of his actual travel experiences comprises only a small portion of Sebald's narrative; instead, it is chiefly given over to tracing the long and sometimes tangential train of associations, thoughts and memories that arise from those experiences. Thus we read of other journeys that the author has undertaken, in other parts of the world, and we encounter also a series of lengthy reflections on topics that often have very little direct connection with Sebald's East Anglian surroundings: these include Rembrandt's painting 'The Anatomy Lesson', intrigues at the Chinese imperial court in the late nineteenth century, and the Holocaust. These diverse narrative threads are woven together smoothly, and Sebald's prose has a slow, meditative rhythm, eschewing the abrupt transitions of subject matter and mood that we find in Sterne. Clearly Sebald is not trying to convey, as Sterne often does in *A Sentimental Journey*, the raw flux of a consciousness caught up in the immediacy of the travel experience. But in a more indirect fashion, the meandering narrative of *The Rings of Saturn* also seems to mimic the drift of the traveller's consciousness, both in the act of travel and also in the act of retrospection, at the moment when the journey is being recalled and recounted.

As well as including more information about how they thought and felt at various junctures of their travels, some modern travel writers also go to much greater lengths than was ever previously the case to situate their journeys in a larger personal history of the self. This self-historicising, or self-narrativising, project, it should be stressed, is not necessarily intrinsic to travel writing even in its more inward-looking form. Yorick and Sebald sometimes recall events prior to their journeys and they explore some of the memories stirred by their travel experiences, but these memories are fairly scattered and unrelated; they do not cohere over the course of the narrative to establish a strong sense of what the traveller was like at an earlier stage of their life. A travelogue like Jenni Diski's *Skating to Antarctica* (1997), however, presents the narratorial self in a very different manner. Diski's narrative is divided fairly equally between an account of a voyage to Antarctica, and an account of her traumatic upbringing and periods of mental illness. Diski's fascination with Antarctica is traced back to an early yearning for some 'place of safety, a white oblivion' (2005: 2) which might offer an emotional respite from her unhappy relationship with her parents, and from the mental instability that ensued. The region's endlessly blank terrain comes to signify the emotional emptiness which Diski feels she has cultivated in life as a coping strategy; and by interpolating this back-story, so to speak, into her travelogue, the voyage to Antarctica takes on immense emotional and psychological significance. The literal voyage, indeed, comes to seem a voyage into the self for this traveller; it constitutes both the culmination of a long-held fantasy and a coming-to-terms with a deeply troubled past.

This is travel writing being put to explicitly autobiographical use, becoming a medium which seemingly enables and articulates an overview of a whole life, or at least, a significant portion of a life, encompassing periods both before and after the journey itself. A similar form of self-historicising occurs in Graham Greene's *Journey without Maps* (1936), an account of a four-week trek through the interior of Liberia. Like many Modernist writers, Greene was profoundly influenced by Freudian psychoanalysis, which taught that the human psyche was fundamentally fissured and not wholly coherent to itself. As a result, Greene offers an account of his past self, and of his motivation for undertaking this African adventure, which is far more fragmentary than Diski's comparatively coherent narrative of her earlier life. Short paragraphs juxtapose incidents from Greene's childhood and more recent past, with Greene himself offering no interpretation or commentary on these images. Readers are left to form their own opinion as to the precise meaning they bear, and the exact narrative logic they create for Greene's journey. Yet that journey is undoubtedly invested with an air of psychoanalytical self-enquiry; and so, like Diski's voyage to Antarctica, Greene's trek through West Africa comes to hold complex layers of emotional and psychological significance.

In some travelogues, then, the journey functions to some extent as a narrative device whereby the author's whole life may be brought into focus. Many travelogues of this type also present the journey as a key stimulus to a new understanding of the traveller's life. In this way, the travel account does not just offer a larger history of the self, it is also plotted as a developmental narrative of growing self-knowledge and self-realisation. It thus becomes a record not just of a literal journey, but also of a metaphorical interior 'voyage' that represents an important existential change in the traveller. This is an autobiographical narrative template that has its origins ultimately in the long Western tradition of spiritual autobiography which begins with Augustine's *Confessions* in the fourth century, yet it seems to have become more prominent in travel writing as a consequence of Romanticism. Spiritual auto-biographies traditionally charted the author's relationship with God, and culminated in episodes that described either conversion to Christianity or else a renewal of Christian faith. With Romanti-cism, however, this narrative pattern was increasingly secularised into one of self-discovery and self-realisation (see Abrams 1971). With Romanticism, moreover, there came an increasing valorisa-tion of travel as a key means by which such **epiphanic** insights into the self might be achieved, and with them the greater degree of authenticity, autonomy and self-realisation that is usually assumed to follow on from such self-knowledge. Much of William Words-worth's poetry, for example, invests travel with this existential significance, repeatedly depicting the poet's rambles and walking tours as journeys that culminate in moments of personal revelation and renovation (see Hartman 1964).

Travel writing in this mode presents the journeys being undertaken as an important rites of passage and as processes of self-realisation. Often, indeed, they are figured as some sort of pil-grimage or quest, since these are traditionally two types of travel that bring about a significant reinvention or renewal of the self. As the examples of pilgrimage and quest will suggest, travel was of course often regarded as an important rite of passage in periods prior to the late eighteenth century: we can assume that both Egeria's fourth-century pilgrimage, as discussed in Chapter 3, and Addison's Grand Tour, as discussed earlier in the present chapter, were undertaken in this spirit. Yet neither Egeria nor Addison organise their accounts so as to present a developmental narrative of personal growth; nor indeed, does Sir Walter Ralegh, although as we have seen he does seem to signal in his preface that his expedition brought about a degree of personal renovation and improvement. After Romanticism, however, there is an increasing tendency, in the more literary branches of travel writing at least, for the travel account to be plotted so that it progresses towards some sort of conclusive, climactic scene, in which the traveller seemingly gains an epiphanic insight into him- or herself.

Borrowing the terminology used by Aristotle to describe narrative structure, we may call these climactic scenes moments of *anagnorisis*, or recognition. One such moment occurs at the end of the penultimate chapter of Jenny Diski's *Skating to Antarctica* (2005). Diski isn't actually able to reach Antarctica, because of thick pack ice that prevents the cruise ship from reaching the continent. But ultimately, this disappointment does not seem to matter very much, as Diski realises that she has in fact completed an interior voyage far more significant than the literal journey she is engaged in. The process of trying to reach the continent, and especially the introspection forced on Diski during the long periods spent in her cabin, enable her to resolve satisfactorily in her mind several key issues relating both to her past and her future. This sense of resolution in turn allows the reader to feel that by the conclusion of *Skating to Antarctica*, the bitter legacies of Diski's past have to some extent been overcome and transcended.

This crafting of the travel account into a narrative of personal development and inner voyaging is today often the hallmark of the self-consciously 'literary' travelogue. Again, however, it is worth reiterating that the modern travel book, as defined earlier in this volume, is not representative of all forms of travel writing over the centuries, or even of all forms of travel writing in the last two centuries. Even in the Romantic period, most travel writers did not craft their accounts according to this developmental pattern. When it does occur, it is usually in a fictive rendering of the travel theme; for example, in poems like Wordsworth's *The Prelude*, Coleridge's 'The Rime of the Ancient Mariner' and Byron's *Childe Harold's Pilgrimage*. A few examples of this narrative pattern may be found in non-fictional travelogues of the era, usually in texts that stand at the intersection of travel writing and spiritual autobiography: John Newton's *Authentic Narrative of Some Remarkable and Interesting Particulars in the Life of ****** (1765), for instance, which recounts a dissolute life of seafaring and slave-trading, before describing Newton's conversion back to Godly ways during a shipwreck. But it is not found in the majority of Romantic-era travelogues, even when they exhibit a pronounced concern with the narratorial self in the sentimental manner pioneered by Sterne. *A Sentimental Journey* itself, significantly, does not so much conclude as simply terminate, with the narrative breaking off mid-sentence. For all that Yorick has been exploring in great detail his responsiveness to the people and places he meets, there is little sense that he has grown in any significant way, or achieved any profound new insights. Similarly, most non-fictional travelogues in this period, even when 'sentimentally' inclined, do not incorporate any sort of climactic, conclusive scene; they simply proceed sequentially, with the traveller recording his or her observations at each stage of the journey. It is arguably not until the twentieth century that the developmental narrative pattern becomes a staple convention, or desired ideal, especially for travel writers who wish to position themselves as 'literary' authors.

In many studies of travel writing, the emergence of more subjectivist travelogues from the late eighteenth century onwards has been characterised as a radical shift from Enlightenment to Romantic values (see, *inter alia*, Parks 1964; Stafford 1984; Cardinal 1997). With this shift, it is suggested, a new 'Romantic' self begins to be articulated, and/or to be fashioned, in travel writing. The Romantic self, or as it is sometimes termed, Romantic 'subjectivity', is assumed to differ in a variety of ways from the Enlightenment self, and the Enlightenment 'subjectivity', that preceded it. Broadly speaking, the assumption is made that Enlightenment travellers prioritise fact-finding and empirical enquiry into the wider world, and that they accordingly fashion themselves on the page principally as observers, and as 'Cartesian' selves or subjectivities, detached from the scenes they survey. Romantic travellers, meanwhile, do not simply observe, they also react to the scenes around them, and record those reactions, and their reflections on them, in their accounts. In many cases, indeed, they seek out situations which arouse strong feelings and sensations of sublimity or spiritual intensity. And by allowing the scenes they observe to impinge upon them in this way, Romantic travellers are seemingly more open than Enlightenment travellers to being changed by their travel experiences and by the others that they encounter. Thus whilst the Enlightenment travelogue will typically present a Cartesian self that does not alter in the course of its travels, the Romantic travelogue ideally records not only a literal journey but also a metaphorical 'inner' journey of self-discovery and maturation.

As this chapter has demonstrated, this is a schema and a terminology that undoubtedly corresponds in some degree to broad changes both in the travel writing genre and in the selves or 'subjectivities' articulated in travel writing. Yet the binary opposition this schema implies between 'Enlightenment' and 'Romantic' styles and sensibilities is perhaps too simplistic. As we have seen, the subjectivism that can be loosely labelled 'Romantic' comes in a variety of forms, which in turn give rise to varying degrees of preoccupation with the self. As a consequence, it is unhelpful to postulate too stark an opposition between Enlightenment and Romantic tendencies in travel writing. Many travel writers from the late eighteenth century onwards avail themselves of the new licence to admit personal thoughts and feelings into their accounts, but they do not all depict themselves as significantly changed by their experiences. Nor, in many cases, do they entirely relinquish travel writing's traditional function of providing important, empirically acquired information about the wider world. Conversely, one also finds from the late eighteenth century onwards many explorers who adopt a more personal, subjectivist style, even as they remain principally committed to the Enlightenment project of data collection and empirical enquiry: conspicuous examples include Mungo Park, George Forster, David Livingstone, H.M. Stanley and Richard Burton. Thus a great many travel accounts, from the late eighteenth century down to the present day, actually sit somewhere between the two extremes conventionally denoted by the terms 'Enlightenment' and 'Romantic'. Or in an alternative critical idiom, many travelogues seek to combine Enlightenment and Romantic **discourses**, and so maintain an agenda that is both scientific/intellectual *and* literary/autobiographical, although the balance struck between these two poles may vary considerably.

THE IMPERIOUS 'I'?

Whether they tend more towards the Enlightenment or the Romantic paradigms outlined earlier, the selves articulated in travel writing usually have an aspirational aspect and perform a rhetorical function. Travel is often undertaken to enhance social status and to accumulate what the sociologist Pierre Bourdieu (1984) has termed 'cultural capital'. When this is the case, any subsequent travelogue is an important part of the traveller's larger bid for authority and social advancement. The image of the self presented in these accounts is usually intended, at some level, to persuade audiences not only that the traveller is a reliable eye-witness, but also that he or she possesses, or has acquired, a range of other desirable attributes and accomplishments, such as cour-age, taste, spiritual enlightenment or a more profound, 'authentic' self-knowledge. In this regard, moreover, the crafting of travel accounts may also serve an important psychological function for their authors: the travelogue is from one perspective a medium in which travellers can reconcile what is likely to have been a welter of disparate, sometimes contradictory experiences into a single coherent narrative, thereby persuading themselves of the essential coherence and integrity of their own identity.

Travelogues, then, usually offer a carefully staged presentation of the self. And for the desired image of the self to be maintained, the travelogue must usually exercise a similar discrimination with regard to everything that is 'other' to the narratorial self: the places that the traveller visits, the cultures that they encounter and the individuals with whom they interact. This is an aspect of travel writing that has prompted considerable ethical unease in many recent critics and theorists of the genre (see, *inter alia*, Pratt 2008; Holland and Huggan 1998; Lisle 2006). For in representing those others, the travel writer is in effect suborning or appro-priating them for his or her own project of identity formation and self-advancement. To this way of thinking, much travel writing entails the traveller achieving a symbolic or psychological mastery over the people and places they describe. Moreover, the travel writer's act of self-fashioning also often proceeds by a logic of differentiation, whereby the Other is constructed in some subtle or unsubtle way principally as foil or counterpoint to the suppo-sedly heroic, civilised and/or cultured protagonist. Or as Debbie Lisle puts it, the selves or subjectivities on show in travelogues are usually 'fashioned over and against a series of others who are denied the power of representing themselves' (2006: 69). As this suggests, there is inherent in almost every travelogue a massive imbalance in the power of representation. And as Lisle and many other critics have emphasised and, as we shall see in more detail next chapter, this imbalance in representational power is often tied to, and helps to sustain, significant socio-economic and political inequalities between travellers and the others they describe.

The self-aggrandising agenda implicit in much travel and travel writing, and the fantasies of empowerment and social advancement that both activities often enable, frequently find expression in what Mary Louise Pratt has called the '**monarch-of-all-I-survey**' **scene** (2008: 197–204). This recurrent trope in travel writing can be illustrated by a passage in Henry Morton Stanley's *Through the Dark Continent* (1878). Climbing to the top of small hill on an island in Lake Victoria, in East Africa, the explorer surveys 'hundreds of square miles of pastoral upland dotted thickly with villages[,] groves of bananas' and 'herds upon herds of cattle' (Stanley 1988: vol. 1, 174). As he lovingly itemises the potentially profitable features of the landscape in this way, Stanley seems to take dominion, in his own mind at least, of the rich tracts of land laid out before him. At one point, indeed, he conceives of himself as sitting 'secure on [a] lofty throne' (vol. 1, 174) as he views the scene. Simultaneously, he elevates himself not only literally but also metaphorically over the local African population. Viewing their movements from a distance, for example, he professes to 'laugh at the ferocity of the savage hearts which beat in those thin dark figures; for I am a part of Nature now, and for the present as invulnerable as itself' (vol. 1, 174). Adopting an epic register, Stanley thus fashions for himself a sublime and transcendent persona. This is a traveller, it seems, whose soul can soar not only above the scenes it surveys, but also above its circumstances more generally; and this is also a traveller, we are clearly meant to infer, who possesses a mind and a sensibility vastly superior to that of the local population.

Stanley essays such an epic self-fashioning in the context of an exploration narrative, but this stylistic register is more usually found in what one can loosely designate the Romantic travelogue. In some cases, moreover, travelogues in this subjectivist vein will use a 'monarch-of-all-I-survey' scene to trigger the epiphanic, and frequently climactic, moments of *anagnorisis* or recognition discussed earlier in this chapter. Such moments further heighten the sense of transcendence, grandeur and/or emotional intensity attaching to the narratorial self; they imply a traveller who has attained a deeper understanding of themselves and of the forces that shaped their personal history. It should be noted, however, that the 'monarch-of-all-I-survey' scene itself may be found as frequently in travelogues that evince a more objectivist or Enlightenment sensibility. An earlier traveller like Ralegh, for example, may not rhapsodise explicitly about the emotions and fantasies that are stirred as he surveys the fertile landscapes of the Orinoco basin, but there are nevertheless several passages in *The Discoverie* in which Ralegh seems to take imaginative possession of the environment, whilst simultaneously encouraging his reader to do the same.

Travel writing's tendency to empower and elevate the narratorial self at the expense of a denigrated Other is especially apparent in a text like Stanley's *Through the Dark Continent*. In a travelogue like Greene's *Journey without Maps*, however, the local population is arguably appropriated in a more subtle fashion to the travel writer's self-dramatising, and self-aggrandising, project. As discussed earlier, Greene seems to regard his journey through Liberia almost as a form of psychoanalytic self-analysis. Although the fragmentary narrative never spells this out explicitly, the reader soon comes to understand that through visiting Africa Greene wishes to access, and to understand, some primal core of his own being, and to reach down to a layer of the self that supposedly sits below consciousness, rationality and civilisation. The narrative then charts an ordeal of exhaustion, discomfort and fever, which is ultimately productive of a moment of epiphanic insight in which Greene discovers in himself 'a passionate interest in living'. Previously, he suggests, he had always assumed, 'as a matter of course, that death was desirable'; the new self-knowledge therefore seems 'like a conversion, and I had never experienced a conversion before' (2006: 201).

Greene returns from Africa, then, with a heightened authority and mystique, since like a pilgrim he can claim that he has acquired a profound existential insight from his journey. Arguably, however, he achieves that existential authority only by subtly exploiting the Africans whom he describes. From one perspective, Greene's is a surrogate pilgrimage that valorises many aspects of African culture, and of African lifeways, over their European equivalents; the account is generally scathing, for example, about European claims to be morally and culturally superior to the 'uncivilised' tribes of Liberia. At the same time, however, the Africans Greene meets are usually rendered more as emblems of the 'primitive' than as fully rounded human beings, and they often seem the embodiments of fears and fantasies that Green himself is projecting on to the region. For this reason, many of the accusations lodged by the Nigerian critic Chinua Achebe against Joseph Conrad's *Heart of Darkness* (1901) are equally pertinent to *Journey without Maps*. Conrad's novella is clearly a major influence on Greene's travelogue, and like his predecessor Greene is arguably guilty of using Africa simply 'as setting and backdrop which eliminates the African as human factor', reducing the continent and its native inhabitants 'to the role of props for the break-up of one petty European mind' (Achebe 1990: 124).

The 'others' that travellers use to define their difference, and implicitly their superiority, may also be drawn from their own culture. Even in the context of 'home travels', the traveller is by definition a more mobile figure than many of the 'locals' he or she encounters, and on the basis of that fundamental difference travel writers often claim for themselves a greater breadth of knowledge, or a greater degree of sophistication, open-mindedness and/or modernity. Another recurrent strategy for self-promotion in travel writing, meanwhile, is for travel writers to contrast themselves with the other travellers they encounter on their journeys. Often these fellow-travellers will be classified as mere 'tourists', whilst the writers ascribe to themselves the attributes and activities that are felt to characterise the true or proper 'traveller'. As James Buzard (1993) has demonstrated, this 'traveller'/'tourist' distinction has underpinned many travel accounts since at least the late eighteenth century, when recreational travel began to become more common, although it was not until the mid-nineteenth century that the actual words 'tourist' and 'traveller' acquired a pejorative and an honorific resonance respectively. To this way of thinking, the tourist represents the very worst aspects of modern travel and, indeed, of modernity generally. He or she is assumed to practise a lazy, timid, and superficial version of travel, in which everything is safely pre-arranged by the supervisory apparatus of the tourism industry. A genuine encounter with an alien culture or environment is thus replaced by a commodified, staged and inauthentic simulacrum of such encounters, with the result that tourists do not gain any significant insight into either the Other or themselves. And whilst tourism is generally assumed in this way to be an intrinsically pointless form of travel, it is also usually presented as being far from harmless. Tourists, it is frequently alleged, ultimately destroy the places and cultures they seek out; their laziness creates an infrastructure that spoils previously pristine landscapes, whilst their cultural insensitivity and boorishness works to vulgarise the traditional communities they visit.

Such, at least, is the standard litany of complaints levelled at the tourist, from the late eighteenth century down to the present day. Some influential commentators on travel writing, it should be noted, subscribe wholly to this bleak view of touristic travel, and also to its frequent corollary, the notion that clear and easily identifiable differences exist between deplorable 'tourists' and superior 'travellers' (see Fussell 1980 and 1987; Boorstin 1961). Other critics and theorists, however, suggest that it is necessary to take a more nuanced view both of the allegations customarily made about tourism and of the supposed 'traveller'/'tourist' antithesis. With regard to the latter, for example, it has been persuasively argued that this is a terminology which historically has often served simply as a vehicle for snobbery and class prejudice, allowing travellers and commentators to inveigh against the fact that they now share their customary travel destinations with travellers drawn from lower strata of society than themselves (see MacCannell 1999; Culler 1988; Buzard 1993). It has also been suggested that a strenuous insistence on one's own status as 'traveller' rather than 'tourist' is sometimes a psychological defence mechanism against so-called 'tourist angst', which is the unsettling realisation that one is oneself merely engaged in a form of tourism. Or as Holland and Huggan put it, the pose of 'traveller' may function as 'a strategy of self-exemption' that enables travel writers 'to displace their guilt for interfering with, and adversely changing, the cultures through which they travel' (1998: 3).

Whatever its precise motivation, it is undoubtedly the case that the 'traveller'/'tourist' distinction underpins, either explicitly or implicitly, many of the self-fashionings performed in travel writing. Thus writers frequently adopt an anti-touristic rhetoric that lampoons and/or laments the activities of other travellers, thereby setting themselves apart from, and superior to, those others. On some occasions, moreover, the whole ethos, agenda and even itinerary of a trip can seem strongly driven by a travel writer's desire to prove him- or herself a 'traveller' rather than a 'tourist'. Thus some travellers will make a great show of the extent to which they journeyed 'off the beaten track', thereby avoiding tourists and the infrastructure that supports them. It is only by this means, it is frequently suggested, that one can access the authentically Other and visit places and cultures still untouched by modernity. Moreover, getting off the beaten track in this way often requires self-styled 'travellers' to endure discomfort and danger as they move beyond the security of established tourist itineraries. This element of misadventure may be from one perspective simply a regrettable necessity if travellers are to pursue the quests they have set themselves. Yet an air of conspicuous hardship and peril will also frequently serve a useful rhetorical purpose for travellers and travel writers. By this means, a journey may be presented as a genuine challenge, and so as a genuine learning experience, for the travelling self. This in turn allows the journey to be presented as a form of pilgrimage or exploration, rather than some sort of self-indulgent jaunt. One might suggest, therefore, that dangers and discomforts often function principally as the *markers* of the supposedly 'authentic' travel experience, and that they are therefore sometimes deliberately sought out so as to strengthen the traveller's claim to have acquired a more authentic and insightful knowledge of both self and Other (see Thompson 2007a).

In a variety of ways, then, travelogues are often exercises in self-promotion and the accumulation of cultural capital; this is perhaps especially the case with the self-consciously literary modern travel book, which is frequently little more than a vehicle for the author to present his or her distinctive sensibility and unique outlook on the world. Noting this tendency in the form, Holland and Huggan have suggested that much travel writing is best regarded not as a genuinely autobiographical form, but rather as *anti-* or *pseudo*-autobiographical (17), insofar as many travel writers in fact avoid genuine introspection and self-enquiry, choosing instead to present the self through a series of stock postures and personae. And as we have seen, this exercise in subtle or not-so-subtle self-advancement often arguably exploits to some degree the other individuals and cultures depicted in the travel account. Yet whilst this is undoubtedly an important and problematic aspect of the genre, should we therefore condemn all travel writing as intrinsically or invariably exploitative and self-promoting? Some recent commentators certainly seemed disposed to dismiss the whole genre in this way (see Lisle 2006; Kaplan 1996). Yet as always with a form as protean and heterogeneous as travel writing, any blanket condemnation of the genre on these grounds needs to be tempered with some important qualifications and counter-arguments.

In the first place, it is worth noting that not every travel writer manages, or even seeks, to project the sort of assured, coherent selfhood implicit in both the Enlightenment and Romantic personae described earlier. Much recent scholarship on travel writing has productively mined the genre for moments of apparent contradiction, confusion and discontinuity in the narratorial self, gleaning from these **aporetic** passages interesting insights into the tensions that some travellers have clearly felt as they seek to fashion an identity for themselves (see Mills 1991; Morgan 1996). These tensions in turn may be read as indicative of larger pressures and constraints operating in the writer's culture, pressures and constraints which dictate who is allowed to set themselves up in the public sphere as travellers, with all the authority this brings to make pronouncements on both other cultures and their own. Such tensions are perhaps especially apparent in women's travel writing, and this is accordingly an aspect of the genre that will be discussed further in Chapter 7.

Thus there are travel writers who essay a coherent, authoritative selfhood on the page, yet who for some reason fail to fully achieve this assertive self-fashioning. Other travel writers, meanwhile, seem deliberately to disclaim and/or subvert the authoritative postures more customary in the genre. In the literary travel book especially, there is a long tradition of self-deprecation and playful self-ironising, in which writers mock their own belated or feeble travel efforts in comparison with those of more obviously accomplished or courageous travellers; examples include Sterne's fictional travelogue *A Sentimental Journey* and the genuine travelogues produced by figures such as Peter Fleming and Eric Newby. This self-ironising tendency in the genre seems to have become more pronounced in recent years. Contemporary writers like Redmond O'Hanlon and Tim Cahill, for example, often present themselves principally as clowns and as cowards who have no desire whatsoever to get into perilous situations, rather than as heroic explorers. Others such as Bill Bryson, meanwhile, are happy to acknowledge that they are just as much tourists as their fellow travellers; superficially, at least, they disclaim the status of 'traveller', in the honorific sense of that term. The persona that many of these recent writers fashion for themselves is therefore better described as that of the 'post-tourist'. As defined by Maxine Feifer (1986), the 'post-tourist' is someone who knows that notions of getting off the beaten track, and of being a 'traveller' rather than a 'tourist', are usually self-deluding fantasies and an illusion frequently manufactured by the tourist industry itself. The post-touristic travel writer will accordingly often reject and mock the rhetoric of authenticity that has been so conspicuous in travel writing in the past. Typically they will be far less disdainful of the alleged inauthenticity of mainstream tourist activities and, even when they engage in very different activities, they are often prepared to admit that these are just a variant form of tourism, rather than a radically different and superior type of travel.

In some cases, this 'post-touristic' attitude forms part of what one can more generally regard as a **postmodern** sensibility or tendency in travel writing. Postmodernism is notoriously hard to define, but in the present context it can be defined as a tendency to playfulness and parody, born of a desire to subvert both the conventions and the authority traditionally associated with many Western genres, disciplines and discourses. With regard to travel writing, this can involve writers playing against traditional narrative and stylistic expectations in a variety of ways. For example, some travelogues, such as Bruce Chatwin's *In Patagonia* (1977), fashion quests that seem never to come to a proper conclusion, or else terminate **bathetically** rather than triumphantly. Elsewhere, we encounter in Chatwin's later travelogue *The Songlines* (1987) and in works like William Least Heat-Moon's *PrairyErth* (1991), texts which seem to undercut travel writing's frequent tendency to a monologic imperiousness of vision by fashioning fragmented narratives, comprised in large part of extensive quotations from other authors. And by incorporating into the text other voices and other points of view, this dialogic or **polyphonic** narrative technique arguably works to 'decentre' the narratorial self.

Sebald's highly digressive technique in *The Rings of Saturn* works a similar effect, and in Sebald's case this decentring of the self seems to be bound up with an attempt to suggest that no 'self' is entirely a singular, bounded entity, wholly unique and private to one individual. A recurrent device that Sebald uses is to have other voices, other 'I's, enter his narrative, as he retells stories that he has heard or read. Often, however, it is not clearly signalled in the text when a new narrator has in this way been introduced, and there are thus many moments when readers are left unsure whether they are reading Sebald's words, or someone else's. As the boundaries of the narratorial self thus seem to dissolve, the **inter-textuality** of Sebald's narrative arguably figures an intertextuality, or intersubjectivity, in the self, as the narrator's consciousness comes to seem a medium in which multiple other consciousnesses are mingled and distilled. Further to this, Sebald's interweaving of experience, memory and reflection is not plotted towards any clear conclusions, or towards a climactic moment of *anagnorisis*. In this way, Sebald seems to fashion on the page neither an Enlightenment self, that seems detached from the scenes it surveys and remains unchanged through its travel experiences, nor a fully Romantic self, which achieves a significant and identifiable degree of self-knowledge and self-realisation over the course of its travels. Rather, *The Rings of Saturn* posits a more provisional, picaresque selfhood, conveying a sense that human identity is a fluid, contingent construct, forever being performatively constituted in response to events and circumstances. Here the self seems to have no fixed, stable essence unique to itself, but rather is always evolving dialogically, as it were, or relationally; that is to say, through its interactions with the wider environment and with others.

In such ways, then, some travel writers have sought to counter the pre-eminence habitually given to the narratorial self in the travelogue. At the same time, however, there are important caveats to be issued about many of these apparent strategies of self-deprecation and/or self-effacement. The comic, self-ironising personae developed by writers like O'Hanlon and Cahill, for example, seem from one perspective parodic of travel writing's long history of self-aggrandising heroics, and also of the **masculinist**, imperialist and culturally supremacist attitudes which often accompanied such heroic accounts of the self. At the same time, however, to disclaim heroism and manliness when one is in fact putting one-self in positions of genuine danger, as O'Hanlon and Cahill often are, is to follow a well-established rhetorical strategy of modest understatement, which ultimately only heightens the heroism that attaches to the traveller. It has also been suggested, moreover, that the buffoonery of figures like O'Hanlon and Cahill is in part a way of disclaiming moral responsibilities and of evading awkward questions about the extent to which modern travel writers are still complicit with, and contributive to, the larger structures of power and discourse that maintain present-day global inequalities (see Holland and Huggan 1998: 30–31).

Similarly, attempts to decentre and diffuse the narratorial self in travel writing, by the use of extensive quotations, multiple narrators and so forth, do not necessarily undermine significantly an author's controlling presence in his or her text. As James Clifford has noted, 'quotations are always staged by the quoter', whilst the interweaving of different voices often still involves, and implies, a 'final, virtuoso orchestration by a single author' (1983: 139). Chatwin's comparatively self-effacing style in both *In Patagonia* and *The Songlines*, for example, did not stop the author becoming an iconic figure and a literary celebrity; even an understated, reticent narratorial persona, it seems, will sometimes be the route to acquiring significant cultural capital. Moreover, the controversy created by Chatwin's account of Aboriginal culture in *The Songlines* suggests that even more fragmentary or polyphonic modes of travel writing may sometimes constitute a subtle appropriation of the Other (see Lisle 2006: 61–67). Clearly, the extent to which travelogues often privilege self over other, observer over observed, remains a deeply contentious issue; and this debate is explored further in the next chapter, which examines some of the strategies habitually used in travel writing to depict other peoples and cultures.

6

REPRESENTING THE OTHER

On 9 January 1830, in the snowy wastes of the Canadian Arctic, a British exploratory expedition met a group of Inuit who had never encountered Europeans before. Unlike some first encounters between cultures, this meeting seems to have been entirely amicable. Gifts were exchanged, and when a British officer and one of the Inuit took part in a friendly running race, they did so 'with so much and such equal politeness on both sides that there was no victor to be declared' (Ross 1835: 247). The British also offered the Inuit some of the tinned food they had brought with them, but this exchange was less successful:

> They did not relish our preserved meat: but one who ate a morsel seemed to do it as a matter of obedience, saying it was very good, but admitting, on being cross questioned by Commander Ross, that he had said what was not true; on which all the rest, on receiving permission, threw away what they had received.
>
> (Ross 1835: 246)

More to the Inuits' taste, however, was the seal oil which the British were using as a lubricant, and as a fuel in lamps. As the subsequent British account of the expedition recorded, when 'the same man [was] offered some oil', he 'drank it with much satisfaction, admitting, that it was really good'.

In itself, this reference to the contrasting diets of the British and Inuit may seem amusing but inconsequential. Yet it has perhaps a deeper and ultimately more troubling resonance. Food often serves as a powerful signifier both of cultural self-definition and of cultural difference. And when the description above is situated within the larger account from which it is drawn, John Ross's *Narrative of a Second Voyage in Search of a North West Passage* (1835), it becomes apparent that the issue of diet indeed functions in this way, as a marker of some significant cultural differences between the British and the Inuit. Strange as it may seem today, the British at this date were immensely proud of their tinned food (see Thompson, 2004). First patented in 1812, and not yet mass-produced, the tin can was a comparatively new technology, which seemed to represent a remarkable advance in food preservation. It also played a vital role in enabling the exploratory activity undertaken by the British Navy in the Arctic in the early nineteenth century. The expeditions undertaken by figures like John Ross and William Parry in this period often lasted for several years, and on voyages of this length scurvy was always a threat, due to the difficulty of maintaining a supply of fresh food. Tinned foodstuffs, however, retained their nutritional value to a greater extent than salted meat and other forms of preserved food, and so provided a better safeguard against disease.

In this context, it is unsurprising that Ross makes several admiring references to tinned food over the course of his narrative. On one occasion, indeed, he waxes lyrical on the topic, wondering what foodstuffs might have survived from Rome and Ancient Egypt if the tin can had been invented earlier, and suggesting whimsically that perhaps it will be possible, 'some thousand years hence', to dine on 'hare soup[, ...] *purée* of carrots', and other dishes 'cooked in London during the reign of George the Fourth' (1835: 619–20). Here and elsewhere, Ross seems to regard the tin can as emblematic of British technological and organisational prowess in general. A triumph of human ingenuity over natural processes of decay, to Ross it represents **metonymically** both the attributes that had made Britain the dominant world power at this date, and the benefits that the British liked to think they were bringing to the wider world – namely, 'progress' or, in early nineteenth-century parlance, 'improvement'.

This symbolic investment in the tin can gives a deeper resonance to the episode recounted earlier, in which the Inuit are unable to appreciate the miracle of tinned meat. This in turn contributes to a larger portrait of the Inuit, as developed over the course of Ross's narrative, which defines them very much in terms of what and how they eat. Again and again, Ross and the other contributors to his volume choose to emphasise, in a mixture of bemusement and horror, the Inuit predilection for raw seal meat, the apparently filthy conditions in which they prepare and eat their food, and their extreme gluttony. The prodigious quantities consumed at one Inuit feast, for example, prompt the following exclamation from James Clarke Ross, John Ross's nephew:

> Disgusting brutes! The very hyena would have filled its belly and gone to sleep: nothing but absolute incapacity to push their food beyond the top of the throat could check the gourmandizing of these specimens of reason and humanity.
>
> (Ross 1835: 358)

This is not the only moment in which the younger Ross uses disturbingly bestial imagery in relation to the Inuit and their eating habits; elsewhere, he compares them variously to pigs, vultures and tigers.

In depicting the Inuit in this way, John Ross and his nephew were engaged in a process that is now sometimes called '**othering**'. This is a much-used term in recent travel writing studies, although confusingly it is often used in two slightly different senses. In a weaker, more general sense, 'othering' simply denotes the process by which the members of one culture identify and highlight the differences between themselves and the members of another culture. In a stronger sense, however, it has come to refer more specifically to the processes and strategies by which one culture depicts another culture as not only different but also inferior to itself. All travel writing must, arguably, engage in an act of othering in the first sense, since every travel account is premised on the assumption that it brings news of people and places that are to some degree unfamiliar and 'other' to the audience. More debatable, however, is whether *all* travel writing inevitably 'others' other cultures in the second, stronger sense of the term. Yet it is certainly in this spirit that Ross's narrative focuses so frequently on the issue of diet. For this is a topic which enables the account to posit a seemingly clear distinction between, on the one hand, the British, the representatives of supposed 'civilisation' and, on the other, the Inuit, who are thus made to seem 'savage' and uncivilised, for all that they may be friendly and good-natured. In this way, Ross's account produces an image of the Other which licenses a sense of cultural superiority in both traveller and audience, and many other travelogues historically have worked in the same fashion, thereby helping to generate or reinforce a range of prejudicial, ethnocentric attitudes.

The motives behind such pejorative or patronising portrayals of other cultures may be various; often these motives will be unconscious and **over-determined**, springing from a complex mixture of emotions, such as fear, envy, revulsion, incomprehension and sometimes even desire, when another culture stirs taboo fantasies that travellers wish to repress and disown. Very often, however, instances of pejorative 'othering' in travel writing serve an important justificatory function. They may legitimate the traveller's personal conduct towards the people he or she met; more crucially, perhaps, they also often work to legitimate the conduct of the traveller's culture. The traveller's portrayal of another people or place is often in this way ideologically motivated, seeking at some level to justify and encourage a particular policy or course of action towards those others. John Ross's depiction of the Inuit, for example, seems to have possessed such an ideological dimension. In the early nineteenth century, British explorers in the Arctic were not only searching for a North West Passage that would enable ships to sail from the North Atlantic to the North Pacific, they were also scouting out the natural resources of the region. Yet these resources were arguably the property of the Inuit, the indigenous population. By painting the Inuit as savages, however, Ross's narrative functions as a subtle endorsement of the British presence in the region. Like most explorers in the eighteenth and nineteenth centuries, Ross takes it for granted that the earth and its resources exist to be harvested by man. Viewed through this ideological lens, however, the Arctic clearly cannot be left to its indigenous population, the Inuit. Portrayed by Ross as primitive, improvident, and in thrall to their most base appetites, the Inuit are seemingly in no position to develop the Arctic properly, or to maximise its productive potential. It falls, therefore, to the British to assume the stewardship of the Arctic, since it is only the British, apparently, who have the foresight, self-discipline and technological expertise required to administer the region properly, in ways that will benefit both themselves and the local population. Or so, at least, we are meant to surmise from Ross's narrative.

The ideological dimensions of travel writing, and the larger rhetorical purposes served by the frequent tendency of travel writers to depict other groups and cultures in a hostile or condescending way, are topics that have been much addressed in the recent wave of travel writing studies. In particular, these are issues which have greatly concerned postcolonialist scholars, who have focused their attention especially on the depictions of other people and places offered in Western travel writing, and in Western culture more generally. Leading the way in this regard was Edward Said's seminal *Orientalism* (1978), a foundational text for both postcolonial and travel writing studies. In *Orientalism*, Said explored Western images and accounts, from ancient times down to the late twentieth century, of the so-called 'Orient': that is, the region stretching from Egypt and the Middle East to India, China and Japan. He detected in many of these representations of the 'Orient', regardless of whether they occurred in art and fiction or in ostensibly factual, objective genres such as travel writing and ethnography, essentially the same underlying repertoire of stereotypes and unquestioned assumptions. Thus Orientals were routinely depicted as sensual and cruel, whilst Oriental societies were usually assumed to have a natural tendency towards despotism. These recurrent motifs, Said suggested, were not necessarily an accurate description of the objective reality of the highly diverse cultures and ethnicities of Asia and the Middle East; rather, they were a set of representational conventions which had become pervasive and as it were institutionalised in European and North American culture. In this way, these motifs and images came to constitute a discourse, a concept Said derived from the French theorist Michel Foucault. Glossed by Said as a 'regularising collectivity' (1983: 186), the term 'discourse' denotes an accumulated archive of knowledge and imagery which comes to shape a culture's attitudes and assumptions on a given topic, and which accordingly dictates what is likely to be regarded as true, and as proper knowledge, in that subject area. 'Orientalism' is thus, for Said, a discourse in Western culture which has consistently worked to construct a singular 'Orient' as the antithesis of a supposedly more enlightened West. And this simplistic, negative 'othering' of Asia and the Middle East, Said further suggests, has generally served ideological ends, and has often been used to justify the West's colonial ambitions in these regions.

In the wake of *Orientalism*, numerous critics and cultural historians have investigated the rhetorical conventions and ideological agendas underpinning Western accounts of other regions of the world, and other cultures and races. In this spirit, for example, Christopher Miller (1985), V.Y. Mudimbe (1988), Tim Youngs (1994) and others have explored the discursive construction of Africa in the West, and the practices and policies that have flowed from an 'Africanist', as opposed to 'Orientalist', tradition or discourse. Ronald Inden (1990), Sara Suleri (1992) and others, meanwhile, have addressed similar issues in relation to India, whilst Terry Goldie (1989) and others have explored European and North American attitudes to supposedly 'savage', hunter-gatherer cultures. Few of these studies, it should be stressed, focus exclusively on travel writing. However, the genre often features prominently in postcolonialist enquiries of this sort. For it is usually travellers who bring back the first reports of other cultures, and so first formulate the grounds, and the key markers, by which those cultures are understood to be different to their own society. In addition, since travelogues necessarily depict moments of cross-cultural contact, they are often highly revealing of the so-called 'imaginative geographies' that operate not only in the individual traveller's mind, but also in his or her culture more generally. Thus travel accounts often illuminate the mental maps that individuals and cultures have of the world and its inhabitants, and the larger matrix of prejudices, fantasies and assumptions that they bring to bear on any encounter with, or description of, the Other.

The present chapter views travel writing through what is broadly speaking a postcolonialist lens, and explores some of the ways in which the genre has both contributed to, and also occasionally contested, Western imperialism. To this end, the first section considers the various ways, some subtle, some decidedly unsubtle, in which travel writing has functioned as a mode of what is sometimes dubbed **colonial discourse** (see Spurr 1993). Here I shall explore the rhetorical strategies, and the representations of the Other, typically offered by travel writing when it is in the service of empire; and it should be noted that these representations and rhetorical strategies are also characteristic of colonial discourse more generally, and so may be found in other genres besides travel writing, such as fiction, journalism and visual art, whenever those genres are informed by imperialist attitudes and ideologies. The second section then explores the extent to which modern travel writing keeps alive these imperialist traditions, and continues to deploy tropes and representational strategies associated with colonial discourse, even after the apparent end of European imperialism. That is to say, it examines travel writing's complicity with what is often termed **neo-colonialism**, by which is meant the networks of knowledge, power and representation that currently sustain the West's ongoing political and economic dominance over the rest of the world. This is not to suggest, however, that all Western travel writing is inherently or invariably imperialist and exploitative. As the first section of the chapter will show, there are important qualifications to be made to any blanket condemnation of the genre on these grounds. And as the third and final section will discuss, recent years have also seen a wave of 'postcolonial' travelogues, in which writers seek to reclaim and reorientate a genre long associated with imperialist and colonialist attitudes.

STRATEGIES OF OTHERING I: TRAVEL WRITING AND COLONIAL DISCOURSE

The late nineteenth and early twentieth centuries are often dubbed the age of 'high imperialism'. It was in this period that Britain, France and the other European powers greatly extended their influence around the world, with the result that by 1914 they effectively controlled some 85% of the globe (Said 1993: 6). During the same period, moreover, the USA, an offshoot of European imperialism, consolidated its control over the North American landmass between Mexico and the 49th parallel, added Alaska and Hawaii to the Union, in 1867 and 1898 respectively, and acquired further overseas territories in the Philippines, Puerto Rico, Guam and Samoa. Many Americans, of course, did not regard their nation's growth as a form of imperialism, although it certainly felt that way to some of the indigenous populations absorbed into the republic. But in Europe, this was a time when many espoused an unabashed imperialism, seeing it as the natural order of things that white peoples of European extraction should govern vast tracts of the globe. Such hubristic, ethnocentric assumptions produced, and were simultaneously a product of, a pervasive imagery and ideology of empire, that found expression at many levels in European society, and in a variety of cultural forms.

Travel writing was one such cultural form steeped in imperialist attitudes and imagery. A text that illustrates this aspect of the genre in an especially stark and extreme fashion, and that accordingly exemplifies many of the characteristic tropes and conventions of colonial discourse more generally, is Henry Morton Stanley's bestselling *Through the Dark Continent* (1878). The book is an account of an arduous, three-year trek across central Africa in which Stanley led a party of some 350 porters and guides from Zanzibar in the Indian Ocean to Lakes Victoria and Tanganyika in East Africa, before following the course of the Lualaba and Congo rivers to reach Africa's Atlantic coast. This was not an expedition of imperial conquest; on this mission at least, Stanley himself added no new territory to any of the European empires. Rather, he travelled principally as an explorer, seeking to gather geographical and ethnographical information. Fed back into the circuits of Western knowledge, however, the data he collected would in due course prove immensely useful to European colonial projects in eastern and central Africa. In addition to providing practical assistance in this way, moreover, *Through the Dark Continent* would also prove useful ideologically, by painting a picture of Africa and its inhabitants that seemed to encourage and justify the imperialist enterprise.

Stanley's narrative functions as a form of colonial discourse in a variety of ways. In the first place, his account of Africa, like John Ross's account of the Arctic, is from one perspective an investigation into the natural resources, and the lucrative opportunities for trade, that exist in the region. He reports on 'valuable article[s] of commerce' (1988: vol. 1, 301) such as beeswax and india-rubber whenever he finds them, and rhapsodises about areas in which the land seems especially fertile, and so amenable to agricultural development. Elsewhere, Stanley also fantasises about a 'great trading port' on Lake Victoria, a place where steamships may collect 'the coffee of Uzongora, the ivory, sheep, and goats of Ugeyeya, Usoga, Uvuma, and Uganda', and many other commodities besides, in exchange for 'fabrics brought from the coast' (1988: vol. 2, 175). This last rhapsody occurs in the course of the 'monarch-of-all-I-survey' scene discussed in the last chapter, and in the present context it is worth remembering that when he fashions such scenes, Stanley seems to take imaginative possession of the landscapes in front of him, and encourages the reader to indulge in similarly acquisitive fantasies. And in this way *Through the Dark Continent*, like many accounts of exploration, at one level works simply to whet the appetites of traders and investors in Europe, suggesting numerous possibilities for profit and self-advancement in distant territories.

Commercial ventures, of course, do not necessarily entail empire and colonialism. Nor does Stanley himself explicitly advocate any form of imperial or colonial arrangement in the region. At the same time, however, the account he provides of Africa makes implicitly a powerful case for some sort of administration by an external power. Like John Ross in the Arctic, but in a far more lurid fashion, Stanley emphasises the primitive state, and the savagery and barbarism, of the majority of the cultures he encounters in Africa. The narrative's most memorable passages, for example, are undoubtedly those that recount the pitched battles that Stanley and his men fought with local tribespeople whilst navigating the Lualaba and Congo rivers. Again and again, he declares himself baffled by 'the senseless hate and ferocity which appeared to animate these primitive aborigines' (1988: vol. 2, 193), although native suspicion of a large, well-armed band of strangers, in a region still terrorised by Arab slave traders, was surely far from inexplicable. In describing these clashes, moreover, Stanley utilises literary techniques acquired during his earlier career as a journalist. His account is written mostly in the past tense, but at moments of high drama it slips into the present tense to offer a vivid recreation of events. In the following vignette, for example, Stanley and his men, travelling by boat, have rounded a bend in the Congo only to encounter a flotilla of native boats, headed by a 'monster canoe' carrying more than a hundred warriors:

As the foremost canoe comes rushing down, and its consorts on either side beating the water into foam, and raising their jets of water with their sharp prows, I turn to take a last look at our people, and say to them:-

'Boys, be firm as iron; wait till you see the first spear, and then take aim. Don't fire all at once. Keep aiming until you are sure of your man. Don't think of running away, for only your guns can save you.'

Frank is with the *Ocean* on the right flank, and has a choice crew, and a good bulwark of black wooden shields. Manwe Sera has the *London Town* – which he has taken in charge instead of the *Glasgow* – on the left flank, the sides of the canoe bristling with guns, in the hands of tolerably steady men.

The monster canoe aims straight for my boat, as though it would run us down; but, when within fifty yards off, swerves aside, and, when nearly opposite, the warriors above the manned prow let fly their spears, and on either side there is a noise of rushing bodies. But every sound is soon lost in the ripping, crackling musketry. For five minutes we are so absorbed in firing that we take no note of anything else; but at the end of that time we are made aware that the enemy is reforming about 200 yards above us.

> Our blood is up now. It is a murderous world, and we feel for the first time that we hate the filthy, vulturous ghouls who inhabit it. We therefore lift our anchors, and pursue them up-stream along the right bank, until rounding a point we see their villages. We make straight for the banks, and continue the fight in the village streets with those who have landed, hunt them out into the woods, and there only sound the retreat, having returned the daring cannibals the compliment of a visit.
>
> (1988: vol. 2, 211–12)

As this will suggest, *Through the Dark Continent* frequently presents Stanley himself as an all-action hero, a figure of exemplary courage and manliness who seems to have sprung from the pages of the *Boy's Own* magazine, or from the contemporary adventure fiction produced by authors such as G.A. Henty and Rider Haggard. And this is another way in which Stanley's travel narrative contributes to colonial discourse. Like the fictions of Henty and Haggard, it seems calculated to rouse in some readers fantasies of adventure and heroism; and as Martin Green has noted, such 'dreams of adventure' often led in due course to 'deeds of empire', encouraging young men to travel to distant regions so as to realise their fantasies and ambitions (Green 1980).

As he recounts his many confrontations with what he dubs the 'perverse cannibals and insensate savages' (1988: vol. 2, 199) of the Congo region, Stanley deploys a number of tropes characteristic both of colonial discourse in its most extreme form, and also of any travel account in which another culture is 'othered' in an especially hostile or fearful fashion. Labelling his adversaries in the passage above 'filthy, vulturous ghouls', for example, Stanley dehumanises them. Here and elsewhere, meanwhile, he also frequently depicts his opponents as a frenzied mob, a swirling, undifferentiated mass of humanity seemingly in the grip of irrational fears and superstitions; and again, this is a rhetorical strategy that travel writers often use to dehumanise communities they find threatening or incomprehensible, since it allows both writer and reader to overlook the fact that every supposed 'mob' is actually made up of many unique individuals, each with their own life-story. Finally, in Stanley's routine insistence that just about everyone he meets in central Africa is a cannibal we witness the deployment of what has perhaps been, across all cultures, one of the most common techniques of hostile or fearful 'othering'. A great many societies historically have cast their enemies, and/or other peoples that they find especially repugnant, as cannibals; equally common, moreover, is for those 'others' to be accused of some form of sexual deviancy. Modern anthropologists suggest, however, that we should always be cautious about taking such accusations at face value (see Arens 1979; Boucher 1992; Obeyesekere 1992). This is not to deny that some human societies have almost certainly practised cannibalism, and it is also true that cultures have differed greatly in the sexual practices they consider acceptable (see Hyam 1990). Yet as William Arens (1979) has shown in relation to cannibalism, there is ample evidence that allegations of this type often bear little relation to the actual activities of the community under discussion. Rather, practices that one culture deems taboo will often function as powerful markers of cultural difference, which can be projected on to other cultures so as to emphasise their perceived barbarism and moral inferiority.

This is almost certainly what is happening when Stanley identifies so many of the tribes he encounters as cannibalistic. There are only a few occasions in which he offers any sort of evidence for this accusation, and in every case modern anthropologists would probably suggest that Stanley has significantly misread what he regards as signs of cannibalism. At the same time, however, it would not be entirely fair to accuse Stanley of wilful deceit in this matter. Although one suspects he sometimes used the term 'cannibal' simply to add to the sensationalism of his account, and to heighten his own heroism, it is likely that Stanley did genuinely believe that many of the tribes he encountered *were* cannibals. Rather, what his account demonstrates is the way a culture's dominant discourses, in the Foucauldian/Saidian sense of that term, often shape significantly not just its images and representations of other cultures, but even the very perceptions of its travellers as they venture out into the world. In Stanley's case, he was trained by the dominant discourses of his age to expect cannibalism in central Africa, and this expectation accordingly led him to interpret what now seems erroneous or, at best, highly ambiguous evidence as incontrovertible 'signs' of man-eating. For this was what **Africanist** traditions in Europe had always alleged about the indigenous population of sub-Saharan Africa. Classical and medieval writers such as Pliny and Leo Africanus, for example, had frequently presented sub-Saharan Africa as a place of primitive savagery, and as the monstrous antithesis of the civilised values of the Mediterranean world. And in the late nineteenth century, these age-old accusations had recently gained a new credibility and authority, as a consequence of the emergence of significant new discourse in European and North American culture; namely, the emergence of a supposed 'science' of race.

European and North American racial science had its origins in the Enlightenment quest to catalogue and classify every aspect of the natural world. Initially, scientists sought to chart the physical differences between the various branches of mankind. Very quickly, however, it began to be assumed that anatomical differences had as their corollary different intellectual and moral capabilities. This led in turn to works such as Robert Knox's *The Races of Man* (1850), the Comte de Gobineau's *Essai sur l'Inégalité des Races Humaines* (*Essay on the Inequality of the Human Races*; 1853–55), and J.R. Gliddon and J.C. Nott's *Types of Mankind* (1854), which sought to classify, and to hierarchise, the different human races on the basis of what were supposed to be essential characteristics, inherent in every racial 'type'. In due course, this classificatory agenda would fuse with the evolutionary theory advanced by Charles Darwin, to produce what one might broadly characterise as **Social Darwinist** theories, which claimed to chart the upward evolutionary ascent of some races, and the downward decline, or 'degeneration', of others. Whatever precise form they took, however, these hierarchies and theories invariably posited the intellectual and moral superiority of white peoples of European extraction, assigning black Africans one of the lowest rungs on the developmental ladder. Indeed, from the 1850s, sections of the Western scientific community argued vociferously that blacks were not just a separate race but a separate species. This was not universally accepted, but there was certainly a consensus in Western science at this date that the peoples of sub-Saharan Africa represented humanity in one of its most savage forms, especially in regions where the inhabitants had had little contact with non-African cultures.

This supposed 'science' of race is now regarded as utterly spurious, and as the product of essentially racist presuppositions and methodologies. Yet it was widely accepted in the late nineteenth and early twentieth centuries, this being moreover a period in which, as Robert Young has written, 'theories based on race spread from discipline to discipline, and became one of the major organising axioms of knowledge in general' (1995: 93). Most European and American travellers of the period had accordingly absorbed, to some degree, these theories and axioms, and as a consequence they often interpreted what they encountered in other cultures as the expression of inherent racial traits. Stanley's familiarity with contemporary race science, meanwhile, is frequently evident in *Through the Dark Continent*. Thus he distinguishes at one point between tribes who exemplify respectively 'the truly debased Negro type' and the 'Ethiopic negro type' (1988: vol. 2, 63), whilst elsewhere the first pygmy he encounters is described as an 'ugly, prognathous-jawed creature' (1988: vol. 2, 135); and 'prognathous' here, which signifies a significant elongation of the jawbone, is again part of the technical vocabulary of contemporary race theory.

Stanley was thus predisposed by his training in race science, and by his familiarity with European 'Africanist' discourse more generally, to find evidence of cannibalism and other 'savage', atavistic practices amongst the tribes of central Africa. At the same time, however, he does not espouse the most extreme forms of contemporary race theory, and there is consequently another important dimension to Stanley's representation of Africa and Africans. The people he meets in the 'dark continent' are not all depicted in terms of savagery and irrational violence. He speaks admiringly, for example, of his guides and porters, and also of ethnic groups like the black population of Zanzibar. The latter are described as 'capable of great love and affection, and possessed of gratitude and other noble traits of human nature', and Stanley insists that they can be made 'good, obedient servants' (1988: vol. 1, 37). Here and elsewhere, he takes issue with contemporary commentators who claimed that 'savage' races were incapable of intellectual and moral improvement, and that they were therefore doomed to be supplanted, and possibly driven to extinction, by supposedly superior races. Instead, Stanley sees evidence of a potential for civilisation in some of coastal tribes he encounters, whom he regards as having been improved by their contact with non-African cultures.

Even as Stanley paints a more positive and sympathetic picture of African peoples, however, his tone is often highly condescending. He clearly takes it for granted that whilst 'negro nature ... [is] after all but human nature' (1988: vol. 2, 371), there is nevertheless a huge gulf between the black and white races in terms of their intellectual, moral and cultural development. Thus when they are not presented in a sensationalistic manner, as bloodthirsty cannibals, the black Africans that Stanley meets are typically depicted in a more sentimental and patronising fashion, as child-like figures or as faithful servants. This is a combination of stereotypes and/or representational modes highly characteristic of colonial discourse, and the ideological work it performs, and the contribution it makes to the colonial enterprise, is fairly obvious. The sentimental agenda fashions an Other that is seemingly in need of help from an external power, and deserving of that help: it thus encourages and legitimates the acquisition of colonial territories under the guise of providing tutelage and benign guidance to the indigenous population. The sensationalistic agenda, meanwhile, emphasises the benighted condition from which the local population must saved, and the primitive superstitions and barbaric practices which must be suppressed by the forces of reason and civilisation.

In this way, *Through the Dark Continent*, like many other forms of colonial discourse, ultimately seems to suggest the desirability of European intervention in another region's affairs. Crucially, it presents that intervention as desirable not simply because of the rich economic rewards on offer, but also as a means of providing the indigenous population with humanitarian assistance and a civilising influence. Thus Stanley declares Africa to be in need of a 'band of philanthropic capitalists' who will 'rescue these beautiful lands' (1988: vol. 1, 175) from their current savagery. Like many other explorers from the eighteenth century onwards, Stanley presents himself very much as an emissary of the so-called 'three Cs': civilisation, Christianity and commerce. It was through a combination of these three influences, it was generally assumed in Europe and North America, that 'savage', primitive peoples would be raised to a higher level of material, moral and intellectual development. This was a rationale for empire which was undoubtedly genuinely believed by some agents of colonialism; for many others, however, it was merely a pretext with which to justify the appropriation of territory and natural resources.

Whilst Stanley obviously encourages a sense of cultural superiority in his readers when he depicts Africans as savages or simpletons, his narrative also works in more subtle ways to produce this effect. For example, Stanley undertakes his trek across Africa ostensibly as an explorer, someone principally dedicated to scientific enquiry. This is a rationale for travel that has often possessed an ideological dimension in Europe and America. Scientific exploration from the eighteenth century onwards was generally regarded, both by the explorers themselves and by their readers, as an essentially benevolent, morally worthy incursion into another region or culture. Or as the critic Mary Louise Pratt has put it, explorers and commentators in this period generally sought to emphasise the extent to which exploration was not a matter of conquest, in the manner of earlier European crusaders and conquistadors, but rather of '**anti-conquest**', as the explorer risked life and limb in the selfless pursuit of knowledge rather than territory or booty (2008: 37–83). As Pratt points out, however, this was a claim, and a self-image, often used to suggest a degree of moral and intellectual superiority over indigenous cultures. Thus eighteenth- and nineteenth-century exploration narratives frequently record meetings with tribal leaders who are deeply suspicious of the explorer's claim to be simply gathering geographical and natural-historical information. Readers are meant to smile at the ignorance and backwardness this supposedly reveals; the implication is that only the enlightened citizens of Europe and North America have the largeness of vision to pursue knowledge for its own sake, and for the general good of all mankind. With hindsight, however, one might suggest that it was contemporary readers, rather than the tribal chiefs, who were being naïve here. For European and US explorers in this period were often quickly followed by more acquisitive, and more aggressive, representatives of their culture. Stanley's explorations in Africa, for example, ushered in the notorious 'Scramble for Africa', in which the European powers rushed to carve out colonies for themselves in the continent. Stanley himself later led a further expedition to the Congo which claimed the region as a colony for Belgium, leading to the creation of the notoriously brutal Congo Free State.

Stanley's designation of himself as an explorer or scientific traveller thus carries subtly an ideological resonance. By the same token, even when Stanley abandons his sensationalistic prose style for a more dispassionate, scientific idiom, his narrative techniques still work to position the 'native' as inferior to the explorer and his readers. The most blatantly racist assumptions underpinning much of the supposedly objective science of this era have been discussed already. At the same time, however, contemporary scientific discourse also assisted the colonialist cause, and fostered a sense of cultural superiority, by more subtle means. Like many Western travellers right down to the present day, for example, Stanley regarded the cultures he encountered in Africa in the light of what is sometimes termed a **stadial** theory of cultural development. That is to say, he assumed that human societies evolve naturally through successive stages of social, economic and technological development. A variety of such stadial schema have been utilised by Western commentators over the years. Eighteenth-century philosophers such as Adam Smith thought in terms of an evolution from hunter-gatherer communities, which were assumed to be the earliest and most primitive form of human society, to first pastoralism, then agriculture, and then finally a supposedly fully 'modern', commercial society. In the nineteenth century, meanwhile, this developmental schema was supplemented by the notion of Stone, Bronze and Iron Age cultures, and this is a terminology that Stanley uses at various junctures in *Through the Dark Continent*; for example, he suggests at one point that the 'negroes of Zanzibar' are 'a people just emerged into the Iron Epoch, and now thrust forcibly under the notice of nations who have left them behind by the improvements of over 4000 years' (1988: vol. 1, 38).

As a means of describing different sorts of socio-economic organisation, and/or the different technologies that cultures utilise, labels such as 'hunter-gatherer' and 'Stone Age' perhaps have some usefulness. More contentious, however, is the implicit assumption that these differences should be located in a temporal sequence, as successive stages in a process of cultural advancement that inevitably culminates in Western modernity. For as the quotation above from Stanley demonstrates, this assumption often carries with it the further implication that societies which have not developed in the same way as Western societies have therefore not developed at all, but remain stuck in an earlier historical phase which the West has supposedly outgrown. Thus there occurs in many travelogues, and in many Western depictions of the Other more generally, what Johannes Fabian has termed a 'denial of coevalness' (Fabian 1983: 31; 37–70). That is to say, many Western travellers take it for granted that it is only they and their compatriots who are properly modern. The 'others' that they encounter, meanwhile, are frequently regarded almost as living fossils, and as being to a greater or lesser degree survivals from an earlier epoch. Hence the frequent conflation of geographical and temporal distance in many Western travelogues, as travellers venture to some remote or unfamiliar region and simultaneously present themselves as going back in time, encountering 'Stone Age', 'Bronze Age' or 'medieval' cultures that are assumed to have remained unchanged for centuries.

To attribute historical stasis to another culture in this way is of course a fallacy. All cultures develop and change over time; in the case of supposedly 'traditional' indigenous communities, it is simply that those changes have led in a different direction, and so produced a society which does not conform to the traveller's expectations of 'modernity'. Both traveller and Other in fact inhabit the same historical moment. By implicitly or explicitly denying 'coevalness', however, Western travellers and their audiences can position themselves as the emissaries of modernity and progress, and so subtly claim a superiority over the others they describe. This impression is heightened, moreover, by the frequent use in scientific discourse, and in many scientifically inclined travelogues, of the so-called 'ethnographic present'. This is the term often used for a present-tense, normative voice, which purports to sum up the behaviour and beliefs of an entire culture. It is in this mode, for example, that Stanley informs us that 'the Waganda [tribesman] peels his bananas, folds them carefully up in the form of a parcel, enclosed in green banana-leaves, and putting a small quantity of water in his pot, cooks them with the steam alone' (1988: vol. 1, 322). Note that Stanley does not say that the individual Waganda tribesmen whom he happened to observe cooked their bananas in this fashion; instead, he deduces universal patterns of behaviour on the basis of what he has seen. This use of the 'ethnographic present', it has been suggested, fosters a sense that indigenous cultures are essentially uniform, fixed and unchanging, as if they have a set of core behaviours and beliefs which everyone follows, and which have always existed, without any sort of development over time. This is arguably another means by which indigenous communities can be subtly positioned, in Western discourse, as being somehow 'outside' proper history, or without a history of their own, at least until their first encounter with European or North American travellers (see Wolf 1982; Fabian 1983).

In this way Stanley's account of the indigenous peoples of central Africa weaves together sensational, sentimental and scientific modes of representation. In their different ways, however, all these modes work ultimately to position black Africans as inferior to white Europeans, and thereby help to convey a moral justification for European intervention in African affairs. And these are representational strategies typical of a great many European and US travelogues of the nineteenth and early twentieth centuries, especially those describing encounters with non-white peoples. The travel writing genre thus carries a troubling legacy, being deeply implicated, at both a practical and an ideological level, in the imperialist enterprise. At the same time, however, if the *general* tendency of Western travel writing, from at least the early modern period, has undoubtedly been to assist and encourage European and subsequently US expansionism, that does not mean that every individual traveller and travelogue has been equally complicit in this project. As always, the enormous diversity encompassed by the genre needs to be kept in mind; and as a result, any sort of wholesale condemnation of the genre on the grounds of racism and imperialism needs to be qualified and nuanced in a variety of ways.

All travel writing must be to some degree ethnocentric, since as discussed in Chapter 4, all travellers necessarily see the world and communicate their observations through an interpretative framework, or in Foucauldian terminology, through the 'discourses' provided by their culture. Yet the *extent* to which travellers are ethnocentric in their outlook, and correspondingly, the extent to which they are able to acknowledge, tolerate and/or appreciate other points of view and alien cultural practices, may vary greatly. Similarly, the *intent* with which travellers construct their necessarily partial accounts of other cultures can also vary significantly. Even in the high imperial era, there were travellers who adopted what one might broadly describe as an anti-imperialist position, seeking to oppose European or US territorial ambitions in a given region, or to expose the abuses and suffering inflicted by such interventions. Roger Casement, for example, produced in the early twentieth century powerful accounts of the brutal treatment of the Congolese, and of the Putomayo Indians of Peru, at the hands of European commercial enterprises. Similarly, as Robert Irwin has emphasised in his riposte to Said's *Orientalism*, European and US travellers and scholars have not all universally denigrated the so-called 'Orient', nor have they all sought to assist Western domination of the region; in fact, some produced highly complimentary accounts of 'Oriental' cultures, and championed independence movements in Asia and the Middle East (see Irwin 2006).

Insofar as they critique and rebuke their own culture in this way, such travellers stand in a long tradition of Western travel writing, stretching at least as far back as Bartolomeo de las Casas's *Brief Account of the Destruction of the Indies* (1552). Travel accounts of this type may be regarded, in Foucauldian/Saidian terminology, as a **counter-discourse** running in opposition to the dominant tendency of the travel writing genre in the West. Yet even these seemingly oppositional travelogues will often be entangled in complex ways with the prevailing discourses of the day. A key part of the usefulness of the Foucauldian concept of the discourse is that it encourages us to consider how far travellers may unwittingly draw upon, and contribute to, prevailing assumptions and representational conventions, even when their avowed aim is to contest stereotypes and prejudices. De las Casas, for example, rejects earlier depictions of the indigenous population of America as barbarous savages in thrall to Satan, yet he replaces this pejorative stereotype with a patronising imagery of native Americans as innocent children and 'sweete lambs' (quoted in Campbell 1988: 207). He still assumes, moreover, that they are in urgent need of spiritual redemption from the Christian church. With regard to the anti-imperial Orientalists identified by Irwin, meanwhile, what Irwin sometimes fails to acknowledge is the extent to which the information garnered by these figures contributed to a larger body of knowledge that *was* useful to agents of empire and colonialism, notwithstanding the original intentions of many individual travellers.

There have also been many Western travellers over the centuries who have regarded the cultures that they visit as superior to their own. These travellers will accordingly often 'other' the peoples that they meet in a more favourable and complimentary fashion than Stanley in *Through the Dark Continent*. In some cases, these favourable portrayals of the Other draw upon, and contribute to, the longstanding Western tradition of the 'noble savage'. Although this phrase was only coined in the late seventeenth century, by the English poet John Dryden, it refers to a concept with a much older history. Since at least the time of Michel de Montaigne's essay 'Of Cannibals' (1580), and arguably as far back as the Roman historian Tacitus's account of Germanic tribespeople in his *Germania* (c.98 CE), some Western commentators and travellers have regarded supposedly 'primitive' societies as morally superior to their own. This **primitivism**, or valorisation of the primitive, became especially pronounced in the eighteenth century and early nineteenth centuries, under the influence of Romanticism. Typically it took one of two forms, both predicated on the fundamental assumption that peoples apparently living closer to nature retained virtues that were lost in more complex and sophisticated societies. So-called 'soft' primitivism held up for admiration peoples whose simple lifestyles seemed to recall the 'Golden Age' or Arcadia of classical mythology; the Tahitians, for example, who seemed to live without undue labour off the natural resources of their island. 'Hard' primitivism, meanwhile, celebrated more rugged peoples such as the Maori or the Highlanders of Scotland, who were deemed to embody a manliness and courage that was supposedly lost in more effete, civilised cultures (see Smith 1969).

As the nineteenth century wore on, and as the race science discussed earlier became more influential, many commentators and travellers sought to debunk the notion of the noble savage. Thus Mark Twain in *Roughing It* (1872) dismisses the romanticised account of native Americans given by novelists such as Fenimore Cooper, offering instead the harsh verdict that the 'Red Man' is in fact 'treacherous, filthy and repulsive' (1985: 169). Yet from the late eighteenth century right down to the present day, a primitivist impulse, and a desire to seek some form of moral or spiritual education from supposedly less sophisticated cultures, has been a significant motivation in many forms of Western travel and travel writing. And this impulse has in turn given rise to many admiring accounts of other cultures.

'Othering' in this laudatory form might seem preferable to the sort of denigration of the Other that Stanley engages in. Yet it too is often morally dubious, and epistemologically problematic. Such positive representations of the Other can obviously span a spectrum which runs from conscientious attempts to describe another culture's actual beliefs and practices to fanciful, highly romanticised depictions. The latter, of course, may reduce the people being described to a caricature just as much as Stanley's sensationalistic account of the Congolese. In many cases, the Other here chiefly serves a rhetorical function, having projected on to it attributes and values that the traveller deems missing in his or her own culture. The image thus created of another people will often bear little relation to the actuality of their lives and lifestyles. In some cases, indeed, this romanticised image may be a means by which the hardship and suffering endured by another community or society is conveniently overlooked. As the anthropologist Renato Rosaldo has noted, it is often only when an indigenous culture has been defeated and subdued that an imagery of 'noble savages', supposedly living in harmony with nature,

UNIVERSITY OF WINCHESTER
LIBRARY

begins to circulate in the conquering culture. This imagery therefore sometimes functions as a form of 'imperialist nostalgia' (Rosaldo 1989: 108), which may work to obscure both what was done to these colonial subjects in the process of so-called 'pacification', and the conditions in which they now live. Furthermore, the myth of the noble savage has sometimes contributed to imperial and colonial endeavours in a more straightforward fashion. It is likely, for example, that Fenimore Cooper's idealised depictions of native Americans encouraged some young men and women to seek out frontier regions where they might encounter 'Indians' living traditional lifestyles, and in this way Fenimore Cooper's novels can be said to have promoted the westward drift of European settlers in America.

Even admiring and highly favourable accounts of other cultures, then, may constitute in subtle ways a form of colonial discourse. At the same time, however, it must be remembered that one may represent the Other in ways that are respectful or admiring without necessarily being excessively fanciful and romanticising, and that some travellers have done so in accounts which offer a sharp rebuke to imperial ambitions and colonial practices. Further to this, there is another important qualification to make to the suggestion that travel writing, or at least Western travel writing, has been invariably colonialist in tendency. More specifically, it must be kept in mind that even when Western travellers do engage in the sort of highly pejorative 'othering' found in Stanley's *Through the Dark Continent*, they are not all situated to the same degree as Stanley in larger networks of imperial power. Writing in the high imperial era, Stanley's sense of superiority over the Africans he meets is underwritten by the massive technological, military and economic advantages possessed by the industrialised Western powers at this date. These advantages also enabled Stanley's readers to undertake some of the colonial projects he implicitly outlines in *Through the Dark Continent*. In this way, as Said and other postcolonialist critics emphasise, there is an important linkage in the high imperial era between representation and power: between, on the one hand, the images of the Other produced by travellers and commentators and, on the other, the policies and practices subsequently pursued by their compatriots, both as they acquire and as they administer colonial territories.

However, this linkage is not necessarily to be assumed in every context, and/or in every period. In the medieval and early modern periods, for example, many European travellers and commentators often 'othered' other cultures in a hostile or pejorative fashion on the page, but in many cases they were not in a position to act upon these stereotypes, or to harbour imperial ambitions towards the Other. Until well into the eighteenth century, for example, many Europeans regarded the mighty Ottoman Empire with envy and a profound sense of inferiority, being keenly aware that their own countries lagged far behind this Islamic state in terms of military power and cultural sophistication. As late as 1625, meanwhile, Barbary pirates could raid the English coastline, carrying off men, women and children as slaves. It is perhaps unsurprising, therefore, that hostile 'Orientalist' representations of the Muslim world circulated extensively in British culture in the early modern period, and that many travellers viewed the Muslim societies that they visited through this Orientalist lens. Yet to describe these hostile attitudes and stereotypes as being 'imperialist' or 'colonialist' in tendency is at this date somewhat misleading; in due course these attitudes and stereotypes would underpin and shape colonial policies and ambitions, but in the period they originally circulated they were expressive not so much of the West's power, as of its sense of powerlessness with regard to the Muslim world. This situation was replicated in Europe's dealings with many other cultures in Asia and Africa until well into the eighteenth century. One must accordingly be wary of viewing medieval and early modern travellers anachronistically, and of ascribing to them and their cultures a degree of colonial power, or even colonial ambition, that in some situations they did not yet possess (see Clark 1999: 4–10).

STRATEGIES OF OTHERING II: TRAVEL WRITING AND NEO-COLONIALISM

The vast European empires of the nineteenth and early twentieth centuries were dismantled, for the most part, in the era of decolonisation that followed the Second World War. As a consequence, one might assume that modern travel writing cannot be situated in, or contribute to, the same sort of networks and infrastructures of global power as existed in the high imperial era. Further to this, a cursory survey of recent travel writing would suggest that the genre has also changed dramatically in tone since the end of empire. It is rare today, for example, to encounter the overt racism and cultural supremacism that characterised many European and US travelogues in the imperial era. Instead, modern travel writers from the West are more likely to espouse what Debbie Lisle describes as a 'cosmopolitan vision' (2006: 4). This cosmopolitanism typically seeks not to denigrate but to celebrate alterity and cultural difference; or as Lisle puts it, travel writers today generally 'frame encounters with others in positive ways', so as to 'reveal moments of empathy, [...] realisations of equality, and insights into shared values' (2006: 4). Travel writing, one might accordingly argue, has successfully reinvented itself. For long periods in the West, the genre was undoubtedly closely bound up with the drive to dominate and exploit other regions of the world. Now, however, it arguably assists a project of 'global community', mutual understanding and tolerance, by 'teaching us how to appreciate cultural difference and recognise the values common to all humanity' (Lisle 2006: 4).

After articulating what one might call the cosmopolitan case *for* modern travel writing, however, Lisle goes on to critique sharply these claims for the genre, and in the process paints a more troubling picture of travel writing's role in contemporary Western culture. For her as for many other recent commentators (see, *inter alia*, Sugnet 1991; Kaplan 1996; Holland and Huggan 1998), the genre's imperialist legacy continues in diverse ways, notwithstanding the self-professed cosmopolitanism of many modern travel writers. As these critics point out, the modern travel book remains principally a medium in which Western (and usually white) writers regale Western audiences with tales of their travels. As they do so, Charles Sugnet has suggested, travel writers typically 'arrogate to [themselves] ... rights of representation, judgement and mobility that [are] effects of empire' (1991: 72). For Sugnet, accordingly, much recent travel writing is both predicated on, and generative of, an implicitly imperialist attitude which takes for granted the right of Western travellers to roam the world and pronounce authoritatively on its inhabitants. Furthermore, the pronouncements these travellers make, and the images they fashion of other peoples and places, arguably sustain and legitimate the comparatively privileged position of most travel writers and their readers. Much recent travel writing, it has been suggested, is principally concerned to 'package' the world for easy Western consumption, producing images of the Other that reassure Western readers not only of their superiority over the rest of the world, but also of their moral right to that sense of superiority. To this way of thinking, accordingly, travel writing remains a genre thoroughly enmeshed in, and contributive to, the neo-colonial networks of power and inequality by which the West maintains its current global dominance.

In this context, it is perhaps unsurprising that many of the characteristic tropes of colonial discourse, and many of that discourse's strategies for representing the Other, have survived in contemporary travel writing, albeit often in subtly reinvented forms. That said, sometimes the use of these rhetorical strategies is decidedly unsubtle. Take the example of Peter Biddlecombe's *French Lessons in Africa* (1993), which describes the author's experiences whilst conducting business in French-speaking West Africa in the 1980s. Here we encounter comments such as the following:

> 'I've spent nearly thirty years in Africa. I love Africa ... But, honestly, it can be the most inefficient, corrupt, impossible place on earth. You do everything you can for them [that is, Africans]. You give your life for them. And what do they do? They steal the money from right under your nose.' He sighed a big sigh. 'But I still can't help loving them. They're like children, they don't know they're doing wrong.'
>
> (Biddlecombe 1993: 159)

The speaker here is not Biddlecombe himself, but a French financial adviser working in the Congo. Yet in context, and from the tenor of his travelogue generally, it is clear that Biddlecombe wholly endorses this patronising and paternalistic attitude. He does meet Africans who are enterprising, self-reliant and honest, but over the course of the whole narrative these come to seem isolated figures, struggling ineffectually against the general tendency of their culture. Thus it is ultimately a predictable, and highly stereotypical, picture that Biddlecombe paints of post-independence Africa and its inhabitants, one that defines the region chiefly in terms of superstition, tribalism, mindless petty bureaucracy, and massive corruption in both political and economic affairs. And it is seemingly these factors that are the principal cause of the extreme poverty and suffering everywhere apparent in the continent, which Biddlecombe also documents in some detail.

It is not only Africans who are depicted in a clichéd, stereotypical fashion in *French Lessons in Africa*. A German woman is lampooned as an 'enormous Brunhilde' (Biddlecombe 1993: 95), whilst the French people Biddlecombe meets are generally portrayed as epicures obsessed with fine dining. For Biddlecombe as for his nineteenth-century predecessor Stanley, it seems, the peoples of the world may be easily differentiated according to a well-established set of national and ethnic characteristics, and individuals will for the most part conform to their national and ethnic 'type'. In this way travelogues like *French Lessons in Africa* convey to their readers a reassuring sense that cultural identities may be easily defined, and that there are clear demarcations to be drawn between 'us' and 'them', 'home' and 'abroad'. When the 'abroad' in question is a region as troubled as Africa, moreover, this rhetoric of cultural differentiation is doubly reassuring, since it usually works to distance the traveller from the problems besetting the Other. Those problems come to seem indigenous to the region, as it were, and chiefly the fault and responsibility of local circumstances and the local population.

In many cases, however, it is highly simplistic for Western travellers and their readers to ascribe the suffering and turmoil they encounter elsewhere in the world entirely to local causes. To do so, moreover, often constitutes a significant evasion of their own culture's complicity in the scenes they are witnessing. For example, Biddlecombe has plenty of stories to tell of political corruption and tyranny amongst Africa's political elite, and also of the many bloody coups and civil wars that have racked the continent since independence. Yet these episodes are seldom put in a larger historical and geopolitical context. There is little reference, for example, to the problems created in Africa, sometimes deliberately, when departing colonial powers left behind them arbitrarily constructed nation-states that often yoked together hostile tribes or cultures. Nor is there any discussion of the extent to which modern tribal animosities in Africa are the product of colonial policies that sought to 'divide and rule' subject populations. Finally, the instability of many African regimes since independence, and the despotism of some of them, is also partly a consequence of Cold War politics, as the continent became an arena in which the West and the former USSR could do battle by proxy. Again, however, there is little detailed discussion of this geopolitical background in *French Lessons in Africa*.

With regard to the poverty and economic backwardness he observes in Africa, similarly, Biddlecombe seldom pauses to consider to what extent the continent's present condition is the result of a long history of exploitation and appropriation by external powers. The slave trade is briefly mentioned, but tellingly Biddlecombe seems more concerned to emphasise that Africans themselves were just as responsible for this atrocity as Europeans and Arabs (1993: 9–10). The restructuring of local economies enforced by European colonialism receives little consideration, nor does Biddlecombe ever address in detail the constraints and handicaps imposed on many African nations in the world economy today: the unfair trade agreements which protect Western farmers and manufacturers, for example, or the liberalisation policies imposed on African nations by Western-dominated institutions like the World Bank and the International Monetary Fund (IMF). For many commentators, these are the mechanisms that create the modern, neo-colonial world order. Biddlecombe makes much of the fact that he is in Africa as a business traveller; indeed, as an ardent **Thatcherite**, he is often keen to assert that 'business', left to its own devices and freed from undue regulation, will ultimately provide the panacea to Africa's many problems. One presumes, therefore, that Biddlecombe was in a position to gauge something of the success, or otherwise, of IMF austerity measures and similar Western-imposed economic programmes, yet he offers few observations on these matters; moreover, there is a significant lacuna in his account when it comes to explaining just what his own business was in the region, and how precisely it impacted on local populations.

This is not to say, of course, that the problems currently besetting Africa were wholly created by outside forces. Nor is it to suggest that every policy pursued by Western nations in Africa, in either the colonial or postcolonial era, has worked to the detriment of the indigenous population. Yet one must be deeply wary of any travelogue that gives no consideration to these issues, ascribing the continent's suffering instead solely to internal factors such as tribalism, residual savagery and corruption. Once again, the ideological work such travelogues perform seems obvious. They enable a Western audience in the first place to disclaim any responsibility for Africa's problems, thereby evading the troubling possibility that their own affluence may be predicated on unjust networks of trade and power, either in the past or the present, that have inflicted hardship elsewhere. Simultaneously, they foster a sense of moral and cultural superiority in the Western reader, insofar as they suggest implicitly that it is only the developed nations of Europe and North America that are genuinely modern, civilised and enlightened.

Africa is not the only region of the world typically depicted in this way by Western travel writers and their readers. The themes developed by Biddlecombe in *French Lessons in Africa*, and the imagery he uses, can be paralleled in a great many recent accounts of Afghanistan, the Balkans, the Middle East and other similarly troubled or dangerous parts of the globe (see Lisle 2006: 152–64). Such regions are routinely presented as being in thrall to atavistic, irrational attitudes, and consequently prone to tribalism and internecine feuding. In that well-established, temporalising trope of dismissive 'othering', meanwhile, they are routinely regarded as somehow not inhabiting the same time period as the traveller and his/her culture, and as being anachronistic survivals from an earlier, more barbarous era. Thus much contemporary travel writing still works, either implicitly or explicitly, to position the West at the forefront of modernity and progress. This in turn helps subtly to legitimate the current world order, and the global dominance of the West, since the further implication of these accounts of the Other is that it is only the West which possesses the expertise and moral vision to administer global affairs. And some recent travelogues in this vein, it should be noted, have more directly influenced Western policy towards other regions of the world. A notorious example is Robert Kaplan's *Balkan Ghosts: A Journey through History* (1993). Kaplan visited the Balkans during the Bosnian–Serbian war of 1992–95, and like many Western visitors to the region, both before, during and after the war, he attributes the conflict to age-old, 'tribal' animosities. Indeed, like many Western commentators over the years he often seems to suggest that a predisposition to violence is somehow 'hard-wired' in the local population (see Hammond 2009: xvi). This has the effect of obscuring the more precise political circumstances which generated the Bosnian-Serbian war. And this in turn, it has been suggested, influenced the decision of the US President Bill Clinton *not* to send peacekeeping troops to Bosnia in the early 1990s; *Balkan Ghosts* allegedly convinced the President that the country's problems were intractable, and that a peacekeeping force would achieve little.

Biddlecombe's *French Lessons in Africa* is a highly anecdotal travelogue, of the 'easy reading' type, which makes little claim to methodological rigour as it presents its account of Africa. Kaplan's *Balkan Ghosts*, however, demonstrates that the prevailing tropes of Western discourse often permeate travelogues that profess to be far more journalistic and rigorous in their approach. Travelogues with literary aspirations, meanwhile, usually avoid the more obviously clichéd stereotypes that Biddlecombe uses, but they are often just as guilty of 'othering' peoples and cultures in ways that make them seem primitive and atavistic in comparison with the supposedly enlightened West. Often, indeed, a depiction along these lines is essential to the atmosphere of exoticism and/or danger that the writer wishes to generate; it provides the necessary backdrop against which he or she can construct an image of themselves as intrepid adventurer, or as 'traveller' in the heroic sense of that term. Just like Biddlecombe, moreover, many literary travel writers shy away from revealing, or interrogating, their own motives for travel, and the economic and social privileges which enable their travelling. By evading these issues, they omit from their accounts the more complex web of inter-relations, and the historical contexts and present-day economic and political networks, which connect themselves and their home culture to the regions they are visiting. 'Elsewhere' is thus kept safely 'other': abroad is presented not so much as a real place inhabited by fellow human beings who are properly our equals and con-temporaries, but rather as an arena or playground where Western travellers may seek out thrilling adventures, or work through personal psychodramas.

In the neo-colonial as in the colonial era, positive as well as negative representations of the Other may work to sustain the unequal power relations between the West and the rest of the world. The counterpart to accounts such as Biddlecombe's, which emphasise the primitive and uncivilised nature of many troubled regions of the world, are travelogues which unduly romanticise and exoticise other regions and cultures. Often these accounts use tropes of temporalisation and historical stasis similar to those found in accounts of dangerous or barbarous 'others', only here the survivals from the past are valorised rather than vilified by the traveller; they signify a culture supposedly untouched by the worst aspects of modernity. In many cases, travelogues of this sort are a continuation of the 'noble savage' tradition discussed earlier in this chapter, and many of the criticisms made earlier about this tradition remain pertinent today. As Robyn Davidson recognises, many depictions of indigenous communities present those commu-nities as 'quaint primitives to be gawked at by readers who couldn't really give a damn what was happening to them' (1998: 141). Davidson is thinking specifically here of Western media representations, and of magazines such as *National Geographic*. Yet her criticism is also relevant to the representations of the Other found in many recent travelogues. Here one might cite again the controversy occasioned by Bruce Chatwin's *The Songlines* (1987), which was briefly mentioned in Chapter 5. One of the problems with *The Songlines*, for hostile critics, was not just that Chatwin made cultural capital, and ultimately financial profit, out of the spiritual traditions of Australian Aboriginal peoples; it was also that he unduly romanticised modern Aboriginal life by focusing so exclusively on its spiritual dimension. This was an emphasis that may well have produced a highly reverential depiction of ancestral Aboriginal wisdom, yet it also, in the eyes of some commentators, worked more dubiously to obscure the material conditions in which many Aborigines live today, and the pressing political and economic difficulties which they currently face as disadvantaged members of modern Australian society (see Huggan 1991; Shakespeare 1999: 489–90; Lisle 2006: 61–67).

It is not only peoples and cultures in the so-called 'developing world' that are routinely depicted in such a romanticised fashion. A mainstay of recent travel writing has been idyllic accounts of travellers visiting or relocating to regions and rural communities in Europe and North America which offer a slower-paced, more traditional lifestyle. This is the pastoral fantasy provided by such popular travelogues as Peter Mayle's *A Year in Provence* (1989). In this branch of the genre, metropolitan travellers and their audiences often apply much the same imagery to rural or supposedly 'traditional' communities as they do to 'noble savages' in more distant regions of the world. And the consequences are often much the same, as these travelogues underplay the political and economic pressures that many of these communities currently face, and the negotiations they necessarily make with modernity, in order to present a highly idealised account of provincial life.

Contemporary travel writing in this romanticising mode frequently works as an adjunct to the tourist industry, and to what has been termed the 'tourist gaze' (Urry, 1990), notwithstanding the efforts many travel writers make to distinguish themselves from 'mere' tourists. For travel writers may be just as guilty as tourists of regarding other cultures and landscapes chiefly as aesthetic spectacles, which seemingly exist solely for their personal enjoyment and edification. Arguably, moreover, the efforts of many travel writers to get off 'the beaten track' and escape conventional tourist itineraries simply helps to create new destinations and itineraries. As they depict communities and landscapes that are supposedly still authentic, pristine and unspoiled, many travelogues work, often inadvertently, to stimulate touristic interest in those destinations. In the process, the images fashioned by travel writers may become iconic; they are what later travellers expect and demand to find. In this way, travel writing, like the so-called 'tourist gaze', sometimes works a dubious transformative effect on the places and peoples it describes. The iconic features of another culture or landscape become 'sacralized' (MacCannell 1999: 42–48), and in due course fetishised and commodified; they are what the tourist industry then sells to its customers as an 'authentic' experience of the Other. Yet as many analysts have pointed out, the need to meet tourist expectations in this regard will often dramatically affect local landscapes, lifestyles and occupations. In this way, other peoples and places can in a sense be held hostage by the iconography that attaches to them in Western culture. And much contemporary travel writing arguably colludes with this tendency insofar as it works first to establish this iconography, and thereafter to underplay the impact of modernity, and especially of tourism, on many other regions of the world.

OTHER VOICES: CONTESTING TRAVEL WRITING'S COLONIALIST TENDENCIES

It will be apparent that commentators who regard travel writing as invariably a force for good in the world, or simply as a harmless 'medium through which humans celebrate [their] freedom' (Cocker 1992: 260), are being unduly naïve and uncritical. As James Clifford has noted, a 'historical taintedness' clings both to Western travel writing, and to many Western traditions of travel more generally (1997: 39). This has led some commentators to regard the genre as inherently imperialist and exploitative. Yet as Patrick Holland and Graham Huggan note, 'it would be as foolish to claim of travel writing that it is uniformly imperialistic as it would be to defend travel writers as being harmless entertainers' (1998: ix). We have already seen some of the ways in which a blanket condemnation of the genre on these grounds needs to be qualified when dealing with Western travel writing of the colonial and precolonial eras; in this final section, we shall discuss some of the ways in which recent, 'postcolonial' travel writing has sought to throw off the genre's problematic legacy.

In the first place, it is worth noting that whilst modern travel writing in the West is still dominated by white Western writers, the genre increasingly admits other voices, and other perspectives on the world. Recent decades have witnessed, for example, a surge in travelogues written by individuals from formerly colonised cultures, or alternatively, by Western travellers who are the descendants of formerly subject, '**subaltern**' peoples. To a much greater extent than was ever previously the case, accordingly, one may now encounter in travel writing the observations of Indian travellers like Vikram Seth and Amitav Ghosh, African travellers like Tété-Michel Kpomassie, and many more travellers who proudly lay claim to complex, 'hyphenated' identities. Thus Jamaica Kincaid's background is both Antiguan and American, whilst Colleen McElroy is African American; Caryl Philips and Gary Younge define themselves as Black British or British Caribbean; Tahir Shah is a British Afghan; and Pico Iyer presents himself as simultaneously 'a British subject, an American resident and an Indian citizen' (Iyer 1988: 24).

It is the travel writing produced by figures like these, along with that written by travellers descended from the European settler populations in former colonies such as Canada, Australia and South Africa, that is often labelled 'postcolonial' in recent discussions of the form (see, for example, Korte 2000: 150–78). This is arguably a misleading designation; strictly speaking, all travel writing produced from the late 1960s onward is 'postcolonial', whatever the cultural or ethnic heritage of the traveller. Yet the label is useful insofar as it signifies travellers whose backgrounds often make them more alert to the complex legacies of empire, and to the ongoing networks of power and trade that interconnect and order the world today, than travellers like Biddlecombe. As the British-Indian writer Salman Rushdie suggests in his 1987 travelogue, *The Jaguar Smile: A Nicaraguan Journey*, the many travellers today who do not 'have [their] origins in the countries of the mighty West or North' are likely to have in common some experience, either personal or familial, of imperial subjugation, and so are more likely to possess 'some knowledge of what weakness was like, some awareness of the view from underneath, and of how it felt to be there, on the bottom, looking up at the descending heel' (1987: 12). As a result, they are often less disposed to imperialist nostalgia, and less inclined to patronise or vilify other cultures simply because they have not yet emulated Western modernity.

In some cases, this 'postcolonial' travel writing seeks expressly to challenge Western stereotypes and attitudes. In this way, for example, Jamaica Kincaid and Caryl Philips produce a kind of '*counter*travel writing' (Holland and Huggan 1998: 50; emphasis in the original), which seeks in diverse ways to reverse the genre's traditional focus and agenda in the West. Thus Kincaid writes in *A Small Place* (1988) about what may seem to Western eyes an idyllic destination, the Caribbean island of Antigua. As she blends elements of fiction, travelogue and essay, however, Kincaid's narrative voice fluctuates between that of traveller and local, and in the latter role she offers a withering critique of the impact of tourism on the island, and of the bitter legacy of empire and colonial-era racism. Philips's *The European Tribe* (1987), meanwhile, reverses the usual travel trajectory described in Western travel writing. If it is still more common for the genre to record the observations of white Europeans amongst black 'natives', here a black man presents his account of a tour through a Europe that is white-dominated, and largely hostile to blacks. The tone is frequently angry and denunciatory, as Philips seeks to make European readers appreciate how they themselves exhibit the tribalism which is routinely attributed to supposedly more backward cultures. Further to this, *The European Tribe* also makes the European reader of travel writing appreciate what it is like to be the object of the travel writer's gaze. Philips has been criticised for the brief and somewhat cursory accounts he offers of many cultures and communities in Europe (see Holland and Huggan 1998: 51). Yet to be riled by these simplifying or distorting judgements is of course to be put in the position of many subaltern populations around the world, who have often been unable to contest the lazy generalisations made about them in Western travel writing; and in this way, *The European Tribe* is arguably both a continuation yet also a subversion of the Western travel writing tradition.

If Kincaid and Philips in their different ways reverse some of the norms of Western travel writing, other postcolonial travel writers seek to expand and reinvent the genre by exploring viewpoints, histories and cross-cultural connections that have often been overlooked or suppressed in the West. Amitav Ghosh's *In an Antique Land* (1992), for example, relates the experience of an Indian traveller conducting anthropological fieldwork in the rural regions of Egypt. Interwoven with this personal narrative is Ghosh's historical reconstruction of the lives of a twelfth-century Indian slave, Bomma, and his Jewish owner, Abraham Ben Yiju. The chief record of these figures are letters written to Ben Yiju by an Arab merchant, Khalaf ibn Ishaq, and as Ghosh reconstructs the links between Bomma, Ben Yiju and Ibn Ishaq, he offers a moving account of the complex networks of trade, culture and friendship that linked India and the Middle East in the centuries prior to European colonialism. A region of the world which Western 'Orientalist' scholarship has generally regarded as backward and culturally inferior to the West is thus revealed as the site of a sophisticated, cosmopolitan culture. The historical role of the West in this region, meanwhile, comes to seem not the introduction of 'civilisation', as Western travel writers have so often claimed, but rather its destruction. And the present-day portions of the narrative reveal the ongoing legacy of this cata-strophic European intervention, as Ghosh traces the ties and the tensions that exist today between two regions of the 'global south' keenly aware of their comparative powerlessness on the world stage.

Not all so-called 'postcolonial' travel writers seek to challenge Western stereotypes and assumptions in this way. Perhaps the most famous postcolonial travel writer is V.S. Naipaul, a Trinidadian of Indian descent who has lived and worked in Britain for most of his adult life. Naipaul's many travelogues, like his novels, speak eloquently of the sense of homelessness and displacement that can result from a mixed cultural heritage, and from a 'hyphenated' identity. This is a theme he shares with many postcolonial travel writers; unlike most other writers writing from an overtly post-colonial perspective, however, Naipaul has also demonstrated a marked tendency to lambast many of the 'Third World' cultures that he visits, in ways which often endorse prevailing Western stereotypes. In the eyes of many critics, accordingly, Naipaul is an apologist for Western neo-colonialism (see Nixon 1992; Said 1993: 320–21); although there are also critics who argue for a more nuanced response to his work (see Huggan 1994; Dooley 2006). Other readers, meanwhile, claim that Naipaul's travel writing provides a salutary counterpoint to the left-liberal political correctness supposedly dominant in the academy today; this is an argument often advanced by Naipaul's admirers as they defend his work in letters to newspapers and magazines, and in online discussion forums.

Naipaul's career is often invoked by critics who see travel writing as a fundamentally exploitative and imperialist genre, which by engaging in 'the production of difference' (Lisle 2006: 24) necessarily always 'others' individuals and cultures in morally dubious ways. Yet this is surely to overstate matters. As James Clifford has written, in a globalised world 'it is more than ever crucial for different peoples to form complex concrete images of one another, as well as of the relationships of knowledge and power that connect them' (1983: 119). As the present chapter has shown, travel writing both historically and in recent years has not always helped this enterprise. The images and representations provided by the genre have often been grossly simplified, and they have often worked to obscure or deny the 'relationships of knowledge and power that connect' travellers and readers to the peoples and places being described. Yet the examples of Kincaid, Ghosh and others suggest that at its best, travel writing may enlighten and challenge readers, by revealing cultural and historical perspectives which have otherwise been overlooked or suppressed. And one might add that it is not only travel writers from obviously 'postcolonial' backgrounds whose work contributes to this project. One might cite here travelogues as varied as Hugh Brody's account of the Beaver Indians in *Maps And Dreams* (1981), Barry Lopez's account of Inuit tribespeople in *Arctic Dreams* (1986), Peter Robb's account of the Mafia's baleful presence in Italy in *Midnight in Sicily* (1996) and Daniel Everett's account of the Piraha people of Brazil in *Don't Sleep, There are Snakes* (2008). None are without their flaws and distortions, since as we have seen the translation of one culture into other must always be to some degree a mistranslation, and a partial representation.

Without disregarding these flaws, however, these and many other recent travelogues arguably demonstrate that it is possible for travel writing to create images of other cultures which are complex, respectful and (where appropriate) sympathetic, whilst also remaining mindful of the 'relationships of knowledge and power' that operate in the modern world.

7

QUESTIONS OF GENDER AND SEXUALITY

Homer's *Odyssey*, written in the sixth century BCE, is one of the founding texts of Western culture. It recounts the wanderings both of the Greek hero Odysseus, as he struggles to return to his Ithacan home after the Trojan War, and also of his son, Telemachus, as he sets out in search of his missing father. The principal female character in the poem, meanwhile, cuts a far more passive and sedentary figure. Whilst husband and son criss-cross the Eastern Mediterranean, Penelope remains at home, resisting an army of suitors who seek to persuade her that Odysseus is dead. Penelope's destiny, it seems, is not to roam the world; she is instead the destination and safe haven which Odysseus and Telemachus are striving to reach, and the longed-for terminus to their adventures and misadventures.

This is an allocation of roles that reflects deep-seated assumptions in Western culture, and in many other cultures besides, about the gendering of travel. In many societies, in many periods, restlessness, freedom of movement and a taste for adventure have been attributes and activities conventionally associated with men rather than women. According to the **patriarchal** ideology of **separate spheres**, a woman's proper and preferred location is the home, and women have therefore traditionally been associated with immobility or, as it is sometimes dubbed 'sessility', and with domesticity. According to such masculinist notions, moreover, women encountered beyond the domestic sphere are unlikely to be fellow travellers from the hero's own culture; instead, they are usually alluring natives or dangerous temptresses, highly eroticised fantasy figures liable to distract the male hero from the true purpose of his journey. Thus Odysseus must resist the bewitchments of Circe, whilst in the later Roman epic *The Aeneid* (c.19 BCE), Aeneas must reject Dido if he is to fulfil his imperial destiny.

To a very great extent, of course, this received wisdom about the gendering of travel is a myth, an ideological construct that simultaneously assumes and promotes the notion of separate spheres for men and women. Insofar as it is not a myth, but has some historical basis, this is largely because the prevalence of this patriarchal ideology has in many periods created the reality it purports to describe, imposing numerous constraints and limitations on any woman who wished to travel. Notwithstanding these constraints, however, women have always travelled more extensively than the masculinist mythology just outlined would suggest. In every period, women at all levels of society have often accompanied their husbands, fathers and brothers on journeys, although the female presence on these ventures has frequently gone unrecorded by contemporary and subsequent commentators. In this way women have been throughout history migrants and settlers; they have formed part of diplomatic and aristocratic retinues; and they have accompanied men to war as camp followers, nurses and sometimes even as soldiers and sailors. In many cultures, meanwhile, women have often availed themselves of the travel opportunities provided by traditions of religious pilgrimage, a form of travel which frequently enabled women to travel independently of men, either individually or in female-only groups (see Morrison 2000). And finally, as tourism became from the late eighteenth century onwards increasingly widespread and popular, so opportunities for women to travel solely for pleasure and recreation steadily increased.

Whilst practices such as pilgrimage have sometimes allowed women to travel without male company, patriarchal societies have generally required women to travel with chaperones. Restrictions in this regard began to be relaxed in the nineteenth century, in Western culture at least, and it became increasingly acceptable, although still not entirely unproblematic, for women to travel on their own. For the most part, however, such independent travel was only possible within the standard, supposedly safe tourist circuit of the day, but as that circuit extended over time, so the travel options available to women became less geographically circumscribed. By the late 1800s, for example, European and American women were able to tour Egypt and the Middle East, as well as the more traditional destinations in Europe and the United States of America. There is also a long and impressive roll-call of eighteenth- and nineteenth-century women who travelled independently well beyond the conventional tourist itineraries of their day: examples include Hester Stanhope in the Middle East, Mary Kingsley and May French Sheldon in Africa, and Marianne North and Isabella Bird, whose travels took them all around the world. Far-flung destinations might also be visited in this period by women accompanying their husbands as they travelled in an official or professional capacity. Thus Lady Mary Wortley Montagu visited Istanbul in the early eighteenth century as the wife of the British ambassador there, whilst a century later, Maria Graham, like Jane Austen's fictional Mrs Croft in *Persuasion* (1817), accompanied her Naval officer husband on a tour of duty to Latin America.

These travelling women have produced over the centuries a vast body of travel writings. Prior to the late seventeenth century, it is probably fair to say, women travellers were much less likely than men to record their experiences and reflections in writing; this was largely due to the more limited educational opportunities available to women, and the correspondingly lower levels of female literacy in this period. Accounts of female travel from the ancient, medieval and early modern eras do survive, however, by figures such as Egeria and Margery Kempe. Thereafter, as female literacy increased dramatically in the late seventeenth and eighteenth centuries, so a growing number of women travellers became also travel *writers*. Often, however, their accounts of travel occur in forms of writing intended for private rather than public consumption, such as letters and diaries. Celia Fiennes, for example, completed in 1701 a lively travel memoir which recorded a series of journeys around Britain in the late seventeenth century, whilst the diary of Sarah Kemble Knight recounts, in a similarly vivid style, the writer's arduous journey from Boston to New York in 1704. Both texts, however, were originally intended only for circulation amongst friends and family; in both cases, it was not until the nineteenth century, when the authors were long dead, that these accounts were published.

Where female-authored accounts of travel did find their way into print in the seventeenth and early eighteenth centuries, it was usually in the context of forms like the captivity narrative and the spiritual autobiography, which sit at the margins of the travel writing genre: an example is Mary Rowlandson's *The Sovereignty and Goodness of God. Being a Narrative of the Captivity and Restoration of Mrs Mary Rowlandson* (1682). It was only in the latter part of the eighteenth century that women such as Mary Wortley Montagu, Mary Wollstonecraft and Ann Radcliffe began publishing travelogues, although it has been estimated that only about twenty such texts appeared in print before 1800 (Turner 2001: 127). By the mid-nineteenth century, however, the number of published travelogues by women had risen dramatically, and from that date down to the present day, women writers have made an extensive and substantial contribution to the travel writing genre, in all its different modes and forms.

Since the 1970s, feminist scholars have been much concerned to recover and re-evaluate the various forms of travel writing that women have produced historically, and this has been one of the main stimuli to the growth of travel writing studies in recent decades. One aim of the feminist project in this regard has been to counter stereotypical assumptions about travel and travel writing being principally masculine enterprises. As many critics have pointed out, these assumptions are reflected and perpetuated in several influential studies of travel writing, such as Paul Fussell's *Abroad: British Literary Travelling Between the Wars* (1980), Eric J. Leed's *The Mind of the Traveller* (1991) and Larzer Ziff's *Return Passages: Great American Travel Writing, 1780–1910* (2000), all of which largely ignore female travellers. Feminist scholars have accordingly sought to correct this skewed literary history. At the same time, they been greatly interested in the autobiographical aspects of travel writing, using female-authored travelogues to explore the ways in which female subjectivities were formed and articulated in different periods and cultures. Further to this, they have also paid much attention to the differing perspectives that women travellers often provide on the countries and cultures they visit, in comparison with male travellers visiting the same destinations. This in turn has prompted some scholars to ask whether men and women travel in fundamentally different ways, and whether they produce intrinsically different types of travel writing. The travel writer and critic Mary Morris, for example, believes this to be the case, insisting in her introduction to the *Virago Book of Women Travellers* (first published 1994) that 'women ... move through the world differently than men' (Morris 2007: 9). Like many editors of anthologies of women's travel writing, moreover, Morris also seems to take it for granted that female-authored travelogues will usually share distinctively 'feminine' characteristics that set them apart from travel accounts produced by men. In this spirit, for example, she suggests that women travel writers are typically more concerned with the 'inner landscape', and 'the writer's own inner workings', than their male counterparts (2007: 9). Another anthologist, Jane Robinson, meanwhile, claims that 'men's travel accounts are to do with What and Where, and women's with How and Why' (1990: xiv).

Other feminist critics have been troubled by such generalisations, and by the 'separatist' view that women's and men's travel writing is in some way fundamentally different. Susan Bassnett, for example, has insisted that 'the sheer diversity of women's travel writing resists simple categorisation' (Bassnett 2002: 239), and so implicitly questions how far it is possible to identify distinctively feminine attributes that are shared by *all* female-authored travelogues. Shirley Foster and Sara Mills similarly argue for a more nuanced understanding of the role gender plays in the shaping first of a traveller's identity, and thereafter of their travel account. In both regards, they suggest, gender is only one variable amongst many, interacting constantly with other factors such as 'race, age, class, and financial position, education, political ideals and historical period' (Foster and Mills 2002: 1). In many contexts, accordingly, the similarities between male- and female-authored travel accounts greatly outweigh any dissimilarities; and by the same token, there are few tendencies or characteristics in travel writing which are so uniquely feminine that they are never found in male-authored accounts. That said, Foster and Mills also stress that within any given period and society one can usually detect broad patterns of difference between men's and women's travel writing (2002: 4). And as Mills elsewhere points out, even when men and women produce more or less identical forms of travel writing, their travelogues will often be received very differently by the reading public, on account of the author's gender (Mills 1991: 30). Thus a travel writer's gender may sometimes play a more important role in the reception, rather than the production, of a travel account.

This chapter will tease out in more detail some of the gender codes, and the patterns of expectation, constraint and prejudice, that have historically underpinned and shaped the travel writing produced by both men and women. The chapter will focus chiefly on women's travel writing, so as to reflect the burgeoning of interest in this topic in recent years. Yet it will begin with some further observations on the gendering of men's travel writing. This is partly to illustrate the matrix of stereotypical assumptions and expectations against which women have had to define themselves as travellers and travel writers, and partly to make the point that gender norms and expectations affect men, and men's writing, just as much as women. Usually, of course, those norms and expectations have worked greatly to the advantage of men, yet they have also in some regards constituted a form of constraint, delimiting how a male travel writer may or may not present himself; and as we shall see, this applies especially to the issue of sexuality.

MASCULINITY, TRAVEL AND TRAVEL WRITING

As the preceding discussion will have suggested, travel has often been regarded as an important mode or rite of masculine self-fashioning.

The journey is thus construed as a test or demonstration of manhood, or in some variants, such as the eighteenth-century Grand Tour, as a rite of passage from boyhood to full, adult masculinity. In these circumstances, one function of any subsequent travel account will usually be to consolidate the traveller's claim to full or proper masculinity. The precise attributes judged desirable in a man, and the itineraries and types of travel undertaken in order to demonstrate those attributes, have of course varied across different periods and cultures. In their efforts to present an image of exemplary manliness, however, travellers and travel writers have often drawn on a broadly similar stock of motifs, personae and narrative paradigms. It is very common in this context, for example, for male travellers to invoke the tradition and ethos of the quest, thereby drawing on conventions and imagery that stretch at least as far back as the *Epic of Gilgamesh* (c.1000 BCE), but which in the West derive especially from the chivalric romances of the medieval and early modern periods. In this Christian inflection of the quest tradition, the traveller's ordeal was depicted as a test not only of their physical strength, resourcefulness and guile, but also of their virtue and religious faith. Many male travellers have accordingly laid claim to these desirable attributes by identifying themselves as some form of questing knight. This is a heroic self-fashioning central to many accounts of conquest and crusade, for example, since it implicitly confers a moral legitimacy on what might otherwise be regarded as merely acts of aggression and rapacity. Crusaders and conquistadors, of course, have usually set off with the intention of literally slaying adversaries and acquiring treasure, in direct imitation of the heroes of quest romances. Many other travellers historically, however, have understood themselves to be questing knights in a more metaphorical fashion; they have set out in search of useful knowledge, new trading opportunities or some other goal, and used the imagery of the quest to lend a greater heroism and grandeur to their activities.

The goal travellers and travel writers most commonly set themselves, of course, is to bring back knowledge of other places, and this is an agenda that has often been subtly (and sometimes not so subtly) gendered in a variety of different ways. In the first place, in many periods it has been incumbent on male travellers to demonstrate that they have made some useful contribution to contemporary commercial, intellectual or strategic concerns. Travellers who failed in this requirement were often dismissed by reviewers and commentators as frivolous and trivial, and frivolity and triviality were in turn often construed as feminine attributes, and as the hallmarks of the female rather than the male traveller. The picturesque tourism pioneered by William Gilpin in the late eighteenth century, for example, was often lampooned by contemporary critics as a distinctly feminised form of travel and travel writing, since it encouraged travellers to consider the landscapes through which they moved principally in an aesthetic rather than a practical or scientific light. Satires such as William Combe and Thomas Rowlandson's *The Tour of Dr Syntax* (1812) accordingly caricatured male devotees of the picturesque as effeminate, emasculated figures, and this in turn became an accusation that many male picturesque tourists sought to counter or deflect in their travel narratives.

These stereotypical associations between, on the one hand, men's travel and intellectual seriousness and, on the other, women's travel and intellectual shallowness or frivolity, have historically operated in a highly normative fashion, influencing both the differing modes of travel writing adopted by men and women, and also the reception that male- and female-authored travelogues received from reviewers and readers. The obstacles thus facing women travel writers who wished to make meaningful contributions to contemporary debates, and the textual stratagems by which they negotiated these obstacles, will be discussed later in this chapter. For men, however, these gender norms and expectations have in many periods constituted both a licence, and also to some degree an obligation, to adopt a range of discourses, postures and styles traditionally marked as masculine. Matters of politics, commerce and science, for example, and the public affairs of both one's own and other nations, have traditionally been regarded as topics that only men were equipped to discuss, and indeed, that they *ought* to discuss, if they wished to evince an appropriately masculine seriousness of purpose. Similarly, a pose of dispassionate rational enquiry, and a narrative voice that eschewed excessive emotionalism and introspection in favour of precise, empirical observation, was in many periods held to be both the preserve of the male traveller, and also a requirement of him, if he wished to cut an appropriately masculine figure (see Cohen 1996; Chard 1999). Scientific discourse, equally, has in many periods been strongly marked as a masculine domain, and has consequently been a route to intellectual authority traditionally more available to the men rather than the women.

In many cultures, a common yardstick for demonstrating and asserting masculinity in travel has been the degree of danger and discomfort involved in the journey. The greater the risk and the difficulty, obviously, the more manly and heroic a traveller seems; in the quest tradition outlined earlier, moreover, the mis-adventures and hardships endured by the protagonist are usually construed as a key means by which strength of character and virtue are both formed and tested. Of course, women travellers over the centuries have endured physical and psychological ordeals every bit as harrowing as those endured by male travellers. Yet women have often had to be much more circumspect with regard to how far they subsequently publicised these distressing experiences. In many periods, any hint of sexual molestation or impropriety might be enough to tarnish a woman's reputation irrevocably, and one reason why it has often been culturally unacceptable for women to travel beyond the standard pilgrimage and tourism circuits of their day has accordingly been the anxiety that they might find themselves in such sexually perilous pre-dicaments. Male travellers, however, have historically been less restricted in this regard, and whilst excessive recklessness has seldom been admired in travellers, a readiness to countenance some degree of danger and discomfort has usually been valorised as a laudable attribute in men.

There has often been a strongly nationalistic and/or imper-ialistic dimension to this construction of travel as a masculine rite of passage. For many travel writers and commentators, for example, dangerous, difficult journeys in remote regions have been pre-sented as a key means of teaching a nation's youth important lessons of manliness, and so of countering a perceived decline in national or imperial prowess. Thus Washington Irving, in his

Tour on the Prairies (1835), laments that so many young American men are sent abroad 'to grow luxurious and effeminate in Europe' (1835: 69); he suggests that they should rather be sent west, to the frontier regions of the United States, so as to learn 'manliness, simplicity and self-dependence' (1835: 70). Anxieties of this sort, about a supposed crisis in contemporary masculinity, have frequently been put to the service of expansionist ideologies, and thus have often formed a key strand of colonial discourse. Works such as Irving's *Tour on the Prairies*, and subsequently Mark Twain's *Roughing It* (1872), for example, encouraged young men to seek out adventures on the frontier, through their depiction of the 'Wild West' as a place where manliness could be demonstrated, and a range of male fantasies fulfilled. In imperial Britain, meanwhile, explorers such as Henry Stanley and Richard Burton, travel writers such as A.W. Kinglake, and writers of adventure fiction such as Rudyard Kipling and Rider Haggard played a similar role, by depicting the freedoms apparently available to young men in regions such as Africa, India and the Middle East (see Green 1980; Bristow 1991; Phillips 1997). In all these writers, and in Twain and Irving as well, regions at or just beyond the edge of supposed civilisation often seem to represent an escape from a smothering femininity, and from domestic ties and mundane chores. These frontier regions are typically constructed as male-only spaces, where men can form intense, **homosocial** bonds; and when women do appear in these accounts, they are often depicted in a highly exoticised, and eroticised, fashion. Witness, for example, the fantasy entertained by the narrator of Tennyson's poem 'Locksley Hall' (1842), as he plans an expedition to Africa: 'I will take some savage woman, she shall rear my dusky race.'

An imagery of sexual possession has also often been applied by male travellers to the regions that they visit, and to the objects of their quests. Sir Walter Ralegh concludes his *Discoverie of Guiana* (1596), for example, with the observation that:

> *Guiana* is a Countrey that hath yet her Maydenhead [that is, virginity], never sackt, turned, nor wrought, the face of the earth hath not been torne, nor the virtue of the soyle spent by manurance ... It hath never

been entered by any armie of strength, and never conquered or
possessed by any Christian Prince.

(Whitehead 1997: 196)

This is an especially striking instance of the gendered **lexis** or
imagery used in many male-authored accounts of exploration and
discovery, as the traveller depicts himself as successfully penetrating 'virgin' territory, and so to some degree taking possession
of it, either literally or metaphorically. In this way many male-
authored travelogues have displayed a striking convergence of
patriarchal and colonialist attitudes. Often their implicit if not
explicit narrative is that of the heroic male traveller taking literal
or symbolic possession of a feminised Other, which might variously be a landscape, a region, or some specific aspect of the
natural world, such as a region's flora and fauna. In some
cases, indeed, it may be a whole culture or ethnic group that is
feminised in this way: thus the so-called 'Orient' and its inhabitants, Edward Said (1995) has argued, have been routinely
depicted as passive, inert and indolent, in comparison with the
more vigorous and virile Western traveller. And it is not only in
exploration and discovery, which are of course typically constructed as very 'manly' forms of travel, that male travellers adopt
this imagery and agenda. As we have seen, the picturesque tourism of the late eighteenth and early nineteenth centuries was
often derided by contemporaries as a feminised mode of travel.
Even here, however, as Robin Jarvis has pointed out, 'the over-
arching sexual symbolism' is often that 'of a desiring male subject
chasing the "woodland nymphs" to their "secret haunts", and
"penetrating" the "undiscover'd shade" of a dense and variegated
landscape' (1997: 60).

Not all male travellers have been colonialists, of course, and
they have not all universally espoused such a possessive and/or
sexually aggressive style of masculinity. There is a long tradition
of comic travel writing by men, for example, in which the overtly
macho posturing strongly associated with accounts of exploration
and adventure is parodied and undermined. Recent exponents
of this comic mode include Eric Newby and Redmond O'Hanlon.
That said, one should not assume that the bathetic, self-deprecating

style of these writers, and their frequent mockery of Victorian notions of manliness, necessarily constitute some sort of radical subversion of traditional masculine codes. Playing down the dangers and discomforts attendant on one's travelling is of course a well-established rhetorical strategy that can be used to convey more powerfully a traveller's heroism and courage; and insofar as travellers like O'Hanlon make a joke out of what were clearly genuinely dangerous situations, they arguably continue this tradition.

A more significant subversion of the gender codes conventionally exhibited in men's travel writing arguably comes from gay travellers, and from the tradition of overtly gay travel writing that begins to emerge in the twentieth century. There were of course homosexual, or bisexual, travellers and travel writers prior to the twentieth century: notable examples include William Beckford, Lord Byron and Roger Casement. Some travellers, indeed, travelled precisely to seek out same-sex liaisons in cultures with more permissive attitudes to sexuality than their own; and this was probably for some an attraction of the homosocial frontier environments depicted in imperialist adventure literature (see Hyam 1990). When these travellers produced accounts of their experiences, however, they had necessarily to elide any reference to homosexuality, or else could only allude to it in a coded fashion. In this way men's travel writing has traditionally had a strongly **heteronormative** aspect, assuming and requiring a heterosexual persona from the male writer. This assumption, and some of the masculine stereotypes that often accompany it, have been challenged in the twentieth century by travelogues such as Edmund White's *States of Desire: Travels in Gay America* (1980), Tobias Schneebaum's *Where the Spirits Dwell: An Odyssey in the Jungle of New Guinea* (1988) and Aldo Busi's *Sodomies in Elevenpoint* (1992), and by anthologies such as Raphael Kadushin's *Wonderland: Good Gay Travel Writing* (2004). That said, however, gay travelogues are not necessarily exempt from the 'orientalising' and exploitative tendencies evident in many other forms of Western travel writing, as Patrick Holland and Graham Huggan demonstrate in their excellent introduction to this branch of the genre (1998: 133–55).

PERFORMING FEMININITY ON THE PAGE: WOMEN'S TRAVEL WRITING IN THE EIGHTEENTH AND NINETEENTH CENTURIES

If the female traveller contravenes the patriarchal ideology of separate spheres by quitting her home and venturing out into the world, the female travel writer, or at least, the woman who *publishes* a travel account, contravenes that ideology twice over. Not only does she travel, she then positions herself a second time in the public sphere, as an author; and a reluctance to take up the latter role is a further reason why there are so few published travelogues by women prior to 1800. Even in the nineteenth century, when female authorship generally had become more acceptable, it remained common for women travel writers to adopt an epistolary or diary format, and by this means to suggest that their observations were never originally intended for publication. Thus Harriet Beecher Stowe announces in the preface to *Sunny Memories of Foreign Lands* (1845) that 'the following letters were written by Mrs Stowe for her own personal friends, particularly the members of her own family' (Stowe 1845: 1.xi). This is highly disingenuous. The letters in *Sunny Memories*, each of which is conveniently the length of a book-chapter, have clearly been carefully crafted by Stowe, and reveal great expertise in the use of dialogue and other literary devices. Like many other eighteenth- and nineteenth-century women travel writers, however, Stowe maintains the pretence that these are essentially private communications made public, so as to forestall the criticisms liable to be levelled at women who trespassed too conspicuously on a supposedly masculine domain.

Disclaimers of this sort, and the use of forms such as the letter or diary, are of course also found in male-authored travelogues in this period. Yet they are a more common feature of women's travel writing, and reflect the problems faced by women travel writers in patriarchal cultures, as they try to reconcile their travelling with highly restrictive norms of femininity. In the first wave of the feminist rediscovery of women's travel writing, there was perhaps a desire to see all earlier women travellers as proto-feminists who set out deliberately to flout convention, and who were accordingly unconcerned if they scandalised contemporary sensibilities. More recent scholarship has suggested, however, that this is too simplistic a view (see Mills 1991: 29; Foster and Mills 2002). Whilst women's travel may always have represented an *implicit* challenge to patriarchal attitudes, most female travellers and travel writers historically have sought to negotiate the gender norms of their day, rather than confront them head on. Nor was every woman traveller and travel writer necessarily feminist, or proto-feminist, in their declared beliefs and political allegiances. Whilst some women travellers, such as Mary Wollstonecraft and Flora Tristan, have espoused overtly feminist attitudes, others have set themselves squarely against contemporary movements for female emancipation and equality. Mary Kingsley and Gertrude Bell, for example, sought strenuously to disassociate themselves from the contemporary 'New Woman' movement, and did not support the campaign for women's suffrage.

In the case of Kingsley and Bell, one senses almost an over-compensation, and a psychological need to balance the implicit transgressiveness of their remarkable travel achievements with an ostentatious display of conventionally 'feminine' attitudes. And for a great many women travel writers, there has certainly been a rhetorical need to balance the fact of their travelling with the adoption of an appropriately feminine persona on the page. Some sort of *rapprochement* in this regard was usually necessary, on the one hand, simply to get published in the first place and, on the other, to avoid hostile criticism from reviewers and commentators. To this end, accordingly, women writers were usually keen to stress the extent to which they conformed to contemporary codes of female propriety in the course of their travels. Hence the reluctance of many female travellers to abandon the often highly restrictive clothing prescribed for American and European women in the eighteenth and nineteenth centuries. Hence also a recurrent need to explain how female 'modesty' was maintained even in the most unusual or irregular settings and situations. Notions of female modesty, equally, also often required women to downplay any dangers, and especially any threat of sexual attack, that they may have faced during their journeys.

This need to demonstrate femininity on the page influenced both the topics a woman travel writer might discuss, and the style and tone she could adopt in discussing them. As outlined earlier, some subject areas were strongly marked in the eighteenth and nineteenth centuries as masculine domains. Sex was of course 'a taboo subject for middle-class Western women' (Foster and Mills 2002: 17), whilst issues relating to politics, economics and public affairs were generally regarded by reviewers and commentators as more properly the preserve of men rather than women. Discussing Fanny Trollope's *Domestic Manners of the Americans* (1832), for example, her son Anthony noted that whilst his mother had highlighted 'with a woman's keen eye' what she perceived as the 'social defects and absurdities' of the American way of life, she had not felt it appropriate 'to dilate on the nature and operation of those political arrangements which had produced the social absurdities which she saw' (Trollope 1987: vol. 1, 2). This was a topic, Anthony suggested, 'fitter for a man than for a woman'. Mindful of such gender demarcations, and the censure that might follow if they contravened them, many women travel writers either avoided these topics, or else attributed reflections on these themes to husbands and other male companions. Ann Radcliffe, for example, prefaced her 1796 account of a European tour with the disclaimer that 'where the oeconomical and political conditions of countries are touched upon [...], the remarks are less her own than elsewhere' (1796: v). The implication is that these parts of her narrative derive instead from her husband, with whom she undertook the tour.

Science was another subject area and discourse that women travel writers were well advised to approach with caution. What was frequently at issue here, it should be stressed, was not so much the thematic content of the female-authored travelogue, as its style, tone and register. For example, an amateur enthusiasm for plants, which might encompass the collecting and sketching of plant species together with some degree of technical botanical knowledge about those species, was a wholly acceptable pastime for female travellers (see Shteir 1999; George 2007). It was more problematic, however, for a woman to lay claim in print to a specialised, expert knowledge of contemporary botanical science, or to present herself as engaged in any form of rigorous scientific enquiry and debate. Yet there were certainly women travellers in the eighteenth and nineteenth centuries who made significant contributions to the scientific debates of their day. For the most part, however, these women were careful, when fashioning their 'on-page' persona, to play down the extent of their expertise. Technical, scientific terminology is often used sparingly, whilst passages that address scientific themes in any detail are often hedged cautiously with disclaimers as to the author's lack of competence in the field. In her *Journal of a Short Residence in Chile* (1824), for example, Maria Graham issues the following apology when describing the most interesting plant species she encountered in Chile:

> I am sorry I know so little of botany, because I am really fond of plants. But I love to see their habits, and to know their countries and their uses; and it appears to me that the nomenclature of botany is contrived to keep people at a distance from any real acquaintance with one of the most beautiful classes of objects in nature. What have harsh hundred syllabled names to do with such lovely things as roses, jasmines, and violets?
>
> (Hayward 2003: 35)

Graham thus positions herself as a hobbyist, as someone who simply relishes the beauty of plants rather than taking a rigorous scientific interest in them. Once again, however, this is a woman travel writer being disingenuous in the way she presents herself in print. An attentive reading of the passage in which this disclaimer appears makes it clear that Graham actually has a far more sophisticated and advanced knowledge of botany than she admits. In her descriptions of plants, for example, Graham uses those 'harsh hundred syllabled names', by which she means the binomial classificatory system developed by Linnaeus, on enough occasions to show that she is thoroughly conversant and comfortable with them: thus the plant known locally as 'mayu' is identified as belonging 'to Linaeus's natural order, Lomentacea' (Hayward 2003: 35). Referenced in her footnotes, meanwhile, are texts such as James Smith's *Introduction to Physiological and Systematical Botany* (1814), which as the title suggests was a fairly technical contemporary treatise on the topic. Further to this, Graham was also engaged, during her time in Chile and Brazil, in assiduously collecting, drying and sketching plant and seed specimens, although she only makes a few passing allusions to these activities in her published narratives. The specimens she accumulated were subsequently sent to leading figures in the botanical world such as Sir William Hooker, director of the Botanical Gardens at Glasgow University (and later director of Kew Gardens in London). Much like the male explorers of her day, then, Graham supplied vital information to some of the key centres of calculation driving contemporary scientific enquiry. This information would in due course be cited in specialist scientific texts such as Hooker's *Exotic Flora* (1822–27) and Carl von Martius's *Flora Brasiliensis* (1840), both of which pay tribute to Graham's diligence and expertise as a plant collector (see Hagglund 2011).

There was thus a serious scientific dimension to Graham's travelling in Latin America which is barely evident from the persona she fashions for herself in her published travelogue. Graham's reticence in this regard, it should be noted, is symptomatic of a more general problem facing women travel writers in the eighteenth and nineteenth centuries: namely, how to establish any sort of narrative authority in their texts. Science was by no means the only subject area or discourse in which it was risky for a woman to adopt an authoritative persona, or to intervene too assertively in ongoing public debates. It was widely assumed that women were not equipped to make meaningful observations on a broad range of topics, this dismissive attitude being partly a consequence of the fact that it was seldom possible, prior to the twentieth century, for women to receive the academic and/or professional training that marked one out as a properly accredited expert in any given discipline. Simultaneously, for a woman travel writer to become too magisterial in her opinions, or too coldly logical, or indeed too strident and impassioned, was to risk censure from critics, reviewers and readers for being 'unfeminine'. As a consequence, there is a marked tendency in women travel writers, even when they are discussing topics in which they clearly have considerable expertise, to advance observations and opinions cautiously, in a provisional, conjectural manner. By the same token, there has also been a strong tendency historically for women travellers to address topics, and to adopt modes of travel and travel writing, in which a personal, subjective response is prioritised over a more intellectual and ostensibly 'objective' attitude. This is one reason for the popularity of picturesque and so-called sentimental travel amongst women in the eighteenth and nineteenth centuries, since in both cases, what the journey and any subsequent account of that journey required from the traveller was not so much academic or factual knowledge, but rather an intensity of personal response. By this means, the female travel writer can claim for herself a sort of 'subjective' authority; at issue in her text, it seems, is not so much the accuracy or otherwise of her observations about the external world, but rather the strength and appropriateness of her own feelings.

It is for this reason that women travel writers in the eighteenth and nineteenth centuries often favour modes of travel writing which prioritise feeling over intellect, and subjectivism over objectivism. In the picturesque or sentimental travelogue, for example, the writing style is usually more emotive and impressionistic than in other types of travel writing where the principal agenda is to relay factual information accurately and efficiently. The narrative form may also be more disjointed and fragmentary, as in the case of Fanny Parks's *A Pilgrim in Search of the Picturesque* (1850), which jumps from one topic to another, without following any clear organising thread. It has sometimes been suggested that this emotive register and digressive, fragmentary tendency are the hallmarks of a distinctively feminine approach to travel writing, and indeed, to writing in general. Yet one should exercise caution before making such a generalising, and essentialising, assumption. As Shirley Foster and Sara Mills suggest, we need always to keep in mind that:

> nineteenth-century critical opinion created a set of criteria for 'appropriately' feminine writing, which included emotional and moral directives about 'feeling' and 'women's sensibility' as well as confining women's writing within certain prescribed areas. Representations which might be considered typically female, then, may be the result of strategic policy – especially if the writers wanted to get published – rather than a specifically gendered orientation. 'Womanly' subject

> matter must not be used as proof of gender specificity nor must it be
> seen as solely biologically derived.
>
> (2002: 11)

One must also remember that such 'feminine' tendencies and topics in travel writing are sometimes found in travelogues written by men. From Laurence Sterne and William Gilpin onwards, for example, there were many male travellers who adopted the sentimental and/or picturesque modes in travel writing, even though this brought with it the risk of being dismissed as 'unmanly' by reviewers.

One must keep these caveats in mind, therefore, before assuming that any particular subject matter or style is intrinsically or essentially feminine. That said, however, one can identify some general tendencies which are highly characteristic of women's travel writing in the eighteenth and nineteenth centuries. As many critics have remarked, for example, there is a greater tendency for women travellers to concern themselves with domestic details, and with the minutiae of everyday living arrangements such as food preparation, child care and the laundering of clothes (see Russell 1986; Romero 1992; Foster and Mills 2002: 95). This narrative focus is often closely bound up with a keen interest in the conditions of life for women in the cultures that they visit, an interest which can embrace topics ranging from the fashions adopted by foreign women through to the social roles they must perform, and their legal and political status. These interests may from one perspective be construed as compliance with the prevailing ideology of separate spheres, since they seemingly confirm the expectation that a woman's special area of insight and expertise will be the domestic sphere. Yet they were also often an important means by which women could claim an authority unavailable to men. These were areas of foreign cultural life that men generally did not comment on, or even, in some cases, that they were prohibited from observing. This was especially the case with certain female-only practices and/or spaces, the most famous example here being perhaps the harem or 'zenana'. These terms refer to the custom, amongst some Middle Eastern and South Asian elites, of reserving some areas of the household for women only. This was of course a practice that greatly fascinated Western travellers, becoming emblematic of so-called 'Oriental' culture and giving rise, amongst men especially, to some highly eroticised imaginings. Unlike their male counterparts, however, women travellers from Mary Wortley Montagu onwards were able to actually visit harems, and to report upon them. Their reports, unsurprisingly, generally puncture the lurid fantasies of Western male commentators, painting a much more mundane picture of life in this seemingly exotic setting (see Foster and Mills 2002: 14–18; and also Melman 1991; Lewis 1996; Grewal 1996).

Even working within the highly restrictive parameters prescribed for them, then, women travel writers might claim a degree of authority, and present themselves as making valid contributions to their culture's knowledge of other cultures. That said, working within these parameters arguably trapped women in a double-bind, since in the eyes of many contemporary commentators, the areas of expertise credited to women were too inconsequential to count as real 'knowledge', or as genuinely useful contributions to ongoing debates. Sympathetic commentators, however, suggested that male and female travel accounts complemented each other, producing in combination a more complete picture of the world and its inhabitants. Some writers even suggested that women travellers offered a more perceptive and accurate account of other cultures than many men, by focusing on domestic details and the minutiae of everyday life. Harriet Martineau, for example, makes this claim in her travelogue *Society in America* (1837), when she insists that 'the nursery, the boudoir, [and] the kitchen, are all excellent schools in which to learn the morals and manners of a people' (1837: 1.xiv), whilst simultaneously pointing out that she has a more extensive knowledge of these domestic settings than any male traveller. Writing anonymously in the *Quarterly Review* in 1845, meanwhile, Elizabeth Rigby asserted that women possessed a

> power of observation which, so long as it remains at home counting canvass stitched by the fireside, we are apt to consider no shrewder than our own, but which once removed from the familiar scene, and returned to us in the shape of letters or books, seldom fails to prove its superiority.
>
> (Rigby 1845: 98–99)

Notice, however, Rigby's use of the pronouns 'we' and 'our': it is symptomatic of the gendered assumptions of the time that Rigby had to write this vindication of women's travel writing not only anonymously, but also posing as a man.

Some women travel writers, then, worked within the para-meters prescribed for them by their culture, but turned this restriction into a source of authority and empowerment. Others, meanwhile, flouted the restrictions placed upon them, or else sought subtly to circumvent them. Maria Graham, for example, may have been cautious about displaying her proficiency in science, but she felt no such reticence about proffering her observations and analyses of political and economic affairs in both Chile and Brazil, two nations which had only recently won independence, from Spain and Portugal respectively. This earned her censure from some reviewers, with one insisting that she was 'unqualified to write *political* disquisitions' (quoted in Hayward 2003: xix, emphasis in the original). Elsewhere, meanwhile, Graham as we have seen provides a degree of scientific information to her readers whilst simultaneously surrounding that information with numerous apologies about her own scientific ignorance. At these moments, Graham's travel writing arguably exhibits a 'double-voiced' aspect that is often found in eighteenth- and nineteenth-century travel writing by women. On the one hand, the writer protests her ignorance of a given topic; on the other, she reveals that she does indeed have a highly sophisticated grasp of that topic, and pro-vides useful information and insights in relation to it. By this means, the female travel writer puts a *cordon sanitaire* around her participation in ongoing cultural and intellectual debates, as expertise is simultaneously demonstrated and disclaimed. A similar rhetorical stratagem is at work in the ironising humour deployed by a writer like Mary Kingsley, in which a recurrent tendency to self-deprecation never entirely masks the fact that the writer is clearly engaged not only in serious scientific research, but also in a decidedly dangerous and arduous mode of travel. And when women travel writers attribute opinions on 'masculine' topics to their male companions, as we have seen Ann Radcliffe doing, their protestations in this regard are not necessarily to be taken at face-value: again, this is sometimes another device by which the women writer could circumvent the gendered cultural prescriptions of her day.

One should accordingly not underestimate the extent to which travel and travel writing constituted an important route to self-empowerment and cultural authority for women in the eighteenth and nineteenth centuries, notwithstanding all the constraints they laboured under both when travelling and when writing. Travel certainly enabled some women to escape the dreary and restrictive responsibilities associated with being, in Victorian parlance, the 'Angel in the House'. For those women who produced accounts of their travels, meanwhile, the travelogue form enabled a further degree of self-fashioning, as the writer crafted and presented to the reading public her own image of herself. Few women travel writers in the eighteenth and nineteenth centuries presented themselves to the reading public as heroic figures engaged in some sort of epic quest, yet the female-authored travelogue might still affirm and demonstrate remarkable instances of female agency and accomplishment. Maria Graham is again a case in point. It should be noted that she had arrived in Chile in 1822 a recently widowed woman, her husband having died at sea during the voyage to Valparaiso. It was assumed she would want to return immediately to Britain, but Graham had other ideas, staying in the country for ten months whilst she gathered the information that would subsequently form the basis of her published travelogue. This travelogue has for the most part a highly **objectivist** tenor, being principally concerned to communicate useful information about Chilean society: there are comparatively few passages of introspection or self-description. Yet there are enough of the latter passages to ensure that the reader always keeps in mind that Graham is a widow, and to some degree surviving on her own in a foreign country.

Graham's *Journal of a Residence in Chile* becomes in this way implicitly a record of female independence and literary professionalism. There is moreover one climactic episode in which the more heroic self-fashioning implicit in Graham's narrative becomes briefly, and tantalisingly, explicit. The last pages of her account describe a visit to the island of Juan Fernandez, famous for being the place where Alexander Selkirk had survived alone as a castaway, inspiring Daniel Defoe's *Robinson Crusoe* (1719). Signifying self-sufficiency and survival against all odds, Selkirk and Crusoe are figures often invoked in male accounts of heroic travel. Women travel writers, however, were usually more cautious about making such grand comparisons, and Graham is no exception in this regard. Scrambling alone across the mountainous terrain of Juan Fernandez, she describes how she:

> reached a lonely spot, where no trace of man could be seen, and whence I seemed to have no communication with any living thing. I had been some hours in this magnificent wilderness; and though at first I might begin with exultation to cry–
>
> > I am monarch of all I survey,
> > My right there is none to dispute,
>
> Yet I very soon felt that utter loneliness is as disagreeable as unnatural; and Cowper's exquisite lines again served me–
>
> > Oh solitude, where are thy charms
> > That sages have seen in thy face?
> > Better dwell in the midst of alarms,
> > Than reign in this horrible place.
>
> And I repeated over and over the whole of the poem, till I saw two of my companions of the morning coming down the hill, when I hurried to meet them, as if I had been really 'out of humanity's reach'.
>
> (Hayward 2003: 183–84)

Here Graham cites the poet William Cowper's famous lines about being 'monarch of all I survey' only to reject them, valuing company and community over solitude and self-sufficiency. One might read this apparent renunciation of a heroic, Crusoe-esque self-image as a woman's deliberate rejection of a hubristic, masculine stereotype; alternatively, one might suggest that it is a rejection required of Graham by the gender norms of her day, for all the reasons outlined earlier. Either way, however, it is important to note that even if the Selkirk/Crusoe comparison is ultimately rejected, it is nevertheless also invoked, and briefly dangled in front of the reader as a heroic self-image this female writer might claim. Here again, we detect the 'double-voiced' quality which seems to characterise so much of the travel writing produced by women in the eighteenth and nineteenth centuries: a sense that even as Graham works within the prescriptive parameters imposed by her culture, so she simultaneously circumvents and subverts those prescriptions.

WOMEN TRAVELLERS AND COLONIALISM

As discussed in Chapter 6, much European and American travel writing in the eighteenth, nineteenth and early twentieth centuries was simultaneously enabled by, and worked to enable, colonialist structures of knowledge and power. A key area of debate in the recent feminist recovery of women's travel writing has accordingly been the relationship of the female traveller, and the female-authored travelogue, to this larger imperial context. And if there was a strong desire in much of the early scholarship on women's travel writing to regard all women travellers as proto-feminists, so equally was there often an assumption that all women travellers must have opposed empire and its injustices, and that their accounts accordingly constitute a form of counter-discourse which contests the colonial discourse of their day (see, for example, Birkett 1989; Mills 1991). Women travellers, it was pointed out, necessarily stood in an ambiguous relation to the colonial or expansionist projects pursued by their nations, being simultaneously 'colonized by gender, but colonizers by race' (Ghose 1998: 5). The familiarity with oppression bred by the former predicament, it was assumed, created an affinity with subaltern peoples; and this affinity, even when it did not manifest itself in overt critiques of colonialism, at least generated a greater openness towards other cultures, and a greater sympathy with the plight of indigenous populations. Thus for Sara Mills, women's travel narratives are frequently characterised by a greater degree of 'interaction with members of other nations', and also by forms of interaction and description whereby the people encountered come to seem 'not ... representatives of the race, as in male-authored accounts, but ... individuals' (1991: 99).

More recent scholarship, however, has sought to emphasise that the woman traveller's relationship with contemporary structures of power was more complex, and included a broader spectrum of perspectives, than early 'feminist wishful thinking' (Korte 2000: 125) would suggest (see, *inter alia*, Suleri 1991; Morgan 1996; Blunt 1994; Foster and Mills 2002). This spectrum includes many women travellers who endorsed wholeheartedly the imperial order that enabled their travelling, and many who used highly racist or ethnocentric strategies of 'othering' in their depiction of other cultures, along the lines discussed in Chapter 6. Thus Janet Schaw, in a journal of a voyage to the Caribbean undertaken in the 1770s, describes the slaves in Antigua as 'brutes' (Bohls and Duncan 2005: 325) and their children as 'monkeys' (320). She goes on to justify the whippings administered by slave-drivers as a 'merely corporeal' punishment which 'inflicts no pain on [the slave's] mind'. '[Their] natures', Schaw claims, 'seem made to bear it, and [their] sufferings are not attended with shame or pain beyond the present moment' (325). Schaw's journal was unpublished in her lifetime, yet there were women travellers who adopted similar ideas and imagery in published travelogues, thereby both evincing and contributing to the racist and ethnocentric assumptions of their age. And in this way the female-authored travel account just as much as the male-authored account has sometimes constituted a form of colonial discourse.

Women travel writers could assist the colonialist enterprise in other ways as well. They could not, of course, be explorers or leaders of military expeditions, and so contribute directly to European and US expansionism; these roles were in this period a male preserve, although as discussed earlier, there were women who travelled in a spirit akin to exploration, making significant contributions to the accumulation of Western knowledge. Yet the picturesque and sentimental travel accounts typically produced by women in this period also served an important function in colonial discourse. As Sara Suleri has argued, the depiction of picturesque scenery in both writing and visual art often served an ideological function, insofar as it typically worked to render an alien landscape and its potentially unruly inhabitants more familiar and welcoming (see Suleri 1991: 75–110). As Suleri puts it, 'a dynamic cultural confrontation' was thus transfixed 'into a still life' (1991: 76) which elided any sense of discord or threat. The aesthetic pleasure this afforded, she suggests, worked to reassure colonial readers and spectators of their safety in a sub-jugated landscape. Moreover, by suppressing from the view any hint of native discontent or resentment, the picturesque scene also implicitly reassured audiences as to the benevolence and moral legitimacy of the colonial enterprise.

Many women travel writers in the imperial era take up a more conspicuously humanitarian position than their male counterparts, evincing in their travelogues a greater concern with the plight of native peoples, and especially with the plight of native women. Yet these expressions of sympathy with the 'native' are not always to be construed as opposition to empire. A greater capacity for feeling, and a greater concern with moral standards, was a key part of an appropriately 'feminine' sensibility in this period, and the taking up of humanitarian causes was accordingly one of the few means by which women might acquire a degree of political agency and moral authority. It has been suggested, however, that in claiming to speak for colonial subjects, or in the American context, for black slaves, many middle-class, white women tra-vellers were actually engaged in another, more subtle form of appropriation and exploitation, whereby the suffering of others became a route to self-empowerment (see Morgan 1996: 256). Furthermore, the expressions of sympathy made by women tra-vellers, and the humanitarian campaigns that they launched, were most commonly directed towards the victims of indigenous, 'native' practices, such as suttee, polygamy and concubinage. Here female compassion towards the Other is arguably of a piece with what Vron Ware describes as 'the dominant ideology of imperialism: that it is only through contact with Western civili-zation that the "natives" had any chance of being delivered from their own tyrannical customs' (Ware 1992: 147). When women travellers did target injustice and suffering produced specifically by the colonial order, meanwhile, the agenda underpinning these complaints was in many cases not so much the overturning or undermining of that order, as simply an amelioration of its more pernicious consequences.

We should not assume, then, that women travellers from the age of empire will automatically or 'naturally' exhibit opposition to colonial power, nor that they will necessarily demonstrate a greater openness and sympathy towards other cultures. That said, the colonial **contact zone**, and the cross-cultural encounters it inevitably involves, was certainly inflected differently for Western women than for men, by virtue of their subordinate status in their home culture. For example, exposure to other cultures might alert the woman traveller to rights and liberties she lacked at home. Thus Mary Wortley Montagu confuted conventional Orientalist depictions of Turkish women as virtual slaves, pointing out that they had the right to own property, unlike British women at that date. She also suggested that the wearing of veils, so often seen in the West as a symbol of female repression, in fact gave Turkish women great freedom, since it ensured they could meet their lovers without being recognised. Other women travellers, meanwhile, were struck by the unsettling comparisons that could be made between their own social status and the conditions of life for women in supposedly more backward, repressive cultures. Such comparisons, like the contrasts identified by Montagu, often worked to complicate and problematise imperialist assumptions about the moral superiority of the traveller's culture. In some cases, accordingly, women travellers were indeed provoked to explicit critiques of the imperial project and/or their own culture's norms. More commonly, however, the situation of being simultaneously 'colonized by gender but colonizers by race' (Ghose 1998: 5) seems to have produced in women an unconscious unease, and a psychological anxiety that finds expression in various forms of discursive uncertainty and contradiction in the female-authored travelogue (see Mills 1991; Morgan 1996). Thus Sara Suleri detects in the superficially serene, picturesque depictions of India offered by many women travellers 'patterns of a hysteria all too secretively aware of the dangers in an unrelenting assumption of cultural and psychic safety' (Suleri 1991: 76). And insofar as women's travel writing in the imperial era often manifests such moments of textual and narratorial instability, which in turn ask awkward questions of the imperial project, it often possesses implicitly, if not explicitly, an oppositional aspect, and so constitutes a form of counter-discourse.

WOMEN'S TRAVEL WRITING TODAY

In the late twentieth and early twenty-first centuries, women have continued to make a significant contribution to the travel writing genre, just as they have done since at least the early nineteenth century. Unlike earlier eras, however, there are today few, if any, overt restrictions on the topics that women address in their travelogues, or on the literary styles and narratorial personae that they adopt. As educational and professional opportunities have become more available to women, in the West at least, so women have increasingly been able to travel, and to publish, in the sort of authoritative roles that were once the preserve of men: as scientists and anthropologists, as news reporters, political commentators and economic analysts. Thus Joan Didion's *Salvador* (1983) deals explicitly with that nation's political situation, whilst Christina Dodwell's *Travels with Fortune: an African Adventure* (1979) and *Travels in Papua New Guinea* (1982) provide a blend of adventure and ethnographic discovery that is very much in the tradition of the nineteenth-century male explorer. Writers such as Irma Kurtz and Chelsea Cain, meanwhile, have offered feminised versions of the picaresque 'road trip' narratives more usually associated with male writers such as Jack Kerouac (see Smith 2001; Paes de Barros 2004). The traditional taboo on women travellers writing about sexual matters has also been lifted, as evidenced in travelogues such as Dea Birkett's *Serpent in Paradise* (1997) and Fiona Pitt-Kethley's *Journeys to the Underworld* (1991); in this regard, moreover, it should be noted that many gay women as well as gay men have been able to cast off the heteronormative constraints imposed on earlier travel writers, to produce collections such as Gillian Kendall's *Something to Declare: Good Lesbian Travel Writing* (2009).

It would be naïve to assume, however, that women travel writers today face no constraints, and that there are no gender expectations which they have to negotiate, either as they travel or as they write. The fear of violence, and especially of sexual violence, arguably remains a more pressing concern for female than for male travellers; as Mary Morris writes, 'the fear of rape [...], whether crossing the Sahara or just crossing a city street at night, most dramatically affects the ways women move through the world' (2007: 9). The cultures that they visit, equally, will sometimes require different conduct and costume from women. The reception they receive back home may also be significantly different from that received by men. Women mountain climbers who lose their lives on dangerous climbs, for example, are much more likely than their male counterparts to be censured for recklessness by the popular press, especially if they are mothers. Robyn Davidson, meanwhile, found that a thousand-mile camel trek through the Australian outback had transformed her, in the eyes of the media, into 'the camel lady', a term she bitterly resented:

> [A] myth was being created where I would appear different, exceptional ... Had I been a man, I'd be lucky to get a mention in the *Wiluna Times*, let alone international press coverage. Neither could I imagine them coining the phrase 'camel gentlemen'. 'Camel lady' had that nice patronizing belittling ring to it. Labelling, pigeonholing – what a splendid trick it is.
>
> (1998: 237)

Thus women who undertake major feats of travel are still often depicted, in the Western media and in popular culture, in terms of their exceptionalism and eccentricity, notwithstanding the long tradition of women travellers and travel writers that has been traced in this chapter. The result of these stereotypical media images, Davidson suggests, is that many women come to believe they are not capable of such journeys; taught from an early age to 'build fences against possibility, daring', they remain 'imprisoned inside ... notions of self-worthlessness' (1998: 237).

In this way, women still find themselves confronted with cultural expectations and stereotypes which assume some types of travel and travel writing, and arguably the very notion of travel *per se*, to be more commonly a masculine rather than a feminine activity. Accordingly, a recurrent theme in much recent women's travel writing has been the author's negotiation of this weight of expectation, and her deliberate intrusion into traditions, modes of travel, and geographical and institutional spaces still strongly marked as male. Notable examples include Dea Birkett's *Jella: From Lagos to Liverpool – A Woman at Sea in a Man's World* (1992), which recounts Birkett's time as the only female member of the crew of an ocean-going cargo vessel, and Sara Wheeler's *Terra Incognita: Travels in Antarctica* (1996). The latter offers a female perspective on the long tradition of polar exploration associated with figures like R.F. Scott, Roald Amundsen and Ernest Shackleton. As Wheeler notes, this has historically been a hyper-masculine tradition which regarded the Antarctic as 'a testing ground for men with frozen beards to see how dead they could get' (1996: 1). And this masculinist legacy lives on in the overwhelmingly male scientific communities that Wheeler encounters on the continent, giving rise to a travelogue that combines penetrating social commentary with a lyrical evocation of the beauty of the Antarctic landscape.

Travellers such as Birkett and Wheeler set out deliberately to contest the gendered expectations that still surround many aspects of travel and travel writing. Many other women travellers, meanwhile, find themselves required to reflect on those expectations, and on their own position specifically as *female* travellers, by virtue of the reception they receive at home and abroad. Recent women's travel writing can thus to some extent be distinguished from the travel writing produced by men by the writer's greater awareness of, and sensitivity to, gender issues. Beyond this, however, it is perhaps more difficult than it has ever been to identify any clear, demonstrable differences between the travel writing produced by men and that produced by women. The argument that gender is the most significant determinant of an individual's travel and travel writing is also undermined by the career of Jan Morris, whom Susan Bassnett regards as 'probably the greatest woman travel writer of the twentieth century' (Bassnett 2002, 238). Yet Morris began her travel writing career as a man, James Morris, before undergoing a sex-change operation in 1972. As Bassnett notes, one can detect no changes in Morris's travel writing after her gender realignment, 'other than occasional references to clothing' (238). It should be acknowledged that Morris writes a distinctly impersonal mode of travel writing, in which the focus is overwhelmingly on the place being visited rather than the narratorial self. That said, however, Morris's narrative voice, and his/her perspective on the world, seems to be shaped most profoundly not by gender but by class and nationality, working in tandem with the author's historical moment. Upper middle class, Anglo-Welsh, and born in the 1920s, Morris has watched British imperial power recede in the aftermath of the Second World War; and whilst she is not uncritical of the British Empire, the most recurrent strain in her writing is arguably an **elegiac** lament for the passing of what she terms the 'pax Britannica', a period in which Britain emulated Rome by bringing peace and stability to much of the world.

The example of Jan Morris also confirms Holland and Huggan's observation that recent 'women's travel writing is not insulated from the criticisms levelled at its male counterpart', and that 'more specifically, it is not immune from imperialist and ethnocentric nostalgia' (1998: 20). As in the colonial era, women travel writers today adopt a broad spectrum of perspectives on other cultures. Female-authored travel accounts just as much as male-authored accounts may work, either by design or inadvertently, to foster neo-colonial attitudes in their readers. Yet by the same token many women travel writers have also helped to provide 'complex concrete images' of other cultures, and of 'the relationships of knowledge and power' that connect communities (Clifford 1983: 119); and as they do so, they continue like their eighteenth- and nineteenth-century precursors to use travel writing as a medium in which to affirm some remarkable instances of female agency and authority.

Glossary

Africanism. A term derived from Edward Said's use of the term **Orientalism**, to denote the Western **discourses** which have collectively shaped Western attitudes and imagery relating to Africa.

Alterity. A term sometimes used in academic discourse to denote 'otherness'; that is to say, at a personal level, whatever is beyond and different from oneself, and at a cultural level, whatever seems alien and strange in another culture.

Anti-conquest. The term used by the literary critic Mary Louise Pratt (2008) to describe the image usually presented by European explorers, and of European exploration in general, from the eighteenth century onwards. From this date exploration became a more overtly scientific activity, whose practitioners were keen to dissociate themselves from the more aggressive activities of many earlier European voyagers and conquistadors. See Chapter 6 for a fuller discussion.

Anti-tourism. The rhetorical strategy whereby a traveller or cultural commentator laments or lampoons the activities and influence of a class of unworthy or disgraceful travellers, who are customarily labelled mere 'tourists'.

Aporia (adj. 'aporetic'). In discussion or argument, an impasse or moment of contradiction and self-doubt, in which a speaker seems to falter as he or she recognises the inconsistencies in their own position.

Bathos (adj. 'bathetic'). The rhetorical technique of deflation or 'falling', as apparent seriousness gives way to absurdity, ineptitude or ridiculousness.

Centre of calculation. Term used by Bruno Latour (1987) to describe those individuals or institutions that coordinate and drive the scientific research process, by receiving data, reflecting on it to produce new theories and models, and then instigating new lines of research which yield new data.

Colonial discourse. The **discourse(s)** operating in a culture to foster, enable and sustain colonial politicies and attitudes.

Contact zone. Term used by Mary Louise Pratt (2008) to denote the space or region in which two cultures encounter each other and interact.

Counter-discourse. See **discourse**.

Discourse. In the specialised sense developed by the French theorist Michel Foucault, an accumulated body of knowledge and imagery which works within a culture to shape what people think and feel about a given topic. For Foucault, there is always a significant correlation between a culture's dominant discourses and the larger patterns of power in that culture; thus in any given period, a culture's dominant discourses will usually confirm and enforce the dominant **ideologies** (see later) of the day. Yet it is also always possible for individuals to contest and resist these discourses, and so to establish (or position themselves within) a 'counter-discourse'.

Elegy. A form of writing which mourns the loss of someone, or something.

Empiricism. The belief that knowledge should be acquired experientially, through experiment and personal experience, rather than through abstract reasoning and deduction; also, the practice of acquiring knowledge in this fashion.

Epiphany. A sudden moment of revelation or profound insight.

Epistemology. The branch of philosophy that explores what knowledge is, and how we arrive at what we perceive to be knowledge. 'Epistemological' concerns are therefore those that relate to the nature, validity and reliability of knowledge.

Ethnography. In a broad sense, a description of another culture or community, and/or the practice of producing these descriptions. In this sense, most **travelogues** (see later) have an **ethnographic** aspect, to a greater or lesser degree. However, the term is also frequently used in a more specialised sense to denote specifically the accounts of other cultures produced by academic anthropologists, from the later nineteenth century onwards, in which a social-scientific methodology and style is used.

Free indirect discourse. A form of narration which blurs the distinction between on the one hand the narrator's thoughts and words, and on the other hand, the thoughts and words of the characters/ individuals he or she is describing. In recent theoretical work on **ethnography**, the term has also come to mean the **narrative** device whereby the collective opinions and attitudes of a whole tribe or culture are seemingly voiced, in formulations like 'The Piraha say that ... ', or 'The Dowayo think ... '.

Globalisation. The process by which the different regions of the world have become increasingly integrated, both culturally and (especially) economically.

High-brow. See **'middle-brow'**.

Heteronormative. Taking heterosexuality as the norm, and/or requiring a demonstration of heterosexuality from an individual; and so implicitly working to promote heterosexuality and to make homosexuality seem 'abnormal'.

Homosocial. Involving social (rather than sexual) relationships between persons of the same sex.

Hypotactic. Utilising a complex syntactic structure, incorporating numerous subordinate clauses and phrases.

Ideology. A group or community's shared system of beliefs, and their shared outlook on the world, which to some degree will inevitably serve to legitimate and promote their own needs and aspirations.

Induction. A mode of intellectual enquiry in which the accumulation of information or data precedes the attempt to arrive at larger theories or conclusions about the phenomenon in question. This contrasts with 'deduction', in which a theory is first postulated, and then data is sought which will either prove or disprove the theory.

Intertextuality. The relationship between texts; and more specifically, the relationship between any one individual text and the many precursor texts which it necessarily draws upon, alludes to and adapts, either implicitly or explicitly.

Lexis. Vocabulary or discursive register.

Life writing. A collective term sometimes used to denote all the forms of writing which an individual may use to give an account of themselves, and to project an image of the self to a wider audience; so autobiography and memoir, most obviously, but also letters, journals and many other genres as well.

Low-brow. See **'middle-brow'**.

Masculinist. Assuming the superiority of men over women, or working to foster a sense that men are superior in this way, and so seeking to legitimate and promote **patriarchy**.

Metonymy. A figure of speech or rhetorical device in which something associated with a particular phenomenon is used as an emblem of that phenomenon. So the term 'the press', meaning the printing

UNIVERSITY OF WINCHESTER LIBRARY

press, is a metonym for the entire range of modern printed news media: newspapers, journals, magazines and so forth.

Middle-brow. A dismissive label, derived from a critical schema which categorises literary works, and cultural products more generally, as either **'high-brow'**, 'middle-brow', or **'low-brow'**. According to this somewhat elitist schema, **'high-brow'** works possess genuine intellectual or aesthetic merit, and will therefore be challenging to many readers, whilst **'low-brow'** works are unchallenging intellectually, often highly sensationalist or **sentimental**, and therefore highly popular. The term 'middle-brow', meanwhile, denotes works which are judged to flatter their readers with pretensions to 'high-brow' status, when in fact they offer little more than superficial, easy reading.

Modern travel book. The term used in this volume to describe the more self-consciously 'literary' travelogues which begin to appear in the eighteenth century, and which are today what many people regard as 'travel writing' or 'travel literature'. See Chapter 2 for a fuller discussion of this term.

Monarch-of-all-I-survey scene. A term used by Mary Louise Pratt (2008) to denote the many scenes in travel writing in which the traveller surveys a landscape, and in the process seems to claim imaginative possession of it. The phrase is taken from William Cowper's famous poem, 'Verses supposed to be written by Alexander Selkirk' (1782), in which Selkirk is made to declare, 'I am monarch of all I survey, / My right there is none to dispute.'

Narrative. A text or passage of writing structured so that it recounts a sequence of events. The novel, for example, is usually a narrative form; encyclopaedias, gazetteers and maps, meanwhile, present information in a non-narrative fashion.

Nature writing. Writing that describes the natural world. Obviously this covers a huge array of texts, encompassing many different genres; the collective term 'nature writing' accordingly tends to be used of works in which 'nature' is not only described, but also constitutes a principal theme or focus of the text.

Neo-colonialism. The term sometimes used for the modern world order, in which the developed nations of the West have for the most part given up overt forms of colonial domination, but nevertheless continue to exercise enormous power over the rest of the world by economic and cultural means.

Non-narrative. See **narrative**.

Objectivism. As used in this volume, this term denotes a tendency in travel writing to prioritise the presentation of information about the wider world over any self-presentation on the part of the traveller. It also refers to the various rhetorical strategies that can be used to make the information presented in a travelogue seem more 'objective' and reliable. See also **subjectivism.**

Orientalism. Traditionally, a term used to denote the academic study of the cultures of Asia and the Middle East. Since Edward Said's (1995) influential critique of this scholarly tradition, however, the term has taken on a more pejorative aspect; now it often denotes the prejudicial tendency in much Western scholarship and art (or in Foucauldian terms, in the West's orientalist **discourses**), whereby so called 'Oriental' cultures are typically presented as inferior in some way to Western culture.

Othering. The process by which one culture constructs its sense of another culture as different and 'other' to itself; alternatively, the rhetorical strategies used to emphasise the difference of another culture or people.

Over-determined. Possessing multiple, and possibly contradictory meanings; or alternatively, springing from multiple, possibly contradictory, motivations.

Paratactic. Utilising a simple syntactic structure in which sentences, clauses and phrases are simply aggregated one after the other, rather than being linked in a more complex pattern of subordinate or relative clauses. See also **hypotactic**.

Pastoral. A form of writing which celebrates nature, or alternatively, the supposedly simple lifestyles of traditional communities, who are regarded as more in tune with nature than modern, industrialised society.

Patriarchy. A society in which political, economic and cultural power is exercised by men, and in which women are accordingly subordinated to men. Or alternatively, the **ideology** (see earlier) which promotes the power of men over women in this way.

Picaresque. A **narrative** which relates episodically a sequence of adventures and misadventures. Typically, the protagonist is somewhat disreputable or inept, and he or she does not learn from their experience, but simply stumbles from one precarious or comical situation to the next.

Polyphonic. Containing multiple voices.

Postcolonialism/postcolonial studies. A loosely-defined, umbrella term that refers to the recent upsurge of interest, across many branches of the humanities and social sciences, in the complex and often bitter legacy of European imperialism.

Postmodern. A term often used to describe a shift in taste and style that occurred in Western culture in the mid to late twentieth century, in reaction to the 'Modernism' of the early twentieth century. So-called 'postmodernism' is highly eclectic, and therefore hard to categorise precisely, but works manifesting a 'postmodern' style or sensibility usually manifest an ironic playfulness and self-referentiality. Typically, moreover, they suggest that truth is relative, and that moral absolutes and grand **narratives** of progress and historical development are merely fictions.

Primitivism. The valorisation, and celebration, of the supposedly primitive over the modern.

Romance. A form of fiction, drama or story-telling which tends to utilise fantastical or mythical settings and situations, rather than more mundane and realistic characters and scenarios. Often contrasted with the 'novel', a form of extended prose fiction which becomes popular in the eighteenth century, in which much greater emphasis is put on realism and plausibility.

Sentimentalism. The term often used to denote a major shift in Western attitudes and tastes from the eighteenth century onwards, as feeling and emotion were increasingly valorised, and literature, art and other forms of cultural representation accordingly began to explore and depict the inner, affective world of the individual. In due course, the term 'sentimental' would take on a pejorative aspect, and come to denote an excessive, mawkish emotionalism. Yet the word did not have this negative aspect when it was first coined in the eighteenth century; and even if the word 'sentimental' eventually fell out of favour in this way, many 'sentimentalist' tendencies in Western culture have continued down to the present day.

'Separate spheres' ideology. The name sometimes given to the belief that men and women have different roles and responsibilities in society, with work, politics and public affairs being the province of men, and the home and the family the proper domain of women.

Showing. See **telling**.

Social Darwinism. The belief, highly fashionable in the late nineteenth and early twentieth centuries, that the behaviour and morality of individuals was largely the result of inherited family traits, and that many of society's problems could accordingly be solved by preventing the breeding of undesirable 'types', and promoting reproduction amongst the more respectable classes.

Spiritual autobiography. A form of autobiographical writing which charts the narrator's spiritual development and growth. In the Christian tradition, these accounts will often focus especially on the events that led up to the narrator's conversion to Christianity, and/or on events leading up to an **epiphanic** rediscovery of faith.

Stadial. Proceeding or developing by stages.

Subaltern. A term sometimes used in **postcolonial studies** to denote the colonial subjects who have imperial or colonial rule imposed upon them.

Subject position. The identity which is imposed upon or required of an individual, by the larger structures of power and **discourse** operating in their society. Or alternatively, the identity which an individual is able to fashion for him- or herself whilst negotiating these larger structures and discourses.

Subjectivism. As used in this volume, this term denotes a tendency in travel writing to prioritise the travelling self, and the personality of the traveller, over information about the external world through which he or she moves. It refers also to the various rhetorical strategies and **narrative** techniques that can be used to make the narratorial self a more conspicuous presence in the text. See also **objectivism.**

Sublime. 'Sublimity' or 'the sublime' are terms used to denote a feeling of awe, in which aesthetic pleasure is mingled with apprehension, and possibly even terror. Thus mountains and stormy seas (or paintings and verbal representations of these scenes) are liable to generate a sense of the sublime in viewers.

Synecdoche. A form of **metonymy** in which the emblem used to denote a phenomenon, entity or process is a *part* of that larger whole. So workers or sailors are sometimes referred to synecdochically as 'hands'.

Taxonomy. A classificatory system, and/or the practice of classifying entities according to some such system.

Telling. A **narrative** mode in which events are recounted briskly, and usually retrospectively, rather than being 'shown', or re-enacted in some detail on the page. Thus in the sentence 'We heard the latest news from London', we are simply told the action. But in a passage like: 'Simon came in. "I have news from London", he said. We gathered round excitedly ... ', the narrator adopts a more 'showing' mode of narration.

Thatcherite. A supporter of the former British Prime Minister Margaret Thatcher, and of the free-market, neo-liberal policies associated with her. The American equivalent would be 'Reaganite'.

Travelogue. Originally a term used to describe television programmes with a travel theme; in recent travel writing studies, however, it has come more generally to mean simply a travel account or travel **narrative**.

Trope. A figure of speech, or rhetorical device, or discursive strategy.

Voyages and travels. From the sixteenth to the nineteenth century, the most common generic label for what we would now call 'travel writing'. However, the category 'voyages and travels' arguably encompassed a much broader range of travel-related writings than our modern term 'travel writing'; for further discussion, see Chapter 2.

Bibliography and further reading

The principal academic journals concerned with travel writing are *Studies in Travel Writing* and *Journeys: The International Journal of Travel and Travel Writing*.

Abrams, M.H. (1971), *Natural Supernaturalism: Tradition and Revolution in Romantic Literature*, New York: Norton and Co.

Achebe, Chinua (1990), 'An Image of Africa', in *Joseph Conrad: Third World Perspectives*, ed. Robert Hamner, Washington DC: Three Continents Press. First published in 1977.

Adams, Percy G. (1962), *Travelers and Travel Liars, 1660–1800*, Berkeley: University of California Press.

——(1983), *Travel Literature and the Evolution of the Novel*, Lexington, KY: University Press of Kentucky.

Addison, Joseph (1705), *Remarks on Several Parts of Italy*, London.

Adickes, Sandra (1991), *The Social Quest: The Expanded Vision of Four Women Travellers in the Era of the French Revolution*, New York: Lang.

Amirthanayagam, Guy (ed.) (1981), *Writers in East-West Encounter: New Cultural Bearings*, London: Macmillan.

Andrews, Malcolm (1989), *The Search for the Picturesque: Landscape, Aesthetics and Tourism in Britain, 1760–1800*, Stanford: Stanford University Press.

Arens, William (1979), *The Man-Eating Myth: Anthropology and Anthropophagi*, Oxford: Oxford University Press.

Baepler, Paul (ed.) (1999), *White Slaves, African Masters: An Anthology of American Barbary Captivity Narratives*, Chicago: University of Chicago Press.

Barker, Francis, Peter Hulme, Margaret Iversen and Diana Loxley (1985), *Europe and its Others*, Colchester: University of Essex Press. 2 vols.

Barrow, John (1801), *Travels into the Interior of Southern Africa*, London.

Bassett, Jan (ed.) (1995), *Great Southern Landings: An Anthology of Antipodean Travel*, Melbourne: Oxford University Press.

Bassnett, Susan (2002), 'Travel Writing and Gender', in Peter Hulme and Tim Youngs (eds), *The Cambridge Companion to Travel Writing*, Cambridge: Cambridge University Press.

Batten, Charles (1978), *Pleasurable Instruction: Form and Convention in Eighteenth-Century Travel Literature*, Berkeley and Los Angeles: University of California Press.

Behdad, Ali (1994), *Belated Travelers: Orientalism in an Age of Colonial Dissolution*, Durham, NC: Duke University Press.

Bell, Ian A. (1995), 'To See Ourselves: Travel Narratives and National Identity in Contemporary Britain', in Ian A. Bell (ed.), *Peripheral Visions: Images of Nationhood in Contemporary British Fiction*, Cardiff: University of Wales Press.

Bendixen, Alfred and Judith Hamera (eds) (2009), *The Cambridge Companion to American Travel Writing*, Cambridge: Cambridge University Press.

Biddlecombe, Peter (1993), *French Lessons in Africa*, London: Little, Brown and Co.

Birkeland, Inger J. (2005), *Making Place, Making Self: Travel, Subjectivity and Sexual Difference*, Aldershot: Ashgate.

Birkett, Dea (ed.) (1989), *Spinsters Abroad: Victorian Lady Explorers*, Oxford, Blackwell.

Birkett, Dea and Sara Wheeler (eds) (1998), *Amazonian: The Penguin Book of New Women's Travel Writing*, Harmondsworth: Penguin.

Bishop, Peter (1989), *The Myth of Shangri-La: Tibet, Travel Writing and the Western Creation of Sacred Landscape*, London: Athlone.

Black, Jeremy (1989), 'Tourism and Cultural Challenge: the Changing Scene of the Eighteenth Century', in John McVeagh (ed.), *All Before Them: English Literature and the Wider World, 1660–1780*, London: Ashfield.

——(1992), *The British Abroad: The Grand Tour in the Eighteenth Century*, Stroud: Alan Sutton.

Blackmore, Josiah (2002), *Manifest Perdition: Shipwreck Narrative and the Disruption of Empire*, Minnesota: University of Minnesota Press.

Blanton, Casey (2002), *Travel Writing: The Self and the World*, London: Routledge.

Bloom, Lisa (1993), *Gender on Ice: American Ideologies of Polar Exploration*, Minneapolis: University of Minneapolis Press.

Blunt, Alison (1994), *Travel, Gender and Imperialism: Mary Kingsley and West Africa*, Guilford, New York.

Bohls, Elizabeth A. (1995), *Women Travel Writers and the Language of Aesthetics, 1716–1818*, Cambridge: Cambridge University Press.

Bohls, Elizabeth A. and Ian Duncan (eds) (2005), *Travel Writing 1700–1830: An Anthology*, Oxford, Oxford University Press.

Boorstin, Daniel J. (1961), *The Image: A Guide to Pseudo Events in America*, New York: Harper and Row.

Borm, Jan (2004), 'Defining Travel: On the Travel Book, Travel Writing and Terminology', in Glenn Hooper and Tim Youngs (eds) *Perspectives on Travel Writing*, Aldershot: Ashgate, 13–26.

Boswell, James (1791), *The Life of Samuel Johnson*, London. 2 vols.

Boucher, Philip P. (1992), *Cannibal Encounters: Europeans and Island Caribs, 1492–1763*, Baltimore and London: Johns Hopkins Press.

Bourdieu, Pierre (1984), *Distinction: A Social Critique of the Judgement of Taste*, trans. Richard Nice, London: Routledge.

Brantlinger, Patrick (1988), *Rule of Darkness: British Literature and Imperialism, 1830–1914*, Ithaca: Cornell University Press.

Bristow, Joseph (1991), *Empire Boys: Adventure in a Man's World*, New York: Harper Collins.

Bryant, William C. (ed.) (1986), *Colonial Travelers in Latin America*, Newark: Juan de la Cuesta.

Bryson, Bill (1999), *The Lost Continent: Travels in Small-Town America*, London: Black Swan. First published in 1989.

Burnham, Michelle (1997), *Captivity and Sentiment: Cultural Exchange in American Literature, 1682–1861*, Hanover: University Press of New England.

Buzard James (1993), *The Beaten Track: European Tourism, Literature, and the Ways to 'Culture', 1800–1918*, Oxford: Clarendon Press.

Campbell, Mary B. (1988), *The Witness and the Other World: Exotic European Travel Writing, 400–1600*, Ithaca, NY: Cornell University Press.

Cardinal, Roger (1997), 'Romantic Travel', in Roy Porter (ed.), *Rewriting the Self: Histories from the Renaissance to the Present*, London: Routledge.

Carter, Paul (1987), *The Road to Botany Bay: An Essay in Spatial History*, London: Faber.

Casson, Lionel (1974), *Travel in the Ancient World*, London: Allen and Unwin.

Chaney, Edward P. (1982), *Richard Lassels and the Establishment of the Grand Tour: Catholic Cosmopolitans in Exile, 1630–1660*, London: Warburg Institute – University of London.

——(1998), *The Evolution of the Grand Tour: Anglo-Italian Cultural Relations since the Renaissance*, London: Frank Cass.

Chard, Chloe (1999), *Pleasure and Guilt on the Grand Tour: Travel Writing and Imaginative Geography, 1600–1830*, Manchester: Manchester University Press.

Chard, Chloe and Helen Langdon, (eds) (1996), *Transports: Travel, Pleasure and Imaginative Geography, 1600–1800*, London: Yale University Press.

Chatwin, Bruce (1989), *What Am I Doing Here?* London, Jonathan Cape.

Cheyfitz, Eric (1991), *The Poetics of Imperialism: Translation and Colonisation from 'The Tempest' to 'Tarzan'*, Oxford: Oxford University Press.

Clark, Steve (ed.) (1999), *Travel Writing and Empire: Postcolonial Theory in Transit*, London: Zed Books.

Clifford, James (1983), 'On Ethnographic Authority', *Representations*, No. 2 (Spring), 118–46.

——(1997), *Routes: Travel and Translation in the Late Twentieth Century*, Cambridge MA: Harvard University Press.

Clifford, James and George E. Marcus (eds) (1986), *Writing Culture: The Poetics and Politics of Ethnography*, Berkeley and Los Angeles: University of California Press.

Cocker, Mark (1992), *Loneliness and Time: British Travel Writing in the Twentieth Century*, London: Secker and Warburg.

Cohen, Erik (1988), 'Authenticity and Commoditization in Tourism', *Annals of Tourism Research*, 15.3.

Cohen, Michèle (1996), *Fashioning Masculinity: National Identity and Language in the Eighteenth Century*, London: Routledge.

Cohn, Bernard S. (1996), *Colonialism and its Forms of Knowledge: The British In India*, Princeton, NJ; Princeton University Press.

Colley, Linda (2002), *Captives: Britain, Empire and the World, 1600–1850*, London: Jonathan Cape.

Constantine, David (1984), *Early Greek Travellers and the Hellenic Ideal*, Cambridge: Cambridge University Press.

Corbain, Alain (1995), *The Lure of the Sea: The Discovery of the Sea-Side, 1750–1840*, Harmondsworth: Penguin.

Cronin, Michael (2000), *Across the Lines: Travel, Language, Translation*, Cork: Cork University Press.

Culler, Jonathan (1988), 'The Semiotics of Tourism', in *Framing the Sign: Criticism and its Institutions*, Oxford: Blackwell.

Curtin, Philip D. (1965), *The Image of Africa: British Ideas and Action, 1780–1850*, London: Macmillan.

Dampier, William (1703), *A New Voyage Round the World*, London. 5th edition; first published 1697.

Davidson, Robyn (1998), *Tracks*, London: Picador. First published 1980.

Davidson, Robyn (ed.) (2002), *The Picador Book of Journeys*, London: Picador.

De Certeau, Michel (2001), 'Spatial Stories', in Roberson, Susan L. (ed.), *Defining Travel: Diverse Visions*, Jackson, MS: University of Mississippi Press, pp. 88–104.

De Teran, Lisa St. Aubin (ed.) (1990), *Indiscreet Journeys: Stories of Women on the Road*, London: Faber and Faber.

Dening, Greg (1992), *Mr Bligh's Bad Language: Passion, Power and Theatre on the Bounty*, Cambridge: Cambridge University Press.

Diaz, Bernal (1996), *The Discovery and Conquest of Mexico*, ed. Genaro Carcia, New York: Da Capo Press.

Diski, Jenni (2005), *Skating to Antarctica*, London: Virago Press. First published 1997.

——(2006), *On Trying to Keep Still*, London: Little, Brown.

Dissanayake, Wimal and Carmen Wickramagamage (1993), *Self and Colonial Desire: Travel Writings of V.S. Naipaul*, New York: Lang.

Dodd, Philip (1982), 'The Views of Travellers: Travel Writing in the 1930s', *Prose Studies*, V, 127–38.

Dodd, Philip (ed.) (1982), *The Art of Travel: Essays on Travel Writing*, London: Frank Cass.

Dooley, Gillian (2006), *V.S. Naipaul: Man and Writer*, Columbia, SC: University of South Carolina Press.

Drayton, Richard (2000), *Nature's Government: Science, Imperial Britain and the 'Improvement' of the World*, London: Yale University Press.

Driver, Felix (2001), *Geography Militant: Cultures of Exploration and Empire*, Oxford: Blackwell.

Duncan, James and Derek Gregory (eds) (1999), *Writes of Passage: Reading Travel Writing*, London, Routledge.

Dunlop, M.H. (1998), *Sixty Miles from Contentment: Traveling the Nineteenth-Century American Interior*, Boulder: Westview Press.

Easley, A. (1996), 'Wandering Women: Dorothy Wordsworth's *Grasmere Journals* and the Discourse on Female Vagrancy', *Women's Writing* 3 (1), 63–77.

Edney, Matthew H. (1997), *Mapping an Empire: The Geographical Construction of British India, 1765–1843*, Chicago: University of Chicago Press.

Edwards, Justin D. (2001), *Exploring the Erotics of U.S. Travel Literature, 1840–1930*, Lebanon, New Hampshire: University Press of New England.

Edwards, Philip (1988), *Last Voyages: Cavendish, Hudson, Ralegh*, Oxford: Clarendon Press.

——(1994), *The Story of the Voyage: Sea-Narratives in Eighteenth-Century England*, Cambridge: Cambridge University Press.

Elsner, Jas and Joan-Pau Rubiés (eds) (1999), *Voyages and Visions: Towards a Cultural History of Travel*, London: Reaktion Books.

Euben, Roxanne (2008), *Journeys to the Other Side: Muslim and Western Travelers in Search of Knowledge*, Princeton, NJ: Princeton University Press.

Fabian, Johannes (1983), *Time and the Other: How Anthropology Makes its Object*, New York: Columbia University Press.

Fabricante, Carole (1987), 'The Literature of Domestic Tourism and the Public Consumption of Private Property', in Felicity Nussbaum and Laura Brown (eds), *The New Eighteenth Century: Theory, Politics, English Literature*, London: Methuen.

Fausett, David (1993), *Writing the New World: Imaginary Voyages and Utopias of the Great Southern Land*, Syracuse, NY: University of Syracuse Press.

Feifer, Maxine (1986), *Going Places: Tourism in History from Imperial Rome to the Present*, New York: Stein and Day.

Feldman, Doris (1997), 'Economic and/as Aesthetic Constructions of Britishness in Eighteenth-Century Domestic Travel Writing', *Journal for the Study of British Cultures*, 4, 31–45.

Fish, Cheryl J. and Farah J. Griffin (eds) (1998), *A Stranger in the Village: Two Centuries of African-American Travel Writing*, Boston: Beacon Press.

Fogel, Joshua A. (1996), *The Literature of Travel in the Japanese Rediscovery of China, 1862–1945*, Stanford: Stanford University Press.

Forsdick, Charles (2000), *Victor Segalen and the Aesthetics of Diversity: Journeys between Cultures*, Oxford: Oxford University Press.

——(2005), *Travel in Twentieth Century French and Francophone Cultures: The Persistence of Diversity*, Oxford: Oxford University Press.

Foster, Shirley (1990), *Across New Worlds: Nineteenth-Century Women Travellers and their Writings*, New York: Harvester/Wheatsheaf.

Foster, Shirley and Sara Mills (eds) (2002), *An Anthology of Women's Travel Writing*, Manchester: Manchester University Press.

Franklin, Wayne D. (1979), *Discoverers, Explorers, Settlers: The Diligent Writers of Early America*, Chicago: University of Chicago Press.

Frantz, R.W. (1934), *The English Traveller and the Movement of Ideas 1660–1732*, Lincoln: University of Nebraska Press.

Friedman, John Block and Kristen Mossler Figg (eds) (2000), *Trade, Travel and Exploration in the Middle Ages: An Encyclopaedia*, New York: Garland.

Fulford, Tim and Peter J. Kitson (eds) (1998), *Romanticism and Colonialism: Writing and Empire, 1780–1830*, Cambridge: Cambridge University Press.

——(2001), *Travels, Explorations and Empires: Writings From The Age of Imperial Expansion, 1770–1835*, 8 Vols., London: Pickering and Chatto.

Fulford, Tim, Peter Kitson and Debbie Lee (2004), *Literature, Science and Exploration in the Romantic Era: Bodies of Knowledge*, Cambridge: Cambridge University Press.

Fuller, Mary C. (1995), *Voyages in Print: English Travel to America, 1576–1624*, Cambridge: Cambridge University Press.

Fussell, Paul (1980), *Abroad: British Literary Travelling Between the Wars*, Oxford: Oxford University Press.

Fussell, Paul (ed.) (1987), *The Norton Book of Travel*, New York: W.W. Norton & Co.

Geertz, Clifford (1988), *Works and Lives: The Anthropologist as Author*, Stanford: Stanford University Press.

George, Sam (2007), *Botany, Sexuality and Women's Writing, 1760–1820*, Manchester: Manchester University Press.

Ghose, Indira (1998), *Women Travellers in Colonial India: The Power of the Female Gaze*, Oxford: Oxford University Press.

Ghose, Indira (ed.) (1998), *Memsahibs Abroad: Writings by Women Travellers in Nineteenth-Century India*, New Delhi: Oxford University Press.

Ghosh, Amitav (1992), *In An Antique Land*, London: Granta.

Gikandi, Simon (1996), *Maps of Englishness: Writing Identity in the Culture of Colonialism*, New York: Columbia University Press.

Gilroy, Amanda (ed.) (2000), *Romantic Geographies: Discourses of Travel, 1775–1844*, Manchester: Manchester University Press.

Glaser, Elton (1989), 'The Self-Reflexive Traveller: Paul Theroux on the Art of Travel Writing', *Centennial Review* 33: 193–206.

Glendening, John (1997), *The High Road: Romantic Tourism, Scotland and Literature, 1720–1820*, London: Macmillan.

Goldie, Terry (1989), *Fear and Temptation: The Image of the Indigene in Canadian, Australian and New Zealand Literatures*, Montreal: McGill-Queen's University Press.

Goodman, Jennifer R. (1998), *Chivalry and Exploration, 1298–1630*, Woodbridge: Boydell Press.

Green, Martin (1980), *Dreams of Adventure, Deeds of Empire*, London: Routledge.

Greenblatt, Stephen (1991), *Marvellous Possessions: The Wonder of the New World*, Chicago: University of Chicago Press.

Greene, Graham (1981), *The Lawless Roads*, Harmondsworth: Penguin. First published in 1939.

——(2006), *Journey Without Maps*, London: Vintage Books. First published 1936.

Gregory, Derek (1994), *Geographical Imaginations*, Oxford: Blackwell.

Grewal, Inderpal (1996), *Home and Harem: Nation, Gender, Empire and the Cultures of Travel*, Durham, NC: Duke University Press.

Hadfield, Andrew (1998), *Literature, Travel and Colonial Writing in the English Renaissance, 1545–1625*, Oxford: Clarendon Press.

Hadfield, Andrew (ed.) (2001), *Amazons, Savages and Machiavels: Travel and Colonial Writing in English, 1550–1630*, Oxford: Oxford University Press.

Hagglund, Betty (2010), *Tourists and Travellers: Women's Non-Fictional Writing about Scotland, 1770–1830*, Bristol: Channel View.

——(2011), 'The Botanical Writings of Maria Graham', *Journal of Literature and Science*, 3:1.

Hahner, June E. (ed.) (1998), *Women Through Women's Eyes: Latin American Women in Nineteenth-Century Travel Accounts*, Wilmington: Scholarly Resources Inc.

Hamara, Judith and Alfred Bendixen (eds) (2009), *The Cambridge Companion to American Travel Writing*, Cambridge: Cambridge University Press.

Hammond, Andrew (ed.) (2009), *Through Another Europe: An Anthology of Travel Writing on the Balkans*, Oxford: Signal Books.

Hanbury-Tenison, Robin (ed.) (1993), *The Oxford Book of Exploration*, Oxford: Oxford University Press.

Hartman, Geoffrey (1964), *Wordsworth's Poetry 1787–1814*, New Haven: Yale University Press.

Hartog, Francois (1988), *The Mirror of Herodotus: The Representation of the Other in the Writing of History*, trans. Janet Lloyd, Berkeley: University of California Press.

Hassan, Ihab (1990), *Selves at Risk: Patterns of Quest in Contemporary American Letters*, Wisconsin: University of Wisconsin Press.

Hayward, Jennifer (ed.) (2003), *Maria Graham: Journal of a Residence in Chile*, Charlottesville and London: University of Virginia Press.

Helms, Mary W. (1988), *Ulysses' Sail: An Ethnographic Odyssey of Power, Knowledge, and Geographical Distance*, Princeton: Princeton University Press.

Hibbert, Christopher (1987), *The Grand Tour*, London: Methuen.

Hindley, Geoffrey (1983), *Tourists, Travellers and Pilgrims*, London: Hutchinson.

Holland, Patrick and Graham Huggan (1998), *Tourists with Typewriters: Critical Reflections on Contemporary Travel Writing*, Ann Arbor: University of Michigan Press.

Hooper, Glenn and Tim Youngs (eds) (2004), *Perspectives on Travel Writing*, Aldershot: Ashgate.

Howard, Donald R. (1980), *Writers and Pilgrims: Medieval Pilgrimage Narratives and their Posterity*, Berkeley: University of California Press.

Huggan, Graham (1991), 'Maps, Dreams, and the Presentation of Ethnographic Narrative: Hugh Brody's *Maps and Dreams* and Bruce Chatwin's *The Songlines*', *Ariel*, Vol. 22, No. 1.

——(1994), 'V.S. Naipaul and the Political Correctness Debate', College Literature 21.3, 200–206.

Hulme, Peter (1986), *Colonial Encounters: Europe and the Native Caribbean 1492–1797*, London: Methuen.

Hulme, Peter and Tim Youngs (2002), *The Cambridge Companion to Travel Writing*, Cambridge: Cambridge University Press.

——(2007), *Talking about Travel Writing*, Leicester: The English Association.

Hunt, Stephen (2000), 'Wandering Lonely: Women's Access to the English Romantic Countryside', in John Tallmadge and Henry Harrington (eds), *Reading Under the Sign of Nature: New Essays in Ecocriticism*, Salt Lake City: University of Utah Press.

Hutnyk, John (1996), *The Rumour of Calcutta: Tourism, Charity and the Poverty of Representation*, London: Zed Books.

Hyam, Ronald (1990), *Empire and Sexuality: The British Experience*, Manchester: Manchester University Press.

Inden, Ronald (1990), *Imagining India*, Oxford: Blackwell.

Irving, Washington (1835), *A Tour on the Prairies*, London: John Murray.

Irwin, Robert (2006), *For Lust of Knowing: The Orientalists and their Enemies*, London: Allen Lane.

Islam, Syed Manzurul (1996), *The Ethics of Travel: From Marco Polo to Kafka*, Manchester: Manchester University Press.

Iyer, Pico (1988), *Video Night in Kathmandu*, New York: Vintage.

Jack, Ian (ed.) (1998), *The Granta Book of Travel*, London: Granta.

Jarvis, Robin (1997), *Romantic Writing and Pedestrian Travel*, Basingstoke: Macmillan.

Johnson, Samuel (ed.) (1789), *A Voyage to Abyssinia by Father Jerome Lobo*, London.

Kaplan, Robert (1993), *Balkan Ghosts: A Journey Through History*, New York: St Martin's Press.

Kaplan, Caren (1996), *Questions of Travel: Postmodern Discourses of Displacement*, Durham, NC: Duke University Press.

Kapuscinski, Ryszard (2007), *The Shadow of the Sun*, Harmondsworth: Penguin. First published 2001.

Kiernan, Victor Gordon (1969), *Lords of Human Kind: European Attitudes to the Outside World in the Imperial Age*, London: Weidenfeld.

Kinsley, Zoe (2008), *Women Writing the Home Tour, 1682–1812*, Aldershot: Ashgate.

Knapp, Jeffrey (1992), *An Empire Nowhere: England, America, and Literature from Utopia to 'The Tempest'*, Berkeley: University of California Press.

Korte, Barbara (2000), *English Travel Writing: From Pilgrimages to Postcolonial Explorations*, Basingstoke: Palgrave.

Kowaleswki, Michael (ed.) (1992), *Temperamental Journeys: Essays on the Modern Literature of Travel*, Athens, GA: University of Georgia Press.

Kröller, Eva-Marie (1987), *Canadian Travellers in Europe, 1851–1900*, Vancouver: University of British Columbia Press.

Kuehn, Julia (2008) and Paul Smethurst (eds), *Travel Writing, Form and Empire: The Poetics and Politics of Mobility*, London: Routledge.

Lamb, Jonathan (2001), *Preserving the Self in the South Seas, 1680–1840*, Chicago: University of Chicago Press.

Latour, Bruno (1987), *Science in Action: How to Follow Scientists and Engineers Through Society*, Cambridge, Mass.: Harvard University Press.

Lawrence, Karen R. (1994), *Penelope Voyages: Women and Travel in the British Literary Tradition*, Ithaca, NY: Cornell University Press.

Leask, Nigel (2002), *Curiosity and the Aesthetics of Travel Writing, 1770–1840: 'From An Antique Land'*, Oxford: Oxford University Press.

Lee, Elaine (1997), *Go Girl! The Black Woman's Book of Travel and Adventure*, Portland: Eighth Mountain Press.

Leed, Eric J. (1991), *The Mind of the Traveller: from Gilgamesh to Global Tourism*, New York: Basic Books.

Léry, Jean de (1992), *History of a Voyage Made to the Land of Brazil*, trans. Janet Whatley, Berkeley and Los Angeles, CA: University of California Press.

Lévi-Strauss, Claude (1973), *Tristes Tropiques*, London: Jonathan Cape. First published 1955.

Lewis, Reina (1996), *Gendering Orientalism: Race, Femininity and Representation*, London: Routledge.

Lisle, Debbie (2006), *The Global Politics of Contemporary Travel Writing*, Cambridge: Cambridge University Press.

Low, Gail Ching-Liang (1996), *White Skins/Black Masks: Representation and Colonialism*, London: Routledge.

Lutz, Catherine A. and Jane L. Collins (1993), *Reading National Geographic*, Chicago: University of Chicago Press.

MacCannell, Dean (1999), *The Tourist: A New Theory of the Leisure Class*, Berkeley: University of California Press.

Martin, Alison (2008), *Moving Scenes: the Aesthetics of German Travel Writing on England, 1783–1830*, London: Legenda.

Martineau, Harriet (1837), *Society in America*, London, 2 vols.

Matar, Nabil (1999), *Turks, Moors, and Englishmen in the Age of Discovery*, New York: Columbia University Press.

McKeon, Michael (2002), *The Origins of the English Novel, 1600–1740*, Baltimore: The Johns Hopkins University Press.

Melchett, Sonia (1991), *Passionate Quests: Five Modern Women Travellers*, London: Heinemann.

Melman, Billie (1991), *Women's Orients: English Women and the Middle East, 1718–1918*, London: Macmillan.

Miller, Christopher L. (1985), *Blank Darkness: Africanist Discourse in French*, Chicago: Chicago University Press.

Miller, David and Peter Reill (eds) (1996), *Visions of Empire: Voyages, Botany and Representations of Nature*, Cambridge: Cambridge University Press.

Mills, Sara (1991), *Discourses of Difference: An Analysis of Women's Travel Writing and Colonialism*, London: Routledge.

Moir, Esther (1964), *The Discovery of Britain: the English Tourists*, London: Routledge.

Montagu, Lady Mary Wortley (1906), *Letters*, London: J.M. Dent and Co.

Morgan, Susan (1996), *Place Matters: Gendered Geography in Victorian Women's Travel Books about Southeast Asia*, New Brunswick, NJ: Rutgers University Press.

Moroz, Grzegorz and Jolanta Sztachelska (2010), *Metamorphoses of Travel Writing: Across Theories, Genres, Centuries and Literary Traditions*, Newcastle: Cambridge Scholars Press.

Morris, Mary (1989), *Nothing to Declare: Memoirs of a Woman Traveling Alone*, New York: Penguin.

Morris, Mary (ed.) (2007), *The Illustrated Virago Book of Women Travellers*, London: Virago. First published 1994.

Morrison, Susan S. (2000), *Women Pilgrims in Late Medieval England*, London: Routledge.

Moss, Sarah (2005), *Scott's Last Biscuit: The Literature of Polar Exploration*, London: Signal Books.

Mudimbe, V.Y. (1988), *The Invention of Africa: Gnosis, Philosophy and the Order of Knowledge*, Bloomington: Indiana University Press.

Mulvey, Christopher (1983), *Anglo-American Landscapes: A Study of Nineteenth-Century Anglo-American Travel Literature*, Cambridge: Cambridge University Press.

——(1990), *Transatlantic Manners: Social Patterns in Nineteenth-Century Anglo-American Travel Literature*, Cambridge: Cambridge University Press.

Nichols, Ashton (1989), 'Silencing the Other: the Discourse of Domination in Nineteenth-Century Exploration Narratives', *Nineteenth-Century Studies*, 3, 1–22.

——(1996), 'Mumbo Jumbo: Mungo Park and the Rhetoric of Romantic Africa', in Alan Richardson and Sonia Hofkosh (eds), *Romanticism, Race and Imperial Culture, 1780–1834*, Bloomington: Indiana University Press.

Nixon, Rob (1992), *London Calling: V.S. Naipaul, Postcolonial Mandarin*, Oxford: Oxford University Press.

Nussbaum, Felicity (1995), *Torrid Zones: Maternity, Sexuality and Empire in Eighteenth-Century Narrative*, Baltimore: Johns Hopkins Press.

Obeyesekere, Gananath (1992), '"British Cannibals": Contemplation of an Event in the Death and Resurrection of James Cook, Explorer', *Critical Inquiry* 18: 630–54.

Ousby, Ian (1990), *The Englishman's England: Taste, Travel and the Rise of Tourism*, Cambridge: Cambridge University Press.

Paes de Barros, Deborah (2004), *Fast Cars and Bad Girls: Nomadic Subjects and Women's Road Stories*, New York: Peter Lang.

Pagden, Anthony (1993), *European Encounters with the New World, from Renaissance to Romanticism*, New Haven and London: Yale University Press.

Parker, Kenneth (ed.) (1999), *Early Modern Tales of Orient: A Critical Anthology*, London: Routledge.

Parks, George (1964), 'The Turn to the Romantic in the Travel Literature of the 18th Century', *Modern Language Quarterly*, 25:1, 22–33.

Pemble, John (1988), *The Mediterranean Passion: Victorians and Edwardians in the South*, Oxford, Oxford University Press.

Penrose, Boies (1952), *Travel and Discovery in the Renaissance*, Cambridge, Mass.: Harvard University Press.

Pesman, Ros (1996), *Duty Free: Australian Women Abroad*, Oxford: Oxford University Press.

Pesman, Ros, David Walker and Richard White (eds) (1996), *The Oxford Book of Australian Travel Writing*, Melbourne: Oxford University Press.

Pettinger, Alisdair (ed.) (1999), *Always Elsewhere: Travels of the Black Atlantic*, London: Cassell.

Pfister, Manfred (ed.) (1996a), *The Fatal Gift of Beauty: The Italies of British Travellers: An Annotated Anthology*, Amsterdam and Atlanta, GA: Rodopi.

——(1996b), 'Bruce Chatwin and the Postmodernization of the Travelogue', *Literature, Interpretation, Theory*, 7, 2–3: 57–90.

Philip, Jim (1993), 'Reading Travel Writing', in Jonathan White (ed.) *Recasting the World: Writing after Colonialism*, Baltimore, MD: Johns Hopkins University Press.

Phillips, Richard (1997), *Mapping Men & Empire: A Geography of Adventure*, London: Routledge.

Plutschow, Herbert (ed.) (2006), *A Reader in Edo Period Travel*, Folkestone: Global Oriental.

Polezzi, Loredana (2001), *Translating Travel: Contemporary Italian Travel Writing in English Translation*, Aldershot: Ashgate.

Porter, Dennis (1991), *Haunted Journeys: Desire and Transgression in European Travel Writing*, Princeton: Princeton University Press.

Pratt, Mary Louise (1986), 'Fieldwork in Common Places', in James Clifford and George E. Marcus (eds), *Writing Culture: The Poetics and Politics of Ethnography*, Berkeley, CA: University of California Press.

——(2008), *Imperial Eyes: Travel Writing and Transculturation*, 2nd edition, London and New York: Routledge. First published in 1992.

Raban, Jonathan (1988), *For Love & Money: Writing – Reading – Travelling 1968–1987*, London: Picador.

Radcliffe, Ann (1796), *A Journey Made Through the Summer of 1794*. London: 2 vols.

Rapport, Nigel and Joanna Overing (2002), *Social and Cultural Anthropology: The Key Concepts*, London: Routledge.

Redford, Bruce (1998), *Venice and the Grand Tour*, New Haven: Yale University Press.

Rennie, Neil (1995), *Far-Fetched Facts: the Literature of Travel and the Idea of the South Seas*, Oxford; Oxford University Press.

Richards, Thomas (1993), *The Imperial Archive: Knowledge and the Fantasy of Empire*, London and New York: Verso.

Riffenburgh, Beau (1993), *The Myth of the Explorer: The Press, Sensationalism, and Geographical Discovery*, Oxford: Oxford University Press.

Rigby, Elizabeth (1845), 'Lady Travellers', *Quarterly Review* 76, 98–137.

Roberson, Susan L. (ed.) (2001), *Defining Travel: Diverse Visions*, Jackson, MS: University of Mississippi Press.

Robertson, George and Melinda Mash, Lisa Tickner, Jon Bird, Barry Curtis and Tim Putnam (eds) (1994), *Travellers' Tales: Narratives of Home and Displacement*, London: Routledge.

Robinson, Jane (1990), *Wayward Women: A Guide to Women Travellers*, Oxford: Oxford University Press.

Rojek, Chris (1993), *Ways of Escape: Modern Transformations of Leisure and Travel*, London: MacMillan.

Romero, Patricia (1992), *Women's Voices in Africa: A Century of Travel Writings*, New Brunswick, NJ: Princeton University Press.

Rosaldo, Renato (1989), 'Imperialist Nostalgia', *Representations* 26: 107–22.

Ross, John (1835), *Narrative of a Second Voyage in Search of a North West Passage*.

Rousseau, G.S. and Roy Porter (eds) (1990), *Exoticism in the Enlightenment*, Manchester: Manchester University Press.

Rushdie, Salman (1987), *The Jaguar Smile: A Nicaraguan Journey*, New York: Viking.

Russell, Mary (1986), *The Blessings of a Good Thick Skirt: Women Travellers and their World*, London: Collins.

Ryan, Simon (1996), *The Cartographic Imagination: How Explorers Saw Australia*, Cambridge: Cambridge University Press.

Said, Edward (1983), *The World, the Text, and the Critic*, Cambridge, Mass.: Harvard University Press.

——(1993), *Culture and Imperialism*, London: Chatto and Windus.

——(1995), *Orientalism: Western Conceptions of the Orient*, Harmondsworth: Penguin. First published 1978.

Schivelbusch, Wolfgang (1986), *The Railroad Journey: The Industrialization of Time and Space in the Nineteenth-Century*, Hamburg and New York: Berg.

Schriber, Mary Suzanne (1997), *Writing Home: American Women Abroad, 1830–1920*, Charlottesville and London: University of Virginia Press.

Schweizer, Bernard (2001), *Radicals on the Road: The Politics of English Travel Writing in the 1930s*, Richmond: University Press of Virginia.

Sebald, W.G. (1998), *The Rings of Saturn*, London: Harvill Press.

Shakespeare, Nicholas (1999), *Bruce Chatwin*, London: Harvill Press.

Shapin, Steven (1994), *A Social History of Truth: Civility and Science in Seventeenth-Century England*, Chicago: University of Chicago Press.

Sharpe, Jenny (1993), *Allegories of Empire: The Figure of the Woman in the Colonial Text*, Minneapolis: University of Minneapolis Press.

Sherman, William H. (2002), 'Stirrings and Searchings (1500–1720)', in Hulme and Youngs (eds), *The Cambridge Companion to Travel Writing*, Cambridge: Cambridge University Press, 17–36.

Shteir, Ann B. (1999), *Cultivating Women, Cultivating Science: Flora's Daughters and Botany in England, 1760–1860*, Baltimore and London: The Johns Hopkins University Press.

Smith, Bernard (1969), *European Vision and the South Pacific 1768–1850: A Study in the History of Art and Ideas*, Oxford: Oxford University Press.

Smith, Sidonie (2001), *Moving Lives: Twentieth-Century Women's Travel Writing*, Minneapolis: University of Minnesota Press.

Spufford, Francis (1996), *I May Be Some Time: Ice and the English Imagination*, London: Faber and Faber.

Spurr, David (1993), *The Rhetoric of Empire: Colonial Discourse in Journalism, Travel Writing and Imperial Administration*, Durham: Duke University Press.

Stafford, Barbara (1984), *Voyage into Substance: Art, Science, Nature and the Illustrated Travel Account, 1760–1840*, Cambridge, Mass.; MIT Press.

Stanley, Henry Morton (1988), *Through the Dark Continent*, New York: Dover Books. First published 1878. 2 vols.

Stannard, Martin (1982), 'Debunking the Jungle: The Context of Evelyn Waugh's Travel Books, 1930–9', *Prose Studies*, 5, 1: 105–26.

Sterne, Laurence (1987), *A Sentimental Journey*, Harmondsworth: Penguin. First published 1768.

Stevenson, Catherine Barnes (1982), *Victorian Women Travel Writers in Africa*, Boston: Twayne.

Stowe, Harriet Beecher (1845), *Sunny Memories of Foreign Lands*, London.

Stoye, John Walter (1952), *English Travellers Abroad, 1604–1667: Their Influence in English Society and Politics*, London: Cape.

Stummer, Peter O. (1994), 'An-Other Travelogue: Ferdinand Dennis's Journey into Afro-Britain', in Geoffrey Davies (ed.), *Southern African Writing: Voyages and Explorations*, Amsterdam and Atlanta, GA: Rodopi.

Sugnet, Charles (1991), 'Vile Bodies, Vile Places: Traveling with *Granta*', *Transition* 51: 70–85.

Suleri, Sara (1991), *The Rhetoric of English India*, Chicago: University of Chicago Press.

Thomas, Nicholas (1994), *Colonialism's Culture: Anthropology, Travel & Government*, Cambridge: Polity Press.

Thompson, Carl (2004), 'The Heroic Age of the Tin Can: Technology and Ideology in British Arctic Exploration, 1818–35', in David Killingray, Margarette Lincoln and Nigel Rigby (eds), *Maritime Empires: British Imperial Trade in the Nineteenth Century*, Woodbridge: Boydell and Brewer.

——(2007a), *The Suffering Traveller and the Romantic Imagination*, Oxford: Oxford University Press.

——(2007b), *Romantic-Era Shipwreck Narratives: An Anthology*, Nottingham: Trent Editions.

Thubron, Colin (1986), 'Travel Writing Today: Its Rise and Its Dilemma', in *Essays By Divers Hands*, Transactions of the Royal Society of Literature, NS, vol. 54: 167–81.

Trollope, Anthony (1987), *North America*, Gloucester: Alan Sutton. 2 vols. First published 1862.

Turner, Katherine (2001), *British Travel Writers in Europe 1750–1800: Authorship, Gender and National Identity*, Aldershot: Ashgate.

Turner, Victor (1969), *The Ritual Process: Structure and Anti-Structure*, London: Routledge.

Twain, Mark (1985), *Roughing It*, Harmondsworth: Penguin. First published 1872.

——(1997), *A Tramp Abroad*, Harmondsworth: Penguin. First published 1880.

Urry, John (1990), *The Tourist Gaze: Leisure and Travel in Contemporary Societies*, London: Sage.

Van den Abbeele, George (1992), *Travel as Metaphor: From Montaigne to Rousseau*, Minneapolis: University of Minnesota Press.

Vivies, Jean (2002), *English Travel Narratives in the Eighteenth Century: Exploring Genres*, Aldershot: Ashgate.

Von Martels, Zweder (ed.) (1994), *Travel Fact and Travel Fiction: Studies on Fiction, Literary Tradition, Scholarly Discovery and Observation in Travel Writing*, Leiden: E.J. Brill.

Walsh, Alison (ed.) (1991), *Nothing Ventured: Disabled People Travel the World*, Bromley: Harrap Columbus.

Ware, Vron (1992), *Beyond the Pale: White Women, Racism and History*, London: Verso.

Watson, Nicola (2006), *The Literary Tourist: Readers and Places in Romantic and Victorian Britain*, Basingstoke: Palgrave.

Waugh, Evelyn (1930), *Labels: A Mediterranean Journal*, London: Duckworth.

Wheeler, Sara (1996), *Terra Incognita: Travels in Antarctica*, London: Vintage.

Wheeler, Valerie (1986), 'Travelers' Tales: Observations on the Travel Book and Ethnography', *Anthropological Quarterly* 59, No. 2: 52–63.

White, Hayden (1976), 'Fictions of Factual Representation', in Angus Fletcher (ed.), *The Literature of Fact*, New York: Columbia University Press.

White, Jonathan (ed.) (1993), *Recasting the World: Writing after Colonialism*, Baltimore, MD: Johns Hopkins University Press.

Whitehead, Neil (ed.) (1997), *The Discoverie of the Large, Rich and Bewtiful Empyre of Guiana, by Sir Walter Ralegh*, Manchester: Manchester University Press.

Whitlock, Gillian (1993), '"A Most Improper Desire": Mary Gaunt's Journey to Jamaica', *Kunapipi*, 15, 3: 86–95.

Wilkinson, John (ed. and trans.) (1999), *Egeria's Travels*, Oxford: Oxbow Books.

Williams, Glyndwr (1997), *The Great South Sea: English Voyages and Encounters, 1570–1750*, New Haven: Yale University Press.

Williams, Wes (1998), *Pilgrimage and Narrative in the French Renaissance: 'The Undiscovered Country'*, Oxford: Oxford University Press.

Withey, Lynne (1987), *Voyages of Discovery: Captain Cook and the Exploration of the Pacific*, London: Hutchinson.

——(1998), *Grand Tours and Cook's Tours: A History of Leisure Travel, 1750 to 1915*, London: Aurum Press.

Wolf, Eric R. (1982), *Europe and the People without History*, Berkeley: University of California Press.

Wolff, Janet (1993), 'On the Road Again: Metaphors of Travel in Cultural Criticism', *Cultural Studies* 7, No. 2: 224–39.

Young, Robert (1995), *Colonial Desire: Hybridity in Theory, Culture and Race*, London: Routledge.

Youngs, Tim (1994), *Travellers in Africa: British Travelogues, 1850–1900*, Manchester: Manchester University Press.

Youngs, Tim (ed.) (2006), *Travel Writing in the Twentieth Century: Filling in the Blanks*, London: Anthem.

Zacher, Christian K. (1976), *Curiosity and Pilgrimage: The Literature of Discovery in Fourteenth-Century England*, Baltimore, MD and London: Johns Hopkins University Press.

Ziff, Larzer (2000), *Return Passages: Great American Travel Writing, 1780–1910*, New Haven and London: Yale University Press.

Index

UNIVERSITY OF WINCHESTER
LIBRARY

Taylor & Francis

eBooks
FOR LIBRARIES

ORDER YOUR
FREE 30 DAY
INSTITUTIONAL
TRIAL TODAY!

Over 23,000 eBook titles in the Humanities,
Social Sciences, STM and Law from some of the
world's leading imprints.

Choose from a range of subject packages or create your own!

Benefits for
you

▶ Free MARC records
▶ COUNTER-compliant usage statistics
▶ Flexible purchase and pricing options

Benefits
for your
user

▶ Off-site, anytime access via Athens or referring URL
▶ Print or copy pages or chapters
▶ Full content search
▶ Bookmark, highlight and annotate text
▶ Access to thousands of pages of quality research
  at the click of a button

For more information, pricing enquiries or to order
a free trial, contact your local online sales team.

UK and Rest of World: **online.sales@tandf.co.uk**
US, Canada and Latin America:
e-reference@taylorandfrancis.com

www.ebooksubscriptions.com

A flexible and dynamic resource for teaching, learning and research.